L2 WRITING IN SECONDARY CLASSROOMS

D1564664

"There is no question that this volume has a significant role to play in teacher education, both in L1 and L2 settings. One of its most valuable features is that its studies are based on real-life data and experiences of both students and their teachers, as well as their daily, tangible, and realistic school writing. This book will prove to be an indispensable resource for novice and practicing teachers and teacher educators."

Eli Hinkel, from the Series Editor Foreword

Second language writers and the teaching of writing at the secondary level have received little attention compared with other skills such as reading. Addressing this gap, this volume uniquely looks at both adolescent L2 writing and the preparation of secondary teachers to work with this population of students. Part I, on adolescent L2 writers, includes case studies looking at their literacy identities, their trajectories in mainstream content area classes, and their transition from high school to college. Part II looks at academic issues. The focus in Part III is L2 writing teacher education. Taking a theoretically eclectic approach that can support a variety of pedagogies, this book contributes significantly to understanding adolescent second language writers and to educating teachers to address these students' specific needs.

Luciana C. de Oliveira is Associate Professor and Director, ELL Licensure Program, Department of Curriculum & Instruction, Purdue University, USA.

Tony Silva is Professor and Director of the ESL Writing Program, Department of English, Purdue University, USA.

ESL & Applied Linguistics Professional Series
Eli Hinkel, Series Editor

de Oliveira/Silva, Eds. • *L2 Writing in Secondary Classrooms: Student Experiences, Academic Issues, and Teacher Education*

Andrade/Evans • *Principles and Practices for Response in Second Language Writing: Developing Self-Regulated Learners*

Sayer • *Ambiguities and Tensions in English Language Teaching: Portraits of EFL Teachers as Legitimate Speakers*

Alsagoff/McKay/Hu/Renandya, Eds. • *Principles and Practices of Teaching English as an International Language*

Kumaravadivelu • *Language Teacher Education for a Global Society: A Modular Model for Knowing, Analyzing, Recognizing, Doing, and Seeing*

Vandergrift/Goh • *Teaching and Learning Second Language Listening: Metacognition in Action*

LoCastro • *Pragmatics for Language Educators: A Sociolinguistic Perspective*

Nelson • *Intelligibility in World Englishes: Theory and Practice*

Nation/Macalister, Eds. • *Case Studies in Language Curriculum Design Concepts and Approaches in Action Around the World*

Johnson/Golumbek, Eds. • *Research on Second Language Teacher Education: A Sociocultural Perspective on Professional Development*

Hinkel, Ed. • *Handbook of Research in Second Language Teaching and Learning, Volume II*

Nassaji /Fotos • *Teaching Grammar in Second Language Classrooms: Integrating Form-Focused Instruction in Communicative Context*

Murray/Christison • *What English Language Teachers Need to Know Volume I: Understanding Learning*

Murray/Christison • *What English Language Teachers Need to Know Volume II: Facilitating Learning*

Wong/Waring • *Conversation Analysis and Second Language Pedagogy: A Guide for ESL/EFL Teachers*

Nunan/Choi, Eds. • *Language and Culture: Reflective Narratives and the Emergence of Identity*

Braine • *Nonnative Speaker English Teachers: Research, Pedagogy, and Professional Growth*

Burns • *Doing Action Research in English Language Teaching: A Guide for Practitioners*

Nation/Macalister • *Language Curriculum Design*

Birch • *The English Language Teacher and Global Civil Society*

Johnson • *Second Language Teacher Education: A Sociocultural Perspective*

Nation • *Teaching ESL/EFL Reading and Writing*

Nation/Newton • *Teaching ESL/EFL Listening and Speaking*

Kachru/Smith • *Cultures, Contexts, and World Englishes*

McKay/Bokhorst-Heng • *International English in its Sociolinguistic Contexts: Towards a Socially Sensitive EIL Pedagogy*

Christison/Murray, Eds. • *Leadership in English Language Education: Theoretical Foundations and Practical Skills for Changing Times*

McCafferty/Stam, Eds. • *Gesture: Second Language Acquisition and Classroom Research*

Liu • *Idioms: Description, Comprehension, Acquisition, and Pedagogy*

Chapelle/Enright/Jamieson, Eds. • *Building a Validity Argument for the Test of English as a Foreign Language™*

Kondo-Brown/Brown, Eds. • *Teaching Chinese, Japanese, and Korean Heritage Language Students: Curriculum Needs, Materials, and Assessments*

Youmans • *Chicano-Anglo Conversations: Truth, Honesty, and Politeness*

Birch • *English L2 Reading: Getting to the Bottom, Second Edition*

Luk/Lin • *Classroom Interactions as Cross-cultural Encounters: Native Speakers in EFL Lessons*

Levy/Stockwell • *CALL Dimensions: Issues and Options in Computer Assisted Language Learning*

Nero, Ed. • *Dialects, Englishes, Creoles, and Education*

Basturkmen • *Ideas and Options in English for Specific Purposes*

Kumaravadivelu • *Understanding Language Teaching: From Method to Postmethod*

McKay • *Researching Second Language Classrooms*

Egbert/Petrie, Eds. • *CALL Research Perspectives*

Canagarajah, Ed. • *Reclaiming the Local in Language Policy and Practice*

Adamson • *Language Minority Students in American Schools: An Education in English*

Fotos/Browne, Eds. • *New Perspectives on CALL for Second Language Classrooms*

Hinkel • *Teaching Academic ESL Writing: Practical Techniques in Vocabulary and Grammar*

Hinkel/Fotos, Eds. • *New Perspectives on Grammar Teaching in Second Language Classrooms*

Hinkel • *Second Language Writers' Text: Linguistic and Rhetorical Features*

Visit **www.routledge.com/education** for additional information on titles in the ESL & Applied Linguistics Professional Series

L2 WRITING IN SECONDARY CLASSROOMS

Student Experiences, Academic Issues, and Teacher Education

Edited by Luciana C. de Oliveira and Tony Silva

Routledge
Taylor & Francis Group

NEW YORK AND LONDON

First published 2013
by Routledge
711 Third Avenue, New York, NY 10017

Simultaneously published in the UK
by Routledge
2 Park Square, Milton Park, Abingdon, Oxon OX14 4RN

Routledge is an imprint of the Taylor & Francis Group, an informa business

Library of Congress Cataloging-in-Publication Data
L2 writing in secondary classrooms : student experiences, academic issues, and
teacher education / Luciana C. de Oliveira, Tony Silva.
    p. cm. – (ESL & applied linguistics professional series)
    Includes bibliographical references and index.
    1. English language–Study and teaching (Secondary)–Foreign speakers.
    2. Language arts (Secondary) I. De Oliveira, Luciana C., editor of
compilation. II. Silva, Tony J., editor of compilation. III. Ortmeier-
Hooper, Christina, 1972– She doesn't know who I am.
    PE1128.A2L23 2013
    428.0071′273–dc23   2012040367

ISBN: 978–0–415–64060–2 (hbk)
ISBN: 978–0–415–64061–9 (pbk)
ISBN: 978–0–203–08266–9 (ebk)

Typeset in Bembo
by Keystroke, Station Road, Codsall, Wolverhampton

Printed and bound in the United States of America by Publishers Graphics,
LLC on sustainably sourced paper.

CONTENTS

Series Editor Foreword   *ix*
Eli Hinkel
Preface   *xi*
Acknowledgments   *xiii*

1 On the Radar Screen and the Need to Focus on L2 Writing
  in Secondary Classrooms   1
  Luciana C. de Oliveira and Tony Silva

PART I
Student Experiences: Case Studies   **7**

2 "She Doesn't Know Who I Am": The Case of a Refugee L2
  Writer in a High School English Language Arts Classroom   9
  Christina Ortmeier-Hooper

3 Adolescent Writers and Academic Trajectories: Situating L2
  Writing in the Content Areas   27
  Kerry Anne Enright

4 "Doing Like Almost Everything Wrong": An Adolescent
  Multilingual Writer's Transition from High School to College 44
  Amanda Kibler

PART II
Academic Issues
65

5 Preparing English Language Learners for Argumentative
Writing   67
Alan Hirvela

6 The Role of Social Relationships in the Writing of
Multilingual Adolescents   87
Jennifer Shade Wilson

7 Emerging Literacies in Digital Media and L2 Secondary
Writing   104
Melissa Niiya, Mark Warschauer, and Binbin Zheng

PART III
Teacher Education
117

8 Focus on Pre-service Preparation for ESL Writing
Instruction: Secondary Teacher Perspectives   119
Ditlev Larsen

9 ESOL Teachers as Writing Teachers: From the Voices of
High School Pre-Service Teachers   133
Youngjoo Yi

10 Responsive Teacher Inquiry for Learning about Adolescent
English Learners as Developing Writers   149
*Steven Z. Athanases, Lisa H. Bennett, and
Juliet Michelsen Wahleithner*

11 Understanding how Pre-Service Teachers Develop a
Working Knowledge of L2 Writing: Toward a
Socioculturally Oriented Postmethod Pedagogy   166
Lisya Seloni

List of Contributors and Editors   *190*
Index   *191*

SERIES EDITOR FOREWORD

Research on L1 (first language) writing dominated the writing research scene between the 1970s and 1990s, and insights into L2 (second language) writing and its many poignant issues have arrived in full force only in the past two or three decades. At present, however, there are few books on secondary L2 writers, and it seems fair to say that relatively little has been studied in the L2 writing development of adolescents or what specifically they need to learn or what they should be taught or how their teaching and learning is to be accomplished.

This book seeks to find answers to at least some of these questions. The chapters consist of original research by scholars who work directly with school-age learners and their teachers. The authors of the chapters have set out to gain vital understanding of the quandaries specific to adolescent L2 writers and their writing. The theoretical foundations of the work presented look at a range of possibilities with the goal of supporting numerous pedagogies currently adopted in secondary schools.

The book represents a compendium of important, relevant, and practical chapters, based on current research in second language writing in secondary schooling. There is no question that the volume has a significant role to play in teacher education, both in L1 and L2 settings. The findings of the research discussed in each chapter will find many uses in teacher education programs in any English-speaking country where immigrant learners are enrolled. One of the most valuable features of the volume is that its studies are based on real-life data and experiences of both students and their teachers, as well as their daily, tangible, and realistic school writing.

This book will prove to be an indispensable resource for novice and practicing teachers and teacher educators. Specifically, the pedagogical applications of the studies and overviews included in the book are extremely useful. They address a range of prominent issues that continue to confound second language writing in high school classrooms: the perspectives of adolescent L2 writers, the impact of context on their experiences of school writing, content learning, access to advanced academic language skills, the essentials of L2 writing pedagogy, and the acute need for teacher preparation for working with school-age learners. The book successfully builds on foundational elements in second language writing and schooling to contribute to the knowledge base currently available in social frameworks that crucially affect language teaching, classroom instruction, and their countless contextual variables. Taken together, these research perspectives make the book unique, well-grounded, and truly innovative.

The practical and realistic view of second language writing, teaching, and learning discussed in the book provides examples from the application of research to a broad range of teaching and learning contexts.

Unquestionably, the editors are among the top world-class authorities in L2 writing and pedagogy. When it comes to the quality, practicality, and research grounding of scholarship and teacher education materials, Luciana and Tony are truly unique. They are highly regarded book authors, methodologists, teacher-educators and widely recognized experts on L2 writing in the world. The editors' impressive experience in teacher education on second language writing and teacher development shines throughout the manuscript.

Eli Hinkel
Seattle University

PREFACE

Second language (L2) writing in the secondary classroom context has received little attention compared to other skills such as reading. Relatively few publications focus on both second language writing and K–12 issues. This situation has been recognized and commented on by professionals in both disciplines, demonstrating the need for much additional work at this intersection. The aim of this book is to address this need by collecting the original research of scholars combining work in these areas so as to better understand adolescent L2 writers and their writing, to elucidate concepts germane to working with this population, and to consider how all of this might play out in the context of teacher education. The book takes a theoretically eclectic approach that can support numerous pedagogies and is intended primarily for secondary teachers and graduate students and faculty in education and ESL.

In Chapter 1 the editors introduce, motivate, and contextualize the contributions to this collection. The chapters in Part I present case studies done with adolescent L2 writers. Chapter 2 looks at the impact of socio-political history and literacy identity on the academic writing of a 14-year-old refugee L2 writer from Nigeria and examines his conflicts and experiences with writing in his U.S. mainstream English language arts classroom. Chapter 3 focuses on two L2 writers, one in honors classes and one in general classes, to highlight how differences in context impact their experiences of writing, their learning of specific content-based uses of writing, and their access to advanced uses of academic literacy across the curriculum. Chapter 4 presents a longitudinal analysis of a Spanish-speaking student who started high school as a beginning English language learner and later graduated with a competitive university scholarship, only to be placed in, and fail, remedial writing courses in his first year of college.

Part II considers a number of timely and important academic issues for those who work with L2 adolescent writers. Chapter 5 explores key elements of argumentative writing instruction and intercultural rhetoric and reviews research on L2 writers' experiences with argumentative writing. Chapter 6 presents a synthesis of research on how social relationships can support writing development in multilingual adolescents and reviews theory-building work on social networks in language learning, social support for education, and adolescent literacy. Chapter 7 looks at diverse ways that digital media are used in adolescent writing and how these uses affect English learners' writing processes and outcomes.

The chapters in Part III address issues in L2 writing teacher education at the K–12 level. Chapter 8 reports on a study surveying secondary ESL teachers about the writing requirements of their teacher education programs in terms of ESL writing pedagogy. Chapter 9 presents findings on the study of two pre-service ESOL teachers' sense of (un)preparedness to teach L2 writing and challenges for L2 writing instruction during internship, as well as the construction of L2 writing teacher identity. Chapter 10 addresses EL writing issues that pre-service teachers in one teacher education program explored through inquiry and illustrates how this inquiry promoted movement from initial problem-framing to discoveries about teaching writing to adolescent English learners. Chapter 11 looks at pre-service teachers' lived experiences with teaching second language writing within a larger focus on linguistic diversity that includes non-English languages as well as dialects of English.

ACKNOWLEDGMENTS

We would like to thank our contributing authors for making this book possible. We would also like to thank our editor at Routledge, Naomi Silverman, and the ESL & Applied Linguistics Professional Series editor, Eli Hinkel, for their encouragement, support, advice, and wise counsel in helping us assemble this collection.

1

ON THE RADAR SCREEN AND THE NEED TO FOCUS ON L2 WRITING IN SECONDARY CLASSROOMS

Luciana C. de Oliveira and Tony Silva

Adolescent second language (L2) writers are a unique population in secondary classrooms. Despite an increase in the numbers of students categorized as English language learners (ELLs) in U.S. schools, there has been a general lack of attention to the writing needs of this population at the secondary level (Leki, Cumming, & Silva, 2008). According to the National Clearinghouse for English Language Acquisition (2006), more than 10 percent of the K–12 student population in the United States is comprised of ELLs, which represents over five million students. Most of these students are in California, Florida, Illinois, New Mexico, New York, Puerto Rico, and Texas. However, states such as Arkansas, Alabama, Colorado, Delaware, Georgia, Indiana, Kentucky, Nebraska, North Carolina, South Carolina, Tennessee, Vermont, and Virginia have experienced more than 200 percent growth in the numbers of ELLs in schools from 1995 to 2006 (NCELA, 2006). These numbers show a clear need to focus on this population of L2 writers, especially at the secondary level. This was demonstrated in the introduction of a special issue of the flagship journal of the L2 writing field, the *Journal of Second Language Writing*, focused on adolescent L2 writers:

> The need for more scholarship on this group of L2 writers is clear, yet our field has yet to establish a base map for understanding these writers and their writing contexts. As a result, these students often remain outside the purview of many L2 writing specialists and off the radar screen of our disciplinary conversations.
>
> *(Ortmeier-Hooper & Enright, 2011, p. 167)*

This collection aims to place L2 writers and L2 writing in secondary classrooms *on* the radar screen of both L2 writing scholars and educators preparing secondary teachers to work with this student population. To date, L2 writing in the secondary classroom context has received little attention compared to other skills (Harklau & Pinnow, 2009). Few articles and books focus on both L2 writing and secondary school (e.g. de Oliveira, 2011; Kibler, 2010; Yi, 2010). In addition, Hirvela and Belcher (2007) note that little attention has been given to the kinds of preparation that pre-service and in-service teachers have to address L2 writing and call for more work in this area. To address these needs, this book combines a focus on research in adolescent L2 writing and the preparation of secondary teachers to teach L2 writing. The book is divided into three parts. Part I presents case studies of L2 writers in secondary classrooms to show the complexities of their experiences. Part II explores academic issues that are important for adolescent L2 writers. Part III focuses on the preparation and needs of pre-service and in-service secondary teachers to focus on L2 writing and writers in secondary classrooms.

Part I: Student Experiences: Case Studies

In "'She Doesn't Know Who I Am': The Case of a Refugee L2 Writer in a High School English Language Arts Classroom," Christina Ortmeier-Hooper explores the experiences of Wisdom, a 14-year-old refugee from Nigeria, in an effort to open new avenues of inquiry around school-age refugees and their academic writing development. Drawing on qualitative data from a 15-month study of adolescent L2 writers in U.S. schools, she asks: What is the impact of socio-political histories, and the literacy identities that emerge from those histories, on adolescent refugee writers in academic writing and English language arts (ELA) classrooms? She explores the conflicts and tensions that emerge when one student's complex history, his concerns about disclosure, and his academic identity do not fit squarely into the teacher's prevailing models for understanding native-English and L2 writers.

In "Adolescent Writers and Academic Trajectories: Situating L2 Writing in the Content Areas," Kerry Anne Enright explores mainstream classrooms that integrate L2 writers and native English speakers for subject-matter instruction. Specifically, she examines the writing practices and norms of these classrooms through the lens of two bilingual adolescents, Ofelia and Rosalinda, on different academic trajectories. She concludes with guiding questions to help mainstream subject-matter teachers design curriculum and instruction with particular attention to (a) the role of writing in content literacy and learning; (b) the role of students' English language development in their understanding and uses of academic writing; and (c) the role of writing in bilingual learners' academic trajectories within and beyond the subject-matter classroom.

In "'Doing Like Almost Everything Wrong': An Adolescent Multilingual Writer's Transition from High School to College," Amanda Kibler uses a longitudinal interactional histories approach to analyze texts written by Diego, a native

Spanish speaker who started high school as a beginning English language learner and later graduated with a competitive university scholarship, only to be placed in, and fail, remedial writing courses in his first year of college. She shows that opportunities for literacy development are created locally and institutionally through experiences, and that interactions with texts and other tools before drafting can have a decisive impact on how multilingual writers interact with their environment during writing tasks themselves.

Part II: Academic Issues

In "Preparing English Language Learners for Argumentative Writing," Alan Hirvela explores issues related to how L2 writers can be better prepared to engage in argumentative writing. He claims that, with the implementation of the *Common Core Standards* for English Language Arts and other content areas in the United States beginning in 2014, argumentation will play a major role in these new standards, so it will be even more important for L2 writers to know how to write argumentative essays.

In "The Role of Social Relationships in the Writing of Multilingual Adolescents," Jennifer Shade Wilson draws on an understanding of literacy as social practice to review published studies on adolescent literacy in order to explore the social relationships that appear to influence the writing activities, practices, and skills of multilingual high school students. She describes relationships according to the three ecosystems most germane to teenagers—home, school, and neighborhood—and discusses the specific influences of the reported relationships on students' writing.

In "Emerging Literacies in Digital Media and L2 Secondary Writing," Melissa Niiya, Mark Warschauer, and Binbin Zheng consider the role of digital media for L2 writing, in particular for adolescent L2 writers in the United States. They explore diverse ways that digital media are used in adolescent writing and how these uses affect L2 writers' writing processes and outcomes.

Part III: Teacher Education

In "Focus on Pre-service Preparation for ESL Writing Instruction: Secondary Teacher Perspectives," Ditlev Larsen reports on a study that surveyed secondary ESL teachers about the requirements of their teacher education programs in terms of ESL writing pedagogy. He found that less than 30 percent of the teachers were required to take an L2 writing theory and pedagogy course and that only about one in ten felt well prepared to teach ESL writing, reporting that their programs offered very little or no specific instruction with regard to the uniqueness of L2 composition, providing appropriate and effective feedback, responding to errors, and grading students' written work.

In "ESOL Teachers as Writing Teachers: From the Voices of High School Pre-Service Teachers," Youngjoo Yi reports findings from qualitative research that examined English to Speakers of Other Languages (ESOL) teachers' sense of preparedness to teach writing, their challenges for writing pedagogy, and their negotiation of writing teacher identity. Her findings reveal that though pre-service ESOL teachers successfully designed and implemented some writing tasks into lessons, they used writing extensively for assessment purposes. She concludes that, despite their ESOL teacher identity construction, they were not able to afford to pursue their *writing teacher* identity.

In "Responsive Teacher Inquiry for Learning about Adolescent English Learners as Developing Writers," Steven Z. Athanases, Lisa H. Bennett, and Juliet Michelsen Wahleithner show how teacher inquiry provides a means to reflect on L2 writers' needs, plan action, and collect and analyze data to uncover patterns and rethink pedagogy. They report L2 writing issues that pre-service teachers in one teacher education program explored through inquiry, including balancing voice with the demands of testing, deconstructing linguistic complexity of writing prompts, and learning how grammar and punctuation fit within writing process and pedagogy. They illustrate how inquiry promoted movement from initial problem-framing to discoveries about teaching writing to adolescent L2 writers.

In "Understanding how Pre-service Teachers Develop a Working Knowledge of L2 Writing: Toward a Socioculturally Oriented Postmethod Pedagogy," Lisya Seloni explores four pre-service teachers' evolving disciplinary knowledge about teaching L2 literacy in K–12. Drawing on sociocultural and postmethod approaches to teacher education, she conceptualizes the teaching of writing as an experiential and transformative educational issue that emerges from linguistic diversity and critical language awareness. She concludes with some curricular recommendations for including more components of L2 writing theory in teaching English to speakers of other languages (TESOL) courses across all levels of postsecondary education.

These chapters provide an important contribution to the fields of L2 writing and education. Over the past 35 years, the amount of scholarly work on L2 writing has increased dramatically. However, very little work has focused on L2 writing in secondary classrooms. We hope this book will lead to other projects designed to draw attention to work in L2 writing in K–12.

References

de Oliveira, L. C. (2011). *Knowing and writing school history: The language of students' expository writing and teachers' expectations*. Charlotte, NC: Information Age.

Harklau, L., & Pinnow, R. (2009). Adolescent second-language writing. In L. Christenbury, R. Bomer, & P. Smagorinsky (Eds.), *Handbook of adolescent literacy research* (pp. 126–137). New York: Guilford Press.

Hirvela, A., & Belcher, D. (2007). Writing scholars as teacher educators: Exploring writing teacher education. *Journal of Second Language Writing, 16*(3), 125–128.

Kibler, A. (2010). Writing through two languages: First language expertise in a language minority classroom. *Journal of Second Language Writing, 19*(3), 121–142.

Leki, I., Cumming, A., & Silva, T. (2008). *A synthesis of research on L2 writing in English.* Mahwah, NJ: Erlbaum.

National Clearinghouse for English Language Acquisition. (2006). *The growing numbers of limited English proficient students: 1993/94–2003/4.* Washington, DC: U.S. Department of Education, Office of English Language Acquisition.

Ortmeier-Hooper, C., & Enright, K. A. (2011). Mapping new territory: Toward an understanding of adolescent L2 writers and writing in U.S. contexts. *Journal of Second Language Writing, 20*(3), 167–181.

Yi, Y. (2010). Adolescent multilingual writers' transitions across in- and out-of-school writing contexts. *Journal of Second Language Writing, 19*(1), 17–32.

PART I
Student Experiences: Case Studies

2

"SHE DOESN'T KNOW WHO I AM"

The Case of a Refugee L2 Writer in a High School English Language Arts Classroom

Christina Ortmeier-Hooper

> A refugee is someone who owing to a well-founded fear of being persecuted for reasons of race, religion, nationality, membership of a particular social group or political opinion, is outside the country of his nationality, and is unable to, or owing to such fear, is unwilling to avail himself of the protection of that country.
>
> *(United Nations High Commission for Refugees (UNHCR), 1951, p. 16)*

In recent years, the number of refugees relocating to other nations has been on the rise, and approximately half of all worldwide refugees are children and adolescents (UNHCR, 2010). In 2006, approximately 47 percent of the refugees admitted into the U.S. were of school age (International Rescue Committee, 2006). Research on refugee youth completed in disciplines like education, sociology, counseling, and international policy has studied the transition of refugees into schools, the emotional needs of refugees, and the relationships between adult refugees and their children (Kiche, 2010; Hattam & Every, 2010; Sirriyeh, 2010; Hurley, Medici, Stewart, & Cohen, 2011; Morrice, 2009; Perry & Moses, 2011; Roxas, 2011; Weekes, Phelan, Macfarlane, Pinson, & Francis, 2011; Taylor & Sidhu, 2012). These studies serve to inform teachers, community service providers, and social workers about the specific needs of these families as they negotiate the challenges of living in a new country, settling into new jobs/schools, learning a language, and often coping with some levels of post-traumatic stress. Internationally, literacy research conducted in Canada and Australia has examined the educational needs of low-literate refugees in local schools (Kanu, 2008; Dooley & Thangaperumal, 2011).

However, the experiences of young refugees as writers are noticeably absent from these conversations. To some extent, that is because research on adolescent

L2 writers has historically been underrepresented within the field of second language writing (Leki, Cumming, & Silva, 2008; Matsuda & De Pew, 2002; Ortmeier-Hooper & Enright, 2011). But as this collection indicates, research on second language writers in K–12 continues to grow in depth and scope. That growing interest creates new opportunities for scholars and teachers to consider the needs and complexities of young refugee writers.

To begin to understand these complexities, we must first acknowledge that young refugees are different from other immigrant and second language adolescents. In education, for example, scholars note that refugee students and their families encounter school quite differently from other multilingual and immigrant populations. Ruiz-de-Velasco and Fix (2000) noted that refugees, in contrast to voluntary migrants and immigrants, "often arrive with few possessions or financial resources and without a network of relatives in this country who might help them to understand the American education system" (p. 35). Suarez-Orozco (1989) found similar differences in a comparative study of Cuban exiles and refugee youth from war-torn Central America. The refugee students had dealt with far more cultural upheaval and disconnection than their Cuban counterparts, and that level of disconnection was often more difficult to overcome.

We know that adolescent L2 writers are negotiating complex identity issues, while at the same time developing their academic writing abilities in a second language (Ortmeier-Hooper, 2010; Ortmeier-Hooper & Enright, 2011; Yi, 2010). Refugee research studies, like those by Ruiz-de-Velasco and Fix and by Suarez-Orozco, suggest that the sociopolitical histories of refugee students play a significant role in the ways that these students interact and the identities that they are able to forge for themselves in school. Therefore, it would seem that the identity negotiations of these youth and the ways that young refugees bring their pasts to the writing classroom may be especially complex. The goal of this chapter is to open discussion on adolescent refugee writers by exploring that complexity. Specifically, I ask: What kinds of sociopolitical histories and literacy identities can emerge from an adolescent refugee's past? And how is a refugee writer's literacy development impacted when his identities are misread by his writing teacher in the mainstream English language arts (ELA) classroom?

In this chapter, I share the case study of Wisdom,[1] a 14-year-old refugee from Nigeria, who identifies his first language as Gokana and his second language as English. I begin with a discussion of the theoretical framework informing my analysis, followed by a brief discussion of my methodology. I report on my findings, beginning with a look at how Wisdom's academic identity was forged by his refugee experiences. Then I take a closer look at the emergence of cultural dissonance between Wisdom and his writing teacher in the classroom. These experiences of dissonance between the young refugee and his teacher impeded his development as a writer. In particular, Wisdom's identity, forged in his refugee experiences, was tested by his writing teacher's misperceptions and his desire to no longer be identified as ESL. That tension created what I term his "paradox of disclosure," in which he was torn between maintaining a level of privacy and informing his teacher about his sociopolitical past.

Theoretical Framework

Research on academic writing continues to reveal a prominent intersection between writing and identity construction (Ivanič, 1998; Cox, Jordan, Ortmeier-Hooper, & Gray Schwartz, 2010). These intersections often emerge on the written page, but they are also evident in the ways students cast themselves in the writing classroom, their interactions with writing teachers, and in their approaches to their writing processes. In second language writing, the connections between identity and writerly tasks are further complicated by the writer venturing into a target language community that may or may not be receptive to his/her language needs (Norton, 2000). Teachers often represent the target community of language learners, and their perceptions of L2 writers can play a role in students' motivation and investment in their writing development. Chiang and Schmida (1999) and Harklau (2000) are two earlier studies that considered multilingual writers' identities within the framework of teacher perceptions. They noted how teachers' perceptions of students' linguistic abilities and educational aspirations impacted L2 student writers, their approaches to classroom writing, and their overall academic achievement. For example, Chiang and Schmida's study of minority student writers illustrated their complex cultural and linguistic histories. But the authors also found that teachers' sometimes singular ideological definitions for L2 writers made it difficult, if not impossible, for them to see moments when their interactions with students challenged these histories and poorly impacted experiences in the writing classroom. The teacher's role in the development of younger L2 students' writing practices has also been discussed by Blanton (2002, 2005) who argued the critical importance of the teacher–student relationship as a lens for understanding how younger students develop their literacy skills in a second language setting.

In this study, I draw on the frames and terms that emerged from these earlier studies to consider how a young refugee's sense of his own identity as a writer and a student is shaped, in part, by his socio-political past. I consider the consequences that occur when that refugee's student identity is at odds with his teacher's conception of him. Here, I observe how the lack of teacher-student relationship, due in part to the cultural dissonance between Wisdom's sociopolitical identity and her teacher's perceptions of him, led to literacy development "shut-downs" in the writing classroom for him.

The Study

This case study is part of a larger 15-month qualitative study of adolescent L2 writers in U.S. high schools. Wisdom, whom I describe in more detail shortly, was the only refugee student in that larger study, and at the time of the project he was a first-year student at Mill River North High School. Mill River, a mid-size city in the Northeast, had a population of roughly 300,000. There were two high schools in the district, and over 40 languages were spoken by students in the district. Approximately 25 percent of Mill River North students were classified as English language learners (ELL), and many of these were refugee students. There was a large ELL program, but Wisdom had been exited from all ELL services two years earlier due to his English proficiency advancements. The writing classroom that forms the backdrop for this chapter comprised approximately 22 students with about five second language students. Mrs. Jennens had been an English language arts teacher in the district for close to 15 years. She was well respected by her colleagues, and she was a popular advisor to the student yearbook. I initially met Wisdom, a male Nigerian student, through a summer school program, where I worked as consultant.

Over 15 months, I collected data from multiple sources, including field observations (in the ELA classroom, in the public library, and in a summer bridge program), field notes, interviews and transcripts, informal interviews with his peers, and writing samples. Over the course of the study, I met with Wisdom for bimonthly hour-long interviews during the first six months and then monthly for the remaining nine months of the study. I conducted six observations of Wisdom in his ELA classroom, met with his ELA teacher, and collected his writing assignments and progress reports. Data for this chapter were analyzed and triangulated with a particular focus on Wisdom's self-identity and his interactions with his ELA teacher. Specifically, I coded the data for instances of identity assertions, cultural dissonance, and writing "shutdown" or disengagement. Although the initial purpose of the broader study was to examine the student's writing experiences in terms of the actual texts and instruction they produced and received, Wisdom's experiences with his teacher propelled me to become more interested in how his self-identity as a political refugee created certain expectations for himself that began to clash with his teacher's perceptions. In this sense, the focus and question guiding this paper were not pre-determined but these themes emerged as the research continued.

Wisdom

Literacy Background

Wisdom arrived in Mill River at the age of nine, a political refugee from Nigeria. He was the youngest of eleven children, but he had come to the U.S. with only an older sister and brother, both of whom were in their thirties and married. Wisdom's schooling in Nigeria had begun at a young age with preschool and kindergarten programs. Though the schools were considered public, it was difficult for many families to send their children because there were many additional expenses—textbooks, uniforms, exams, paper. In his village, many families were unable to send their children to school due to these costs, and many children who started were unable to finish their schooling due to the financial constraints. Wisdom noted that these inequities in educational opportunities were fueled by government officials who, in his opinion, cared little for the schools and the next generation. In Wisdom's family, the difficulty of making those financial payments to school meant that most of his siblings did not finish their education, though his parents strove to send their children to as many years of schooling as possible.

When I met Wisdom, we both wondered about his participation in this study; he wasn't sure if he met the profile of a typical "English language learner," because English was the national language of his country. But as in many English-speaking countries in Africa, over 50 languages are spoken through Nigeria's various cities and villages. Wisdom's home village had four languages aside from English. For his part, Wisdom identified Gokana as his first language, the one he used with his family. Although he studied some English during his preschool and early elementary school years, he reported that they spoke a mix of English and Gokana in his Nigerian classroom. He could read in Gokana, but he could barely write. When he was six years old, his literacy education in both languages was interrupted by a political conflict in his village. For three years, he lived in a refugee camp in Benin with little to no education. Wisdom described the school at the refugee camp as a covered tent. His sense was that schooling times at the camp were put together to keep the refugee children busy, but there were limited resources to provide good instruction in any language.

Upon his arrival in Mill River, Wisdom was ten years old, and he was placed in a fifth-grade magnet ELL elementary class, where all his instruction was delivered by ELL teachers. By the end of fifth grade, he would prove to be a tenacious learner. When he was promoted to middle school, he exited the magnet program and received services one period a day from a pull-out ELL teacher. By eighth grade, Wisdom had exited all ELL services. He took only mainstream classes and saw his ELL teacher on rare occasions. His eighth-grade progress reports and portfolio comments showed that his mainstream teachers were clearly impressed with his work ethic, his creativity, his intelligence, and his writing abilities.

Wisdom's Sociopolitical History

For the purposes of this chapter, it is important to understand the circumstances that drove Wisdom to the refugee camp in Benin, and eventually to Mill River, particularly because those refugee circumstances are so intrinsically caught up in his identity in school and as a writer. Wisdom's self-identity begins with the story of his father. In Nigeria, Wisdom's father had been a village leader, and a small business owner. As Wisdom described him, he was a man who greatly valued his children and education. His father was a village leader, working with other activists, who led an uprising against the Nigerian government in the 1990s. According to Wisdom, the uprising had been a matter of practical economics, a David-and-Goliath story of a wealthy, corrupt government attempting to take over the oil-rich province that Wisdom's family called home. Wisdom recalled the story of the uprising as one in which the government had tried to take the oil from the village without any compensation for the people. As he explained,

> Basically what we wanted them to do was just to pave the road and just make it to have a better place to live, more organized, and more developed. [pause] They just wanted to take the oil. We weren't pleased with that, so we said no.

> *(qtd. in Ortmeier-Hooper, 2013)*

A bloody civil uprising ensued. The conflict, though it lasted only about six weeks, had dire consequences for Wisdom and his family. During the fighting, Wisdom, his mother, and some of his siblings escaped to the woods. His father was a leader in the village and stayed behind to defend their homes. Because of his leadership role in the community, Wisdom's father was in the most danger, a target of the officials. His father, along with the other leaders, was detained by the officials, and eventually put to death for his involvement in the uprising. As Wisdom quietly explained, "They killed him. They hung him" (Personal communication, August 2004).

Wisdom explained that he was eventually rescued from the woods by an older brother, who smuggled him and two other older siblings out of the village and across the border to a refugee camp in Benin. They had to leave his mother and other siblings behind. They remain in Nigeria, and Wisdom doubted that he would ever see his mother again. As Wisdom told the story of his past to me, he was brief and there was a tone of resignation in his voice. There was a kind of shorthand in the tale itself; he had told this story many times.

Despite his guardedness, he was deeply proud of his heritage, his family, and the rich history and traditions of Nigeria. They shaped who he was and how he saw himself.

Findings and Discussion

Intertwining Threads: Sociopolitical Identity, Academic Aspirations, and a Writer's Identity

Norton (2000) has long noted the important role of identity in acquiring a second language. As she argued, "the role of language [is both] *constitutive of* and *constituted by* a language learner's identity" (Norton, p. 5, my emphasis). The two, language and identity, are inextricably linked. Sociocultural, ethnic, and cultural theories of identity have been based on the assumption that identities are socially constructed by outside forces and then rejected or accepted by the individual. Learning a new language is indicative of this kind of dynamic; such perspectives ask: How do learners approach the target language? What circumstances and motivations are driving them to learn the language? What is the level of support in learning that language? Here, I'll provide a rich description of Wisdom's language and sociopolitical identity, in tandem with what I call his *writerly identity*, in order to contextualize the intertwining and multiplicity of Wisdom's sense of self in the writing classroom.

Wisdom felt a sense of ownership when it came to English, even though he readily admitted that Gokana was his first language, the one that dominated his literacy when he first arrived in the United States. He noted that his homeland's variety of English, sometimes called Nigerian English, sounded somewhat different from the American English he learned in the United States. Wisdom never questioned his need for English-as-second-language instruction and support when he came to the U.S. But he was uncomfortable with the label of *English language learner* which seemed to negate his stake in a language that he saw as part of his homeland. In fact, his Nigerian identity, one so grounded in his family's sacrifices, was deeply ingrained in how he viewed his English learning and his education.

Wisdom's sociopolitical past shaped not only his literacy development, but also his academic drive. He was profoundly concerned with doing well in school and determined to go to college. He put tremendous amounts of pressure on himself, reviewing his report cards and meticulously scrutinizing his teachers' comments. Although his older siblings did not track his test scores or grade report, he felt a level of expectation placed on him by his family, and perhaps even more accurately, an expectation placed on him by his family's losses. As he explained,

> They push me. They put so much pressure on me that it kills me sometimes. [. . .] It works like this. When I have homework, they don't tell me: "do your homework, do your homework." I know I have to do it. [. . .] I know that this is my opportunity, and if I screw it up it will be worse for me. [. . .] I just know it is something that I have to do for my future. [. . .] There is a lot of pressure because they want me to get a better education, especially my mom would be very happy when I finish college and everything. She just wants me to be educated.
>
> *(Personal communication, August 2004)*

This sense of personal responsibility and duty reverberated in his discussions on writing, homework, and his overall academic influences. This sentiment, for example, emerged in other interviews when we discussed how Wisdom identified himself:

C: When you say "Who I am"—what do you mean by that?

W: What I mean by that is that school is very important to me. And I have a lot of pressure on myself. I put a lot of pressure on myself to do good in school. It is one of the things I have to pursue to make sure I do good. I take it [school] very seriously. That it is what I have to do.

(Personal communication, October 2004)

Kiche (2010) had similar findings in her study of older Sudanese refugee adolescents. She found that the refugee students took on roles of recognition for their academic achievements, modeling for younger members of the Sudanese community. As the students in her study graduated from high school, they were openly recognized and praised by community leaders. In recognition of their new achievements, community members brought them presents and praised them for a job well done. This recognition was significant to the young refugee students (p. 80). In Wisdom's case, his role as the youngest member of the family and the only with an opportunity to succeed in the U.S. school system made him a role model, even at the young age of fifteen. He understood and embraced that responsibility.

Wisdom connected this sense of responsibility (political and educational) to his work as a writer. When asked which authors he admired, he immediately identified his writing mentors as Martin Luther King, Jr. and Mahatma Gandhi, noting how they used writing and speeches to create change in their communities. He had read King's "I Have a Dream" speech and excerpts from "The Letter from Birmingham Jail," as well as biographies of the two figures. Their combined use of activism and the written word encouraged Wisdom's own sense of his "writerly" identity. In interviews, he often started sentences with "As a writer, I feel. . . ." In one interview, he commented, "As a writer, you have to express how you feel." He continued,

I write to satisfy myself first. I have to like what I am writing to make it sound entertaining for the person who is going to read it. So I have to put myself in the job that I am doing is good enough for the person who is going to read it. To appreciate it or like it.

(Personal communication, September 2004)

This sense of "writerly" identity also came through as he talked about his process, articulating how he spent ten minutes before writing trying to visualize his goals and his audience. As Wisdom explained,

I think about it [the writing task]. And where is it going to take place and how is it going to take place. How I am going to set it up before I write. I can see what I am writing before I write it.

(Personal communication, October 2004)

He noted that when he wrote for his teachers, his goal was to get good grades, but he also tried to write to interest his teachers as readers. He went on to explain,

"And I do it by putting in hard work and working to improve my writing" (Personal communication, October 2004).

I bring these threads of writer-identity and sociopolitical identity together here because, for Wisdom, they were intensely interwoven. In his free time, he wrote lyrics for songs that questioned political happenings and called for social justice in the U.S. and in Africa. His notebook showcased his knowledge of the Bible and his own testimonials that mimicked the language of sermons. When his sociopolitical identity and academic dedication were called into question by his teacher, the dissonance that occurred between his teacher and his sociopolitical identity caused Wisdom's sense of language identity, "writerly" identity, and literacy development to plummet as well.

A Building Sense of Dissonance

> "The weeks have been going kinda rough but we will survive. It's high school. lol."
>
> *Wisdom (Email correspondence)*

Norton (2000) in her discussion on identity, motivation, and second language acquisition asked us to consider, *How are the learners received (and judged) by the target language-speaking population?* Here, I want to consider this question when the target population is the mainstream English language arts teacher, primarily responsible for a student's literacy and writing development. Blanton (2002) has argued that the writing performance of second language writers is impacted by their relationships with their teachers. In her study of younger children, Blanton found that the "affective-intellectual 'space' between teacher and child" was a critical element in a student's literacy development. Blanton noted the importance of what she termed *synchronicity*, the dynamic created by teacher and child with each other as the place where there were optimal conditions for development and learning (pp. 304–305). In later work, Blanton (2005) added that "the bottom line is this: relationships are fiercely fundamental to all learning, but serve, more specifically, as the critical lynchpin of rapid and successful literacy development" (p. 112).

I contend that the reverse of Blanton's argument is also true. When the synchronicity between teacher and students does not exist, it is possible for a dissonance to emerge and disrupt an L2 writer's development. In the case of Wisdom, this disruption occurred with his English writing teacher who failed to acknowledge and understand Wisdom's sociopolitical past and its impact on his identity and academic goals.

In early September, Wisdom began the semester with Mrs. Jennens optimistically, saying that she was "a nice teacher," "funny," and "knew how to do her job." Wisdom entered Mrs. Jennens' classroom with no label of "ELL" attached to his name. He didn't have an ELL teacher assigned to him anymore, and as he explained, in the mainstream class, no one asked him about his language background. Wisdom noted, "The reason I want to be in mainstream classes is because I see more of a challenge in front of me. It makes me a better student" (Personal communication, September 2004).

But in late October, that initial enthusiasm for his English teacher and the class began to wane. From Wisdom's perspective, it began when he never received any feedback on his writing. Papers were often not returned; sometimes he only got error corrections, but no comments on the actual strengths or content of his written work. Then there were two moments when, according to Wisdom, Mrs. Jennens misheard his use of common words and phrases and mistook his pronunciation for inappropriate language, publicly dishonoring him in front of the class. Then she moved his seat to the back of the class. The rising dissonance between teacher and student soon began to reach deeper into Wisdom's sense of his own identity. Wisdom noted that she seemed to think he didn't take school seriously. As he said, "What she thought of me was that I was a wise guy. Someone . . . like some of the punks. She just doesn't know who I am" (Personal communication, November 2004).

In my conversations with his teacher, she confirmed that she questioned his attitude. She noted that she thought it might stem from his perceptions on women, though in my own dealings with Wisdom I never found that to be the case. Neither had his earlier teachers. In fact, his report card for the same semester revealed that his other teachers found him to be a model student. Mrs. Jennens, however, felt that he was disgruntled because he didn't understand the social dynamics of high school. For example, when Wisdom questioned the lack of respect shown by upperclassmen to younger students, he openly called it unjust. She speculated that his stance was not making him popular socially and that was one reason for the tension in the classroom.

To be fair, Mrs. Jennens was a well-regarded teacher. She had attended training sessions on ELL students in the past, and she had gone to a district-wide workshop on refugee and immigrant children the summer before. But Mrs. Jennens didn't seem to connect those training sessions to Wisdom. In our early discussions about Wisdom, she never commented on his second language or noted any linguistic and/or cultural differences. Wisdom, perhaps since he was not identified as a student in the ELL program, perhaps because he seemed acclimatized to the dominant American culture, or perhaps because his English language was well developed, did not seem to fit the profiles that she encountered in the workshop training.

For Wisdom, this sense of his teacher's depiction of him as a "punk" was made clear in his November progress report. Next to his grade, a C, she included the comment: "Needs more self-discipline." Wisdom was horrified by the comment. First, the comment called into question his integrity and his commitment to his education. Second, it was public. The report card was sent home to his family, and in the classroom his peers readily shared progress notes with one another. Wisdom felt that the teacher had not only misread his intentions as a student, but she had publicly shamed him. Wisdom saw her comment as the ultimate betrayal.

That betrayal would impact his development and engagement as a student writer. What was emerging was what Ybarra (2001) has described as a cultural dissonance between student writers and writing teachers. In his study of Latino writers in a basic college writing class, Ybarra noted the disconnections that emerged between the cultural experiences of the students and their writing teachers in college basic writing classrooms. These disconnections led to fear and often suspicion on the part of the Latino students (Ybarra, 2001, p. 38). Here, borrowing from Ybarra's work, I would argue that the building dissonance between Wisdom and his teacher was also culturally informed, though his teacher was largely unaware of that. Mrs. Jennens, like the writing teachers in Ybarra's study, did not understand her student's refugee past or the sociopolitical identities and aspirations that emerged from those defining experiences. The framework that she might need to understand his past was not in place. Similar to Ybarra's findings, the complete cultural disconnect and dissonance between the teacher and the student's frame of reference led to (often self-induced) disruptions in Wisdom's writing development.

Dissonance and a Writer's Engagement

Over five months, the dissonance between Wisdom and his writing teacher festered and impacted his work in the classroom and as a writer. This dissonance impacted his work in the classroom, particularly his writing. In the classroom, Wisdom tried to be quiet, but he was also clearly trying to disengage. In my earlier observations, his body posture was leaned over his desk, pen ready, and often raising his hand. But as the dissonance unfolded, his eagerness dissipated. At one of our meetings in November, Wisdom took his ELA reading assignment and remarked that he wanted to throw it in the trash: "No point in having it around. Not my problem" (Personal communication, November 2004).

In December, Wisdom explained, "I definitely don't want to be in that class, because of the way she treats me. [. . .] She just doesn't seem to care at all." In his words, Wisdom explained that he stopped "putting his heart" in his writing. Wisdom's response to the dissonance between him and his writing teacher was to "shut down" when it came to his writing. Indeed, in one meeting with me, he rebelliously ripped up a draft of an essay, saying, "She doesn't care anyway. It doesn't even bother her. If she cares or not, I think I should be doing it for myself." And yet a few moments later, he admitted, "I don't feel like doing the work, but I need to raise myself to a good grade" (Personal communication, December 2004). His fear of getting poor grades made this a difficult dance of rebellion for him. But it was still difficult for him to invest in his writing the way he wanted to, the way he felt he should.

Wisdom's response to these tensions mirrors the assertions of Blanton. As Blanton (2002) noted, "it isn't that children can't develop literacy without this boost [this synchronicity between teacher and student], they just don't develop it as smoothly, quickly, or 'naturally'" (p. 305). He was acutely offended by how his teacher had positioned him as a "punk," a depiction that violated his own self-identity as a writer, a determined student, and a concerned community leader, and the result was a stop-motion in terms of his writing development. He disengaged. He didn't stop going to class and he wasn't openly disruptive, but he shut himself down. His motivation and investment in developing his writing skills, which he had valued, fell dramatically.

The Paradox of Disclosure

> I think my language arts teacher treats me differently. She kinda of imposes everything on me. It makes me feel that like she is doing it because of what she sees on the outside, not what's going on the inside.
>
> *Wisdom (Focus group interview, October 2004)*

One of the difficulties for Wisdom in this predicament was that he was unsure how to disclose his pasts and his sense of identity to Mrs. Jennens. I should note that neither Mrs. Jennens, who was Caucasian, nor Wisdom saw race or racism as the primary issue here. Wisdom, for his part, thought it was more about Mrs. Jennens' lack of understanding when it came to his past, or the past of other refugees, and how that fueled the motivations of such students in school. Those were the things that Wisdom thought she couldn't see from the outside, as noted in the quote above. But Wisdom, for his part, never disclosed his refugee past in any form to Mrs. Jennens. He never shared his background as a speaker of Gokana or English as a second language. His language history was not discussed. Indeed, he never disclosed *any aspect* of his sociopolitical past to her.

But Wisdom questioned his decision not to reveal his pasts to her; in light of the ongoing conflict, he wondered about the academic consequences of that decision. In the classroom, he found himself misjudged and misunderstood. Outside the classroom, he noticed that his own disengagement was compounding the situation, but emotionally he couldn't always control the impulse just to give up. After a few months, Wisdom surmised that something had to be done, but he was conflicted about the steps he needed to take. In short, he felt that his teacher needed to know more about him, but at the same time, he was torn about disclosing his identity and his refugee past to her. He was reluctant to share his own story and his motivations for education with his teacher. He declared that his story was "private," adding "I'm kinda sick of it." He explained, "I get tired of it. I don't want to run away from my history, but I get bored writing the same thing over and over again. You know what I mean?" (Personal communication, December 2004).

Ironically, though, despite Wisdom's desire to keep his refugee past private, he was also frustrated that his English writing teacher never extended the invitation for him to write about any part of his personal life. For him, it was a missing component in her teaching of writing. From an interview:

C: Do you think if she'd ask you to write those things and read the things you wrote, you would have had a better relationship in class, among other things?
W: (nods) That shows who we are. That would make it easier for her to approach us.

(Personal communication, January 2005)

For Wisdom, the lack of such an assignment meant that Mrs. Jennens wasn't invested in him as a student writer or as a person. That sense of disengagement and anonymity was compounded by her lack of response to written essays. In Wisdom's mind, the two pieces were factors that made him feel as if he was invisible to her. Still, in our discussions, Wisdom seemed to waver between wanting to share his past and not wanting to. At one point, I asked Wisdom if he would have written about his sociopolitical history if she had assigned a personal narrative to the class. I share this exchange at length due to its relevance:

W: No, I don't think I would have shared it with her.
C: On one hand, you say "I don't want to write about this anymore."
W: Exactly.
C: But on the other hand, you want the teacher to know who you are. Maybe not everything . . . But you want to know about your cultural values and expectations. For schools, etc.
W: She can know about that one. But then if we talked about that, then that one, the other one, might creep in and then we can talk about the other stuff. If it creeps in then, it is okay to talk to about. But not just to jump in on that topic and share. (pauses)
W: The thing is that in order for me to talk to her about things like that, there has to be a relationship there. We ourselves have to build a relationship and talk about things like that. You can't just see a stranger and say, "oh, my family's going through this and that." You have to have something there.
C: And because you were having these problems with her, did you feel like there was no invitation to talk about these things?
W: No, I didn't feel like babbling things out. And she could figure it out. She could understand that kind of background I come from.

(Personal communication, January 2005)

What Wisdom suggested here was that he needed an invitation of sorts from his writing teacher in order for him to begin to disclose his refugee past and its importance in shaping his identity in the classroom. But the teacher never provided him with an opening to share those aspects of his identity with her. There was no relationship there. In his eyes, she was not interested in trying to learn about him.

On one occasion, he tried to create that opening himself. In a journal entry for the class, Wisdom chose to answer the prompt: *Where do you see yourself in 20 years?* In describing his response, Wisdom explained that he wove in pieces of his socio-political past, hinting at his academic aspirations and his need to give back to his community:

> I wrote about where I see my life to be like. Like being at a hospital with patients. Go to college first and then get my degrees as a doctor. And then if that doesn't happen. Then I'll be playing professional soccer. [. . .] And making millions of dollars actually. And distributing it to people that need it.
>
> *(Personal communication, October 2004)*

It was the one time when Wisdom attempted to share a glimpse of his sense of self with his teacher. But the conversation that Wisdom tried to initiate with his writing was one-sided. Mrs. Jennens never responded. One could argue that it would be challenging for any teacher to read the layers of his journal entry without understanding the larger context of his past, but her lack of response to his written text reinforced Wisdom's sense that she didn't care.

In January, when Wisdom came to the conclusion that this conflict couldn't continue, that it was hurting him more than his teacher, he surmised that he needed to do something in order to help Mrs. Jennens better understand who he was. But he was conflicted about the steps he felt he needed to take. Wisdom decided that testimonials by others might be his best choice. Ironically, and somewhat inconsistent to his desire to remain "non-ELL" in the eyes of his mainstream teachers, Wisdom called upon his middle-school ELL teacher to advocate on his behalf at the high school. His former seventh-grade ELL teacher knew him "almost like a mother knows her kid," he explained. She knew his past, and he wanted her to talk to Mrs. Jennens and his guidance counselor about his cultural background. As Wisdom noted, "she knows me. She knows I want to make a change with what I have. Or do the best with what I have in front of me. She knows that" (Personal communication, November 2004). So, his former ELL teacher came to a special school meeting with Mrs. Jennens and a guidance counselor to discuss Wisdom's issues with them. He didn't like the idea of being associated with an ELL program again. But he felt he had no choice.

Conclusion

Wisdom's story suggests that we need to consider more closely how young refugees have been shaped emotionally, and even academically, by their socio-political pasts. We must consider how their experiences can constrain or motivate certain responses and values in the writing classroom. For some students, the impact of their refugee experiences in the classroom and in their development as writers may not be fully visible at the surface, and students may be reluctant to reveal more. That paradox of disclosure may also hold true for other immigrant and multilingual writers, but Wisdom's case suggests that it may be heightened for refugee children with difficult histories. Adolescent refugee writers find themselves caught between their pasts and their futures, and because of their youth, they may be unsure how to articulate their past histories without opening old wounds. They may wish to leave those histories behind them. They may wonder about the appropriateness or politeness of such disclosures. Wisdom himself suggests that the development of trust and rapport between teacher and student is essential to negotiating this difficult terrain of disclosure. He also had concerns that talking about his past would cause teachers to expect less of him academically or define him as a perpetual English language learner, despite his English language experiences or abilities. How teachers receive, judge, and seek to understand the sociopolitical pasts and identities of young refugee writers can encourage or negate the synchronicity that Blanton suggests we need to establish with L2 writers in order to foster their literacy development.

Wisdom's efforts to have his former ELL teacher testify on his behalf did create a truce between him and Mrs. Jennens. Although he never fully embraced the course with enthusiasm again, he did manage to begin to reinvest in his efforts. For example, when Mrs. Jennens introduced a poetry unit at the end of the school year, Wisdom saw it as an opportunity to illustrate his love of writing lyrics and poetic verse. His engagement in this writing unit helped to ease some of the tensions, though he still didn't receive much feedback on his writing. For her part, Mrs. Jennens noted the detente as well. In subsequent discussions that spring, she talked vaguely about his language and family issues. She noted that though his written work received grades in the upper half of the class, his written "accent" was still noticeable and problematic. She began to use the term "ELL" in discussing his classroom work and writing. In some ways, she seemed to be recasting Wisdom into a more narrow definition of an ELL writer, one that fit the definitions that were part of the dominant discourse in the school and one that seemed to focus on his deficits rather than his strengths (Canagarajah, 2002). At the end of the year, Mrs. Jennens did not recommend him for the upper-academic track that he had hoped to access in his sophomore year. It is possible that Wisdom's attempts to reveal more of his literacy and sociopolitical histories to his teacher resulted in a diminished definition of his abilities, thereby limiting his opportunities for more advanced coursework.

The limitations of a case study project like this one are that the findings are not generalizable, but Wisdom's story does give us some insights into how traumatic sociopolitical pasts can shape a young refugee's identity and academic perceptions. It also suggests that further research needs to be conducted in order to illustrate other ways that the sociopolitical histories and trauma experienced by these individuals may influence their writing experiences and processes. In the U.S. and internationally, we still have a great deal to learn about how second language students, who are also refugees, engage with writing and academic literacy demands at various educational levels and institutions.

Wisdom's story reminds us as teachers that young L2 writers do not conveniently fit into a "one size fits all" definition. There is no monolithic definition that can be used as a "box" to understand the range of experiences, histories, and literacies that L2 writers bring into the writing classroom. Likewise, there is no single prescriptive instructional blueprint that can be used to respond to the range of experiences and sentiments that emerge in adolescent L2 writers' text and classroom responses. But Wisdom's experiences do suggest that writing teachers need to become more aware of the experiences that refugee adolescents may bring with them and the ways those experiences shape their sense of identity in the classroom. Working to know the adolescent L2 writers in a secondary class *as individuals* and providing invitations to them as writers to communicate and express themselves—creatively and personally, as well as academically—seems essential. Furthermore, given the paradox of disclosure, teachers may need to initiate their own research in order to fill in the gaps around a student's refugee experiences, either by speaking with local refugee advocates or researching online about the conditions in the countries that their students come from, their literacy histories, and the sociopolitical circumstances that may have driven them from their homelands. Learning more about the multifaceted experiences of refugee L2 writers might provoke scholars and teachers to think beyond the confines of some more narrow descriptions of English language learners and reposition themselves to consider how student writers' experiences, identities, and interactions in the English-dominant classroom may be shaped, not only by their linguistic backgrounds, but also by the sociopolitical and cultural realities of the world.

Note

1   The names of all individuals and schools discussed in this chapter are pseudonyms.

References

Blanton, L.L. (2002). Seeing the invisible: Situating L2 literacy acquisition in child–teacher interaction. *Journal of Second Language Writing*, *11*(4), 295–310.

Blanton, L.L. (2005). Student interrupted: A tale of two would-be writers. *Journal of Second Language Writing*, *14*(2), 105–121.

Canagarajah, A.S. (2002). *Critical academic writing and multilingual students*. Ann Arbor: University of Michigan Press.

Chiang, Y.-S., & Schmida, M. (1999). Language identity and language ownership: Linguistic conflicts of first-year university writing students. In L. Harklau, K. Losey, & M. Siegal (Eds.), *Generation 1.5 meets college composition* (pp. 81–96). Mahwah, NJ: Erlbaum.

Cox, M., Jordan, J., Ortmeier-Hooper, C., & Schwartz, G.G. (Eds.). (2010). *Reinventing identities in second language writing*. Urbana, IL: NCTE Press.

Dooley, K.T., & Thangaperumal, P. (2011). Pedagogy and participation: Literacy education for low-literate refugee students of African origin in a western school system. *Language and Education, 25*(5), 385–397.

Harklau, L. (2000). From the "good kids" to the "worst": Representations of English language learners across educational settings. *TESOL Quarterly, 34*, 35–67.

Hattam, R., & Every, D. (2010). Teaching in fractured classrooms: Refugee education, public culture, community and ethics. *Race, Ethnicity and Education, 13*(4), 409–424.

Hurley, J.J., Medici, A., Stewart, E., & Cohen, Z. (2011). Supporting preschoolers and their families who are recently resettled refugees. *Multicultural Perspectives, 13*(3), 160–166.

International Rescue Committee. (2006). *Refugee children and youth backgrounders.* Retrieved from http://www.rescue.org/sites/default/files/migrated/where/united_states_salt_lake_city_ut/refugee-backgrounders.pdf (last accessed November 6, 2012).

Ivanič, R. (1998). *Writing and identity: The discoursal construction of identity in academic writing.* Philadelphia, PA: John Benjamins.

Kanu, Y. (2008). Educational needs and barriers for African refugee students in Manitoba. *Canadian Journal of Education, 31*(4), 915–940.

Kiche, A. (2010). The educational and occupational aspirations of Sudanese refugee youth in an American public high school in the Midwest. Doctoral dissertation. Retrieved from http://ir.uiowa.edu/etd/527 (last accessed November 6, 2012).

Leki, I., Cumming, A., & Silva, T. (2008). *A synthesis of research on L2 writing in English.* Mahwah, NJ: Lawrence Erlbaum.

Matsuda, P.K., & De Pew, K.E. (2002). Early second language writing: An introduction. *Journal of Second Language Writing, 11*, 261–268.

Morrice, L. (2009). Journeys into higher education: The case of refugees in the UK. *Teaching in Higher Education, 14*(6), 661–672.

Norton, B. (2000). *Identity and language learning: Gender, ethnicity and educational change.* London: Longman.

Ortmeier-Hooper, C. (2010). The shifting nature of identity: Social identity, L2 writers, and high school. In M. Cox, J. Jordan, C. Ortmeier-Hooper, & G.G. Schwartz (Eds.), *Reinventing identities in second language writing* (pp. 5–28). Urbana, IL: NCTE Press.

Ortmeier-Hooper, C. (2013). *The ELL writer: Moving beyond basics in the secondary classroom.* New York: Teachers College Press.

Ortmeier-Hooper, C., & Enright, K.A. (2011). Mapping new territory: Toward an understanding of adolescent L2 writers and writing in U.S. contexts. *Journal of Second Language Writing, 20*(3), 167–181.

Perry, K.H., & Moses, A.M. (2011). Television, language, and literacy practices in Sudanese refugee families: "I learned how to spell English on Channel 18". *Research in the Teaching of English, 45*(3), 278–307.

Roxas, K. (2011). Tales from the front line: Teachers' responses to Somali Bantu refugee students. *Urban Education, 46*(3), 513–548.

Ruiz-de-Velasco, J., & Fix, M. (2000). Overworked and underserved: Immigrant students in U.S. secondary schools. Urban Institute. Retrieved from http://www.urban.org/publications/310022.html (last accessed November 6, 2012).

Sirriyeh, A. (2010). Home journeys: Im/mobilities in young refugee and asylum-seeking women's negotiations of home. *Childhood, 17*(2), 213–227.

Suarez-Orozco, M. (1989). *Central American refugees and U.S. high schools: A psychosocial study of motivation and achievement.* Stanford, CA: Stanford University Press.

Taylor, S., & Sidhu, R.K. (2012). Supporting refugee students in schools: What constitutes inclusive education? *International Journal of Inclusive Education, 16*(1), 39–56.

United Nations High Commission for Refugees (UNHCR). (1951). *Text of the 1951 Convention relating to the status of refugees.* Retrieved from http://www.unhcr.org/protect/PROTECTION/3b66c2aa10.pdf (last accessed November 6, 2012).

United Nations High Commission for Refugees (UNHCR). (2010). Global trends 2010 report. Retrieved from http://www.unhcr.org/4dfa11499.html (last accessed November 6, 2012).

Weekes, T., Phelan, L., Macfarlane, S., Pinson, J., & Francis, V. (2011). Supporting successful learning for refugee students: The classroom connect project. *Issues in Educational Research, 21*(3), 310–329.

Ybarra, R. (2001). Cultural dissonance in basic writing courses. *Journal of Basic Writing, 20*(1), 37–52.

Yi, Y. (2010). Adolescent multilingual writers' transitions across in- and out-of-school writing contexts. *Journal of Second Language Writing, 19*(1), 17–32.

3

ADOLESCENT WRITERS AND ACADEMIC TRAJECTORIES

Situating L2 Writing in the Content Areas

Kerry Anne Enright

As secondary subject-matter classrooms in the United States continue to grow in linguistic diversity, this "New Mainstream" (Enright, 2011) calls for increased attention by scholars and educators to the ways in which routine classroom practices impact the schooling experiences of bilingual and multilingual students of varying English proficiencies. While some secondary schools still educate language minority students in special ESL classes or content courses designed for their language development needs, a growing population of second language writers is being schooled in English-only classrooms designed for native speakers of English. Contemporary accountability policies encourage standardized curricula and prescribed academic outcomes for all students, often with no regard for different learning needs or language proficiency issues (Enright & Gilliland, 2011). While states with a long history of immigration and language diversity have attempted to address these classroom needs by infusing teacher education and professional development programs with special teaching approaches and strategies for educating English learners, writing instruction—particularly content area writing—is one of the least addressed areas in the preparation of new teachers. Content area writing pedagogies with consideration for the needs of second language writers are almost absent from the preparation of teachers (Harklau & Pinnow, 2009).

This chapter focuses on two adolescent L2 writers, one in honors classes and one in general classes, to highlight how differences in context impacted their experiences of writing, their learning of specific content-based uses of writing, and their access to advanced uses of academic literacy across the curriculum. Ofelia's case illustrates many of the opportunities and challenges experienced by L2 learners in high school honors classes. Rosalinda's program of study was more typical of general track classes for students of average academic ability. Her case represents the experiences of many L2 writers in linguistically diverse "New Mainstream" classrooms that integrate bilingual learners with native English speaking peers.

Comprehensive high schools are incredibly complex sites for the study of L2 writing. First, they serve a much broader range of L2 writers than the select populations who ultimately enter college. Also, tracking mechanisms, account- ability policies, and curricular constraints impose a number of contextual factors that can result in vastly different schooling experiences for different L2 writers attending the same school. Many schools, such as the one described in this chapter, integrate L2 writers into mainstream classrooms with native English speakers for subject-matter instruction. The consequences of these classrooms as sites for learning academic literacy in general, and second language writing specifically, are underexplored (Enright & Gilliland, 2011; Harklau, 2011; Ortmeier-Hooper & Enright, 2011). One purpose of this chapter is to illustrate some of these complex contextual factors and their consequences for L2 writers by examining writing practices and norms through the cases of two students on different academic trajectories within the same school and program. Since both students were ninth graders in the same learning community, comparing their experiences can also contribute to a more general understanding of how L2 writing mediated learning across the curriculum for English learners in this linguistically diverse high school.

Theoretical Framework

Recent scholarship has begun to explore the relationships between current accountability policies and various aspects of teaching and learning in linguistically diverse "mainstream" subject-matter classrooms (for examples, see Enright & Gilliland, 2011; Kibler, 2011; Villalva, 2006). While many programs and practices that serve English learners have evolved in the past 15 to 20 years, the dilemmas that they attempted to remedy are still pervasive in secondary school classrooms. The "achievement gap" in standardized test scores, graduation rates, and college attendance between native English speakers and L2 learners of English— particularly from socioeconomically poor backgrounds—is an ongoing challenge. Likewise, the long-standing gap between the kinds of preparation L2 learners receive in specially designed ESL/ELD classes and mainstream or "regular" classes is still evident in nearly all high schools that serve immigrant and other L2 learners of English, suggesting that even as programs and policies change, the educational disparities experienced by bilingual learners have changed little since Valdés (1998, 1999, 2001) and Harklau (1994a, 1994b) described them more than a decade ago.

This inquiry into English learners' experiences of academic writing in high school subject-matter classrooms presumed that context influences classroom writing practices, and that these practices socialize young people into particular norms for academic writing within and across curricular areas. I draw from theories of later language socialization (Baquedano-López & Kattan, 2008; Duff, 2008; Heath, 1983) and academic literacies (Barton & Hamilton, 2005; Ivanič, 2004; Lea

& Street, 1998) to examine the classroom norms and literacy practices related to academic writing in the classes attended by Ofelia and Rosalinda.

Unlike traditional notions of reading and writing, these situated perspectives on literacy combine the social and the particular to understand how language and literacy are construed, performed, and interpreted locally with specific participants, in particular contexts and activities, with particular modes of communication and representation. Situated approaches are especially typical among scholars who focus on linguistic minorities, often in out-of-school or special program settings that impose fewer institutional constraints on language use. These situated approaches privilege the local but sometimes neglect to account for broader contextual influences on local literacy practices. Research on more universally shared norms for academic language and literacy in adolescence is generally school-based, employing either functional linguistic approaches, strategy instruction, or classroom discourse analysis to better understand and therefore equip students and teachers for school-based language and literacy expectations. Studies in these locations, however, often do not address the full range of language skills and understanding of language minority students; this has important implications for the "opportunity gap" between language groups, privileging standard language forms and functions of literacy without seizing opportunities to expand current theories and approaches in ways that might normalize linguistic diversity and multilingualism. By focusing on the cases of two particular adolescents in different curricular tracks, this chapter brings situated perspectives *into* the classroom, to understand how broad literacy norms were locally negotiated by these young people, and to privilege the particular experiences and understandings of these youngsters so that we can better understand how their school-based experiences of literacy, and writing more specifically, shaped and were shaped by their overall academic trajectories and honors track and general track programs.

The Study

Madera High School,[1] the site of the Diverse Adolescent Literacies Project from which data for these cases were drawn, is a comprehensive high school of nearly 1,600 students located less than 30 miles from California's state capital. Typical of many California public high schools, Madera High School is ethnically and linguistically diverse. At the time of the study, more than half (54 percent) of the students were Latino/a, 35 percent were White, and the rest came from a range of ethnic backgrounds. Many students were still learning English or came from homes where a language other than English (usually Spanish) was spoken. Students officially designated as English learners comprised 20 percent of the enrolled students; 15 percent were redesignated (former) English learners, and many more came from bilingual homes.

During the year of the study, the leadership at Madera High School was piloting a smaller learning community within the larger school structure to foster better monitoring of student progress and communication among educators who teach the same students. The small learning community, with 130 randomly selected ninth graders (with the exception of newcomer immigrants) and five teachers (mathematics, science, health, and English), became the educational context in which data from the cases of Ofelia and Rosalinda were situated. Second language writers in this small learning community, including those with low-intermediate English proficiency on standardized measures, received no specialized English as a second language or English language development instruction. There were three levels or ability tracks of instruction for mathematics (Pre-Algebra was remedial; Algebra was general/college prep; Geometry was advanced). Science had two levels (Earth Science for general/college prep students and Biology for advanced); English Language Arts also had two levels (general/college prep and honors for advanced students), and there was one general level of instruction in health education. These academic levels were not as rigid as the tracking mechanisms found in many high schools, where students exclusively enroll in all honors, all remedial, or all general/average courses of study. At Madera High School, it was sometimes possible for a student to enroll in an honors mathematics class, for example, while taking a general English class. Still, to generalize our findings to more typical "tracked" school settings, we identified clusters of students whose course-taking patterns suggested an all-remedial, all-general, or all-honors program of study (which I call "tracks" throughout this chapter), and labeled their schedules remedial, general, or honors. Rosalinda's case represents that of a second language writer in the general/college prep track, whereas Ofelia's case is that of a second language writer in honors classes.

The teachers of the core curricular areas (math, science, and English) were all White native speakers of English with four to fifteen years of teaching experience. The health teacher was a native English speaker of Filipino descent. I gathered data over the course of a full academic year with the help of four graduate research assistants. We each followed a particular class schedule (remedial, general, or honors) in each of the content areas (mathematics, science, health, and English Language Arts[2]) for three days a week, taking extensive field notes focused on literacy and language use (Cazden, 2001; Dyson & Genishi, 2005) in 146 class sessions. In addition, we audio-recorded classroom discourse, small group discussions among focal students, and teacher–student conferences. Finally, we gathered classroom artifacts, copies of curricular materials and student work, and conducted interviews with the teachers and with focal students of various English proficiencies in each curricular track.

As noted in Table 3.1, honors classes enrolled the fewest English learners (with enrollments of 0, 3, 2, and 2), whereas the remedial and general track classes enrolled almost all of the learning community's official English learners (with enrollments of 4–5, 7–13, 10–12, and 10–12, depending on content area). The presence of English learners in English Language Arts classes appears smaller because ninth grade English classes were nearly half the size of other subject classes

TABLE 3.1 Class Demographics

Subject	Track	#EL/ LEP	#Redes	#FEP	Male	Female	Total students
English	Remedial	4	2	1	7	6	13
English	General	5	0	2	8	7	15
English	Honors	0	3	1	7	11	18
Health	Remedial	13	2	2	18	15	33
Health	General	7	4	1	18	13	31
Health	Honors	3	2	1	13	19	32
Math	Remedial	12	1	2	15	14	29
Math	General	10	2	1	21	13	34
Math	Honors	2	7	2	17	14	31
Science	Remedial	12	2	0	15	17	32
Science	General	10	3	2	20	13	33
Science	Honors	2	5	2	16	15	31

EL = English learner
LEP = Limited English Proficient
Redes = former EL, now redesignated as fully English proficient based on standardized tests
FEP = Bilingual student who speaks a non-English language at home but was considered fully English proficient upon beginning education in the district

due to a district-wide class size reduction policy for English Language Arts that year. Regardless of the official English learner designation, all classes had second language writers in them; however, most honors classes enrolled bilinguals deemed fluent in English by the district's measures.

Writing Practices across the Curriculum

Decisions about curriculum and instruction in core subject areas were driven by the high-stakes assessments associated with each course; these assessments were implemented to maintain compliance with accountability mandates determined at the district level and aligned with federal and state accountability policies under No Child Left Behind. In mathematics, the high stakes assessments were statewide standardized tests which involved no narrative writing; as such, very little narrative writing occurred in math classes at Madera High School. The ninth-grade English Language Arts curriculum revolved around six district-wide benchmark assignments that focused on essays and other written texts aligned with the packaged curriculum and state content standards. These benchmark assignments were graded based on standardized rubrics that focused on particular features of the completed text. Biology, as a graduation requirement, also involved benchmark assignments, which included lab reports. Details on the influence of the accountability mandates on these high-stakes writing assignments are reported in Enright and Gilliland (2011). The consequences of the accountability focus on classroom talk in English Language Arts classes are reported in Enright, Torres-Torretti, and Carreón (2012).

All students in the study, regardless of ability track, spent most of their writing time taking notes that denoted guidelines and requirements for major assignments, vocabulary and curricular concepts to be reproduced later in tests, or in the case of mathematics, sample problems and computations with very few words at all. Beyond note-taking, students frequently answered textbook questions, filled in blanks on worksheets, and wrote lab reports for their science classes. In English classes, every ninth grader was required to write six benchmark assignments that were evaluated according to criteria on a standardized district-wide rubric. Lab reports also served as benchmark assignments in Biology, since it was a science course required for graduation at Madera High School. While these writing norms and practices were typical regardless of a student's ability track in the small learning academy, there were distinct differences in how they played out in the daily classroom experiences of honors versus non-honors students.

The following section illustrates how second language writing and norms for academic literacy interacted to frame the academic trajectories of two bilingual Latina ninth graders in different academic tracks: Ofelia (honors track) and Rosalinda (general track). Ofelia was somewhat exceptional as a second language writer in honors track classes. Rosalinda's general track program of study was more typical of bilingual Latino/a students in public U.S. high schools. This chapter focuses on a general track student rather than a remedial track student to compare to the honors case study for two reasons. First, the curriculum, instruction, and general student demographics of general and remedial sections for science and health classes were essentially the same (unlike mathematics and English); whereas the differences between honors and the other tracks were significantly different in all classes except for health. More importantly, it is already widely understood that remedial classes are likely to enroll bored or disruptive students, be taught by burnt-out or underprepared teachers, and employ scripted or reduced curricula with little attention to rigor or advanced literacies (Applebee, Langer, Nystrand, & Gamoran, 2003; Harklau, 1994b; Oakes, Selvin, Karoly, & Guiton, 1992). Fewer comparisons exist of general track classes, ostensibly designed to prepare students for college requirements, with honors track classes, already understood to be rigorous with rich literacy experiences.

Ofelia: L2 Writing Experiences in Honors Classes

Ofelia García was 15 years old at the time of the study, with an honors track program of study: Geometry, Biology, honors English, and health. Although her family was originally from Jalisco, Mexico, Ofelia had been in the United States for eight years. Her schooling, then, had been almost entirely in U.S. schools. Like most other second language writers in honors classes, Ofelia was officially labeled a "redesignated" student according to school records. The "redesignated" label was assigned to students who were currently identified as fluent in English but had been designated as limited in their English proficiency on standardized measures at some point during their schooling within the district. The honors English class had no students officially designated as English learners; Ofelia was one of three bilingual students in the class who were redesignated as fluent at some point during their schooling in the district.

At the time of the study, Ofelia was living with her parents, younger siblings (a sister and brother), and an uncle. Spanish was the dominant language of the home, although she used both English and Spanish with her siblings. Her parents were unable to read and write in English and had limited literacy skills in Spanish, so they felt ill-equipped to help Ofelia and her siblings with their homework. Ofelia recalled the last time her mother tried to help her when she was a small child. "When I was little my mom tried to [help me with homework], but since she couldn't understand English, she couldn't help me and I cried." At the beginning of the study, Ofelia had a computer in the home, but no cellular phone. She relied on the computer to surf the web and for social networking and photo websites. The week of our springtime interview, however, her father had punished her for talking back to him by disconnecting the internet and arranging to sell the computer.

During a group interview with the learning community teachers, Ofelia's honors English teacher remarked that for bilingual learners, "if they were already literate in their home language, it's huge; they seemed to have more of a sense of the language. They seemed to be able to transfer the skills more." Ms. Thompson named Ofelia and one of her classmates as examples of students who were "literate in their home languages" and "able to transfer the literacy skills over to English." She contrasted Ofelia and her classmate with other Latino/a bilinguals in general classes who "can't read and write in Spanish," which she was convinced "hinders them" in their use of English literacy skills. These remarks were particularly interesting given the fact that Ofelia's parents had limited literacy skills in Spanish, and that most of Ofelia's schooling had been in the United States. She was not a late-arriving immigrant student with years of schooling in her home country. Ofelia did have some basic literacy skills in Spanish, however, and reported being more confident writing in Spanish than in English. Of course, Ofelia never needed to produce academic compositions or answer essay questions in Spanish, so the demands of writing in Spanish were not comparable to the writing demands she faced in English.

Writing in Honors Classes

For the first half of the academic year, Ofelia struggled in her classes, earning grades in the "C" range in her core classes of honors English, Geometry, and Biology, and a "B" in her health class. She was able to raise her grades in the winter and spring, however, so that her spring grades were "A" in English and "B–" in Biology. In the winter, her regular English teacher was replaced by a long-term substitute when she left for maternity leave; this changed Ofelia's experience of the class significantly. In describing her English class before the arrival of the long-term substitute, Ofelia complained,

> Well, I didn't like my teacher because she didn't really teach. . . . We never did work. All the people were talking, and I think she was kind of racist because, like, all the quiet people and Mexicans were over here, and all the white people and all the preps were over there. She never picked on the other side; she always picked on *that* side.

In my own observations of the class, I was impressed by the quick verbal wit demonstrated by a handful of the white monolingual English-speaking students. They easily seized the floor as the teacher was lecturing about a point in the literature, snowballing into jokes and insults until the teacher would intervene and resume her lecture. "So nothing worked for you in that class?" I asked Ofelia.

> . . . we had a sub, it was Mr. Robertson, and I really. . . . Like he was more strict. I like more strict teachers because I focus more. So I always did my work, my homework, everything, my folder was all organized and I got an A in that class, with that teacher. . . . Because we had *another* sub, and she didn't pay attention to no one. Well yeah, only to smart people, people that raise their hands. And she based all our grade from them, from their participation on us. So I didn't like that teacher either.

Honors classes enrolled the greatest number of native English speakers and had the most sophisticated writing demands. For example, as students wrote their benchmark essays for honors English, they were expected not only to produce a text that met rubric criteria, but also to understand the functional differences between different types of essays (for example, persuasive versus literary analysis). In science classes, the lab reports in honors classes dealt with high degrees of abstraction and required hypothesizing, synthesizing, and summarizing. The long-term substitute in honors English analyzed a model text and discussed nuances of genre differences with students; however, the science teacher did not explicitly teach students how to handle the writing demands of the lab reports or other science writing assignments. Rather, the gifted students enrolled in the class were expected to have the requisite language and literacy skills already; for these assignments, they were expected to use those skills to demonstrate their under-standing of the key curricular concepts.

Ofelia struggled with writing and other uses of academic English in these classes, and valued explicit instruction by the teacher above all else. Generally, though, she felt that this type of instruction was limited and insufficient. The Biology teacher, for example, would often elicit students' experience with new material or check for understanding of review material by asking an open question to the whole class. This did not work for Ofelia at all. "Because sometimes I don't know the answer and they [students answering the question] don't really explain it," she complained. When I asked her what she really needed in those instances, she replied, "Explanation." She had the same complaint about the instruction in her Geometry class, saying that the teacher would give notes to present new material, but that it didn't work for her, "Because he only says it; he doesn't really explain it." She felt that she learned the most "when we get in groups and we can get help from others," but this happened rarely in her classes. Instruction didn't work for her when it was "just, like the teacher talking, and that's it."

Because of the limited explicit instruction (in writing and in content skills), Ofelia preferred writing tasks that were less formal, with fewer prescribed norms for form and content. When asked what types of classroom activities were most interesting or successful for her, she noted that in English classes, she preferred "writing that could do . . . and write . . . about anything . . . like a free topic." When asked what she wrote during free-writing assignments, she said, "Anything that comes to mind." Free-write assignments were graded for completeness, not content or form, making them a very low-stakes writing activity in English classes. In health class, she preferred posters and assignments that involved visuals. For Biology, she felt that the required and graded notebook was the classroom activity that worked best for her. I asked Ofelia what she did when she didn't understand something in one of her classes. "I have an iPod. I listen to my iPod . . . or I draw, or write," she replied. The culture of these classrooms did not provide a safe space for her to ask questions or seek help. Four or five quick-witted monolingual English-speakers set the pace of instruction as well as the norms for asking questions. Ofelia had trouble keeping up with them.

Rosalinda: L2 Writing Experiences in General Track Classes

Rosalinda Alvarez was a 15-year-old ninth grader in general track classes at Madera High School: Algebra, Earth Science, General English, and health. Her family was originally from Mexico but lived transnationally, or "back and forth," throughout her elementary school years. Like one-third of her classmates in the general track classes, Rosalinda was officially designated an English learner by the school; her score on the California English Language Development test was a 4, denoting intermediate to intermediate/high proficiency in English. Rosalinda said that she was fairly comfortable reading and writing for personal reasons in Spanish. She wrote poems in Spanish regularly, and tried to make them rhyme. While there were no English as a second language or English language development classes for bilinguals in the small learning community, there was a remedial companion English class for students with very low grades in English Language Arts the prior year. Rosalinda was not enrolled in the remedial companion class, an indication that she had not been identified as a student struggling in English Language Arts.

Rosalinda's family provided a complex support system for her educational success. Her parents had limited education in Mexico and worked as fieldworkers in California; they were unfamiliar with the educational practices and policies of U.S. schools. On the other hand, Rosalinda's older sister had navigated U.S. schools very successfully, earning a scholarship to one of the California State University campuses a few hours away. Their father would not permit his daughter to live so far from home, however, and made it clear that his two sons were expected to work in the fields with him. The children only spoke Spanish with their parents, but spoke English and Spanish with each other. Rosalinda did not have a computer in the home but had a cellular phone to keep in touch with friends, watched television and read mystery books in her free time, and went to the local library at least twice a week to use the computers there, a routine she developed with her older sister when her sister had been in high school. At home and at school, Rosalinda was highly attuned to issues of fairness. She and her sister successfully banded together, with their mother's support, to demand that their brothers clean up the kitchen as much as they did, when their father had insisted this was women's work. At school, Rosalinda highlighted this same attention to fairness, particularly with regard to equitable contributions of classmates during group work.

The teachers did not cite Rosalinda as an example of a particularly successful or challenged student during focus group discussions. They did, however, come to some agreement on their characterization of students in the different curricular tracks in comparison to one another. They all nodded enthusiastically when one teacher remarked, "Ya know, the [honors] kids don't need our help, and the [remedial] kids don't want our help. The [general] kids are the ones who really take advantage of the help, though."

Writing in General Track Classes

Unlike Ofelia, Rosalinda had a more consistent performance in her classes throughout her ninth-grade year. Her English Language Arts grade was always in the B range, with A's in Algebra and science. In her health class, she earned a B+ in the fall but an A in the spring. Rosalinda reported that English was her most difficult class, explaining that "I'm not good at essays, and grammar. And science is hard. . . ."

Rosalinda's classes differed from Ofelia's honors classes in several ways. First, enrollments were quite different. One-third of the students in the general mathematics and science classes were officially designated as English learners, not yet fluent in English. Only two out of more than 30 students in the honors sections of math and science were designated as English learners, however. The curricula were different across tracks in mathematics and science, too. Rosalinda was taking Algebra instead of Geometry; her Earth Science class (instead of Biology) was not even a graduation requirement, and was excluded from the benchmark assignments for that reason. Basic classroom routines were similar across the Algebra and Geometry classes, which were taught by the same teacher. However, the honors

Geometry students were allowed to work in pairs more often, and were permitted to interact more informally with the teacher, with occasional tangential comments or personal questions during class lectures. In both classes, notes were generally limited to copying sample problems and the steps required to solve them.

In the science classes, the teacher's routines were more consistent across tracks. The material was quite different, though, with the Earth Science class focusing on concepts that would be more familiar to students (at least if their native language was English), with labs that were activity-based and concrete. On the other hand, the Biology class engaged in more sophisticated content and labs that often involved manipulating abstract concepts rather than hands-on activities (for more details, see Enright & Gilliland, 2011). Rosalinda felt that her science class was one of her most difficult classes. However, she especially liked an activity called "four corners." In her description, she reported that "you like read a paragraph and then you summarize into a sentence, and we read like a whole section. . . ." She appreciated this activity, which involved moving around the room and discussing science concepts with classmates, because students co-constructed what was eventually written on the page. "I kept the page, and with the notes, so I could go back to them and read them for the tests." Rosalinda felt that homework in science class was especially difficult, however, noting, "I don't like writing a lot. So I have to explain, like every question is, has a why do you think that, so I have to explain all myself in." When I noted that she was explaining herself quite well in our interview, she laughed and said that explaining was hard in writing because,

> I think of this word in Spanish, 'cause I'm thinking Spanish, and then I'm translating and writing in English, so sometimes I can't find a word to translate, so I don't know how to explain myself, and then some other people that read it, they think different. 'Cause they, since I used another word, it means like different . . . not like what I wanted to say.

The curricula in the honors and general track English classes were the same, with the same textbook, readings, and benchmark assignment essays. However, the English Language Arts classes were taught by different teachers with very different language and literacy practices and expectations. Rosalinda did not like group work in Algebra class because students got off-task; in English class, however, she preferred groups because "we're actually talking about the subject." She also liked working on group posters, drawing pictures to represent themes in the literature, and writing summaries. When asked when she was most interested or involved in her English class, Rosalinda said, "When we were doing stuff, like that includes like drawings, and not writing 'cause I'm not good at writing, but like, just making summaries." When I asked her to elaborate, she said,

> I don't mind if it's summaries, but I don't like essays . . . 'cause summaries just, you already read like the whole thing . . . you're just, like, taking out

important events, and on an essay you have to like explain a lot of stuff, since it's longer. . . . You have to like write more.

Routine instruction in the general track English class involved the participation of more students than routine instruction in the honors English class. Instead of a handful of students manipulating classroom discussions, the teacher managed carefully controlled I–R–E (teacher Initiates, student Responds, teacher Evaluates response) sequences of talk in which there was almost always one right answer that he was trying to elicit by coaching students through simple questions. This pattern encouraged more students to participate in classroom talk but limited the depth of ideas discussed. With regard to writing instruction, the teacher focused on forms and features of language that needed to appear in the final products, similar to the approach of the honors English teacher. The difference was that most of the honors students were quick to understand the purposes of the various genres and had the English proficiency to produce the features and forms of writing demanded of them. In the general track class, initial instruction and feedback to students on their writing focused on form more than purpose, which made it especially difficult for students like Rosalinda to write competently in any genres beyond the summaries that she preferred.

Ofelia and Rosalinda shared some common struggles as they wrote in content area classes; these struggles suggest some general principles for subject-matter teachers to consider in classrooms that incorporate bilingual learners, even if these learners are like Ofelia, no longer officially deemed limited in their English proficiency. At the same time, the differences in writing norms and expectations across ability tracks have significant consequences for the learning and academic trajectories of bilingual learners, particularly during times of high accountability and assessment. In the final section, I describe these struggles and differences, with recommendations for educators of subject-matter classrooms that enroll bilingual learners of varying English proficiencies.

Academic Trajectories of L2 Writers in Subject-Matter Classrooms

Recommendations for Educators of Bilingual Adolescents

The current accountability climate has had a remarkable influence on the teaching and learning of writing in subject-matter classrooms. Many districts mandate a rigid pacing of instruction, holding teachers accountable to the pacing and content of instruction by imposing inflexible standardized assessments throughout the academic year. This was the case at Madera High School, and these accountability policies had a profound impact on the writing experiences and academic trajectories of bilingual learners in these classrooms. As teachers focus more on aspects of the curriculum that are prescribed by their districts and evaluated by high stakes assessments, uses of writing to learn subject-matter concepts become more constrained. Likewise, instruction in *how* to write to demonstrate subject-matter learning also suffers. These trends are both evident in the complaints of Ofelia and Rosalinda regarding the challenges of *explanations* in their subject-matter classes.

Ofelia's chief complaint was that teachers did not provide enough explicit instruction in her honors subject-matter classes. She didn't want teachers to simply *tell* her something; she wanted them to *explain* it. Concepts were described superficially in class lectures, and when teachers checked for understanding with review questions targeting the whole class, the quickest and most proficient students (conceptually and verbally) determined the pace of the class so that Ofelia's questions remained unanswered. With regard to writing, the evaluation criteria were often shared with students, especially for the English language arts benchmark essays. However, these evaluation criteria focused on forms and content of written texts without explaining how these forms and content were related to genre-norms, communicative purposes, or norms for using writing that were linked with distinct ways of knowing and making sense of the world in each discipline. As a bilingual writer in honors classes, Ofelia was expected to have the tools to create the required products, and the products themselves were generally described explicitly. However, with the exception of some essay instruction from the long-term honors English substitute teacher, Ofelia did not receive instruction in *how* to use writing to craft and support an argument or display her content-specific learning. Most of her native English-speaking classmates appeared to have these skills before enrolling in these ninth-grade classes. Ofelia's case is an important reminder to teachers that we must consistently check the understanding of all students, not count on the first voices and raised hands to signal the understanding of the whole class. While all students in honors classes would benefit from explicit instruction in how to write for various purposes and how to consider purpose, audience, and evidence in writing to display their learning for assessment purposes, bilingual learners are in greatest need of this sort of explicit instruction because they are still being socialized into the norms of academic English within and across school contexts. When Ofelia had a long-term substitute who carefully modeled and explained the purposes of particular uses of language across essay genres, she was able to write successfully and earn an A in the honors English class. In other core classes, she was not as successful, however.

In Rosalinda's general track classes, the subject-matter concepts were less complex. Rosalinda did not want more explicit content explanations from teachers. In fact, she often understood the basic concepts in her classes, finished classwork early, and became bored waiting for her classmates to finish their seatwork. Her complaint, instead, was about the explanations required of students to demonstrate their learning via writing in these subject-matter classrooms. If she could demonstrate her learning with posters, short-answer questions, and summaries, she felt successful. She didn't mind taking notes or writing summaries based on her course readings, but she loathed writing essays because they were longer and "you have to explain a lot of stuff." She understood that these written products, with their tightly defined evaluation criteria, were different from summaries because they involved explanation of concepts that went beyond "taking out important events." Her literacy repertoire in English was not developed enough yet to know *how* to craft those explanations in writing, and instruction in *how* to craft those explanations was entirely missing from the general track curriculum, regardless of the subject-matter area. Genres of writing were only explained in terms of the features and content that each written product must contain. Students did not analyze sample texts to note how writers achieve different purposes with their writing, nor did they have a chance to discuss their choices as writers during conferences with their teachers. The high stakes and need for efficiency encouraged norms in which teachers and tutors suggested writing "fixes" for bilingual learners to help them shift below-standard written texts into texts that met standards according to official criteria. They felt there wasn't time to focus on understanding the processes and purposes of writing, the thinking (linguistic and conceptual) involved in organizing and drafting texts for specific academic purposes.

Whether they intend to or not, teachers of bilingual adolescents are socializing their students into normative ways of understanding content, writing practices, and academic language. In honors classes, these young people are exposed to complex written texts as they read for their subject-matter classes; likewise, they have access to sophisticated oral language norms when they are integrated into classes with academically talented native speakers of English. However, when class discussions leave bilingual learners confused, and written assignments are required but not instructed or supported, bilingual learners are little more than window-shoppers in honors classes: they can observe and admire the more advanced content learning and writing of their peers, but it is not theirs to develop or display if they aren't given the appropriate tools and taught how to use them.

In general track classes, bilingual learners are engaged more fully than window-shopping, but they are essentially experiencing a "five-and-dime" version of instruction and writing norms. They are provided with graphic organizers and explicit evaluation criteria so that they can produce written texts that meet minimum criteria established by the district. However, little time is given to articulating the thinking behind the writing or the purposes behind the required features and forms of text that they produce. In these contexts, students are trained, not taught. The mechanistic approaches to writing only leave them capable of copying notes and writing summaries. Like Rosalinda, many bilingual students understand that their writing should accomplish more important communicative and academic purposes, but they have not been instructed in *how* to write for these purposes.

For educators concerned with the academic trajectories of bilingual youth, one more contextual factor is important to note. While the writing norms were constrained and dismal across both tracks (honors and general), the conceptual rigor of the curriculum was richer in many of the honors classes. Concepts were more abstract and closer to the kinds of content of college classrooms than those in general track classes. However, since students often had to demonstrate their learning via writing, and since writing wasn't explicitly taught for these purposes in the subject-matter classes, bilingual learners' grades suffered significantly if they lacked the proficiency in English to write for these purposes. Over time, this was not only discouraging but also impacted their opportunities to be enrolled in honors classes in future years. In this way, writing served a gatekeeping function that could prevent academically talented bilinguals from having full access to advanced curricula and classes.

Subject-matter teachers of bilingual writers are encouraged to reflect on the following questions as they consider the role of writing for bilingual learners in their own classrooms:

Role of Writing in Content Literacy and Learning

- What kinds of written texts represent knowledge in my content area? How can I integrate more of these texts into our daily classroom routines for students to analyze, imitate, and critique?
- What opportunities do I give students to use writing to reflect on, synthesize, and critique curricular concepts in my classes?
- How can I support the writing of bilingual writers in ways that encourage a focus on thinking and meaningful engagement with content, instead of formulaic products that might conceal conceptual misunderstandings?
- How do I expose and articulate the thinking reflected by my own choices as a writer in my subject-matter area?

Role of English Language Development in Academic Writing

- How might students of different English proficiencies and native language skills demonstrate their learning through writing in my subject area?
- How can I differentiate instruction for students of different English proficiencies so that they are all appropriately supported and challenged to develop greater proficiency as writers?
- How do I facilitate rich oral language activities that involve *all* students to mobilize their linguistic resources prior to, during, and after writing?

Role of Writing in Academic Trajectories

- What writing skills does my current curriculum presume of learners, and how can I ensure that I am identifying and supporting bilingual learners who are still developing these skills?
- What are the high-stakes assessments in my content area, and how does writing proficiency serve as a gatekeeper for bilingual learners who take them?

• What writing skills are needed to be successful in my subject area beyond the grade(s) or level(s) that I teach? How am I preparing my bilingual students to identify and learn these skills, and adapt them appropriately for future contexts?

The current accountability paradigm encourages standardized one-size-fits-all approaches to teaching and learning in subject-matter classrooms. These approaches are harmful to the academic trajectories of bilingual learners like Ofelia and Rosalinda if teachers do not attend to their unique linguistic and academic needs, however (Ortmeier-Hooper & Enright, 2011). Fortunately, the experiences and struggles of these young women suggest that educators can support their content learning, and their writing in particular, by making adjustments that are possible even within the constraints of rigid curriculum and assessment mandates. The cautions articulated in their cases, and the questions noted above, may help teachers to shift our lens as we design instruction and assess learning so that the connections between thinking, writing, and learning are more explicit in the classroom, and the academic trajectories of our bilingual learners are expanded and supported through their experiences in our classrooms.

Notes

1   Names of participants and research site are pseudonyms.
2   Social Studies / History was not offered until students' tenth-grade year.

References

Applebee, A. N., Langer, J. A., Nystrand, M., & Gamoran, A. (2003). Discussion-based approaches to developing understanding: Classroom instruction and student performance in middle and high school English. *American Educational Research Journal, 40*(3), 685–730.

Baquedano-López, P., & Kattan, S. (2008). Language socialization in schools. In P. A. Duff & N. H. Hornberger (Eds.), *Encyclopedia of language and education, volume 8: Language socialization* (2nd ed., pp. 161–173). New York: Springer.

Barton, D., & Hamilton, M. (2005). Literacy, reification and the dynamics of social interaction. In D. Barton & K. Tusting (Eds.), *Beyond communities of practice: Language, power and social context* (pp. 14–35). Cambridge: Cambridge University Press.

Cazden, C. (2001). *Classroom discourse: The language of teaching and learning* (2nd ed.). Westport, CT: Heinemann.

Duff, P. A. (2008). Language socialization, participation and identity: Ethnographic approaches. In M. Martin-Jones, A.-M. de Mejía, & N. H. Hornberger (Eds.), *Encyclopedia of language and education, volume 3: Discourse and education* (2nd ed., pp. 107–119). New York: Springer.

Dyson, A. H., & Genishi, C. (2005). *On the case: approaches to language and literacy research.* New York: Teachers College Press.

Enright, K. A. (2011). Language and literacy for a New Mainstream. *American Educational Research Journal, 48*(1), 80–118.

Enright, K. A., & Gilliland, B. (2011). Multilingual writing in an age of accountability: From policy to practice in U.S. high school classrooms. *Journal of Second Language Writing, 20*(3), 182–195. doi: 10.1016/j.jslw.2011.05.006

Enright, K. A., Torres-Torretti, D., & Carreón, O. (2012). Hope is the thing with metaphors: De-situating literacies and learning in English language arts classrooms. *Language and Education, 26*(1), 35–51.

Harklau, L. (1994a). ESL versus mainstream classes: Contrasting L2 learning environments. *TESOL Quarterly, 28*(2), 241–272.

Harklau, L. (1994b). Tracking and linguistic minority students: Consequences of ability grouping for second language learners. *Linguistics and Education, 6*(3), 217–244.

Harklau, L. (2011). Commentary: Adolescent L2 writing research as an emerging field. *Journal of Second Language Writing, 20*(3), 227–230.

Harklau, L., & Pinnow, R. (2009). Adolescent second-language writing. In L. Christenbury, R. Bomer, & P. Smagorinsky (Eds.), *Handbook of adolescent literacy research* (pp. 126–137). New York: Guilford.

Heath, S. B. (1983). *Ways with words: Language, life, and work in communities and classrooms.* New York: Cambridge University Press.

Ivanič, R. (2004). Discourses of writing and learning to write. *Language and Education, 18*(3), 220–245.

Kibler, A. (2011). "I write it in a way that people can read it": How teachers and adolescent L2 writers describe content area writing. *Journal of Second Language Writing, 20*(3), 211–226.

Lea, M. R., & Street, B. V. (1998). Student writing in higher education: An academic literacies approach. *Studies in Higher Education, 23*(2), 157–172.

Oakes, J., Selvin, M., Karoly, L., & Guiton, G. (1992). Educational matchmaking: Academic and vocational tracking in comprehensive high schools. Santa Monica, CA: The RAND Corporation.

Ortmeier-Hooper, C., & Enright, K. A. (2011). Mapping new territory: Toward an understanding of adolescent L2 writers and writing in US context. *Journal of Second Language Writing, 20*(3), 167–181. doi: 10.1016/j.jslw.2011.05.002

Valdés, G. (1998). The world outside and inside schools: Language and immigrant children. *Educational Researcher, 27*(6), 4–18.

Valdés, G. (1999). Incipient bilingualism and the development of English language writing abilities in the secondary school. In C. J. Faltis & P. M. Wolfe (Eds.), *So much to say: Adolescents, bilingualism, and ESL in the secondary school* (pp. 138–175). New York: Teachers College Press.

Valdés, G. (2001). *Learning and not learning English: Latino students in American schools.* New York: Teachers College Press.

Villalva, K. E. (2006). Hidden literacies and inquiry approaches of bilingual high school writers. *Written Communication, 23*(1), 91–129.

4

"DOING LIKE ALMOST EVERYTHING WRONG"

An Adolescent Multilingual Writer's Transition from High School to College

Amanda Kibler

One fall afternoon, Ms. Gutiérrez was leading a lively discussion about *Parrot in the Oven*, a novel her ninth-grade students were reading in English or Spanish. Although a few had lived in the neighborhood since elementary or middle school, many students had first arrived in U.S. schools within the previous year or two. The class, designated for students whom teachers feared would be unsuccessful in "mainstream" courses because of a lack of English proficiency, took place at South Sierra High School, a small public school serving a majority-Latino population in California. It was there that I met Diego.

Diego was born to Spanish-speaking immigrant parents in the South Sierra community but moved with his family in first grade to a rural *rancho* in Mexico where he had no opportunity to continue his education. Only when he came back to South Sierra at age 12 did he return to an English-speaking environment, and to school. When I met him at the beginning of ninth grade, he was still writing primarily in Spanish, but an excerpt from an end-of-year assessment shows progress he made during that year:

> My importante porsend is my mom she is very nice to me she help me with the materials for the school. My mom is strict, is a good *cocinera*, and a good clin up the house . . .

Even though the cramped conditions in which his family lived made it difficult for him to do schoolwork at home, Diego earned a reputation among teachers and peers early in his high school career as a hard worker and an excellent math student. In what could be considered a remarkable "success story," Diego not only graduated with the credits necessary to enroll in state universities, but thanks to the school's "no tracking" policy, he also secured, with the help of his teachers, a competitive scholarship that would pay his college tuition and living expenses at any university to which he was accepted.

Although Diego struggled to pass the English section of the statewide high school exit exam, he spoke confidently about the writing preparation he received at South Sierra. In an interview just before graduation, he said,

> Now I know how to write in English. In my sophomore year, I was still not that good on writing, but I was writing in English. Then, like, from junior and senior now, I can write bigger paragraphs and more, like, vocabulary, with different details and ideas and knowledge. I couldn't do it before.

He admitted, though, that he might encounter challenges in college, explaining that "on my writing skills, I know that I'm gonna need to, like, to write more than high school and speak more and read more every day." He spoke excitedly about the upcoming school year, his future roommates, and his plans for earning a degree in business finance.

Academic life at Ocean College, the four-year institution he then attended, was a jarring change. Diego was placed in the two lowest remedial English courses offered at the school, both of which were multiple levels below college-level English. The message, for him, was simple: "I went there, now [they're] telling me that I actually didn't learn the basic things on high school about how to write a paragraph or an essay." The placement alone was an unwelcome surprise for Diego, but he was quickly overwhelmed by the difficulty of these courses. He failed both classes and was forced to re-take them the next semester.

Diego poignantly recounts what happened when he returned to his high school to tell his former teachers what had happened:

> I explained to [the college counselor] and another teacher that, no this is what I'm learning, and I think I'm supposed to learn already this on high school . . . I print out one, a paper that I'd got in high school, and it supposedly was like really good. And I showed it to my English teacher over there [at Ocean College], and . . . she just told me, "oh, this is like a D paper." And then I showed them over there at high school, [and said,] "this is an A paper that I got here, and this is a D paper. This is supposed to be a D paper over there, so that means that we're doing like almost everything wrong."

Diego's return to confront his high school teachers is notable in many regards, not least of which is the fact that Diego had the courage to do so. From a pedagogical standpoint, his experiences point toward two provocative questions: Was something going "wrong" in Diego's secondary writing experiences? If so, what was it, and what can it tell us about second language writing and the educational opportunities provided to multilingual students in K–12 schools? In keeping with Pardoe's (2000) contention that analysis of *un*successful writing can provide valuable information about literacy practices and development, this chapter analyzes Diego's problematic writing experiences over time, with a close examination of single writing tasks completed in tenth grade and his first year at college, to explore the following question: How does a student like Diego leave high school as a "successful writer" but arrive in college and quickly come to believe he didn't know the "basic things"? This question, in turn, forces an examination of who "successful writers" are, what counts as "successful writing," and how these texts are created across different contexts, particularly for students writing in their non-primary languages.

Insights from the Literature

At the secondary level and in K–12 schooling overall, scholars find "a continued legacy of paying [immigrant students] little to no attention, or a future of directing only negative attention to their presence" (Rodriguez & Cruz, 2009, p. 2393; see also Ruiz-de-Velasco & Fix, 2000). Transitions to college can be difficult for these students because they have frequently been tracked into high school courses that do not provide sufficient access to the academic discourse or curricular content needed for success in college (Callahan, 2005; Harklau, 1994). In many cases, this tracking can also make students ineligible for university acceptance before taking additional courses at community colleges. At the community college level, however, researchers express concerns regarding placement practices that channel U.S.-educated language minority students into remedial or ESL courses (Bunch & Panayotova, 2008) and overall low rates of progress through such coursework before students are able to take credit-bearing English courses (Moore & Shulock, 2010).

Qualitative studies examining multilingual writers' experiences transitioning from high school to college have found several potential difficulties for students. Allison (2009), for example, discovered that there were very few opportunities for non-native English speaking twelfth-graders in her study to "rehearse college literacy activities" in high school courses. Harklau's research (2000) also suggests immigrant students may be idealized as hardworking and determined by their high school teachers but are viewed as having picked up the "worst" of American habits by teachers at the college level who are more accustomed to working with recently arrived international students (p. 52). Although there is a level of continuity to be found in writing tasks in high school and college settings, multilingual writers often discover significant differences in literacy demands across the two settings (Harklau, 2001).

Conceptual Framing

This analysis proceeds from the notion that literacy is inherently social (Barton, Hamilton, & Ivanič, 2000; Martin-Jones & Jones, 2000; Street, 2003), and that sociocultural theories of learning can help specify aspects of the social practice of literacy. Such a starting point provides a conceptual lens for analyzing who "successful writers" are, what counts as "successful writing," and how these texts are created across different contexts.

Writers are inevitably shaped by their previous experiences with literacy, education, and schooling, bringing complex and contested histories of participation (Rogers, 2002) to any new writing task. These cultural and individual histories include not just the acquisition of literacy skills but also histories of engagement in literacy practices (Street, 2000, 2003), and encompass observable reading and writing events as well as "the social structures in which they are embedded and which they help shape" (Barton & Hamilton, 2000, p.7). Drawing from socio-cultural theory, learning to write can be seen as a process that originates in social activity but that is gradually internalized (Lantolf, 2000a, 2000b; Vygotsky, 1978), although never fully removed from immediate or past contexts (Van Oers, 1998). Further, identities as "good writers" or "diligent students," for example, are not static but rather shaped in practice through social interaction (Holland, Lachicotte, Skinner, & Cain, 1998) as individuals "form as well as perform" such identities (Bartlett & Holland, 2002, p. 14).

A range of writing standards and assessment models have attempted to define what "successful writing" is for various purposes and institutional settings, but there is diversity both within and across institutional contexts as to how teachers and other readers conceptualize this notion (Kibler, 2011b; Pardoe, 2000). From a social perspective, written texts are embedded in literacy practices but do not constitute them in their entirety (Tusting, Ivanič, & Wilson, 2000).

The processes through which a piece of writing is created is a complex matter, both cognitively and socially. Insights gained from activity theory suggest that although students are participating in the same classroom task, such as "write an essay about topic X," they may be engaged in very different goal-directed activities (Lantolf & Appel, 1994; Lantolf & Pavlenko, 2001), depending on their histories and motives. In this way, writing an essay is "a means to some other end" for both teachers and students (Barton & Hamilton, 2000, p.12). Further, the tools available for writers to use—including other people, texts, technology, and language itself—mediate the writing process, and these physical and symbolic resources are embedded in cultures and social relationships (Lantolf, 2000b). From this per-spective, learning to write also involves acquiring cultures (Vásquez, 2006), or what others describe as gaining access to communities of practice (Lave & Wenger, 1991) or Discourses (Gee, 2010). It is difficult, however, to predict trajectories of learning, in this case learning to write, because they depend on material circum-stances as well as the significance learners assign to various activities (Lantolf, 2005; Lantolf & Pavlenko, 2001). Learners "actively engage in constructing the terms and conditions of their own learning" (Lantolf & Pavlenko, 2001, p. 145), but critical sociocultural theorists emphasize that students and teachers are constrained in many ways by power relationships embedded in institutions and society (Moje & Lewis, 2007).

Methodology

This analysis forms part of an eight-year longitudinal study of five writers, which began when students started high school (grade nine) in 2006 and will continue until four years after their high school graduation. Students were selected based on several factors (see Kibler, 2010), but all spoke Spanish as a primary language and, according to ninth-grade assessment data, were at beginning or intermediate English language proficiency in writing. Data for the overall study include writing samples, discourse-based student interviews, and informal observations, with additional audio-recorded ethnographic observations and teacher interviews in grade 10. The current analysis draws upon this history of engagement with Diego and his peers but focuses specifically upon two writing assignments in which Diego engaged during high school and college (see Table 4.1).

These two assignments were chosen because (1) writing samples and extensive interview data were available for both, (2) they were, respectively, the oldest and most recent writing tasks in the data set for which interview data were available, and (3) they represented the primary extended writing tasks for the given grading periods in which they occurred.

The approach to data analysis used in this chapter, which I call an interactional histories approach, was first developed for documenting writing processes in ethnographic contexts (Kibler, 2010, 2011a). I have modified this three-part framework for use in longitudinal interpretative studies that include interviews and writing sample collection but not a consistent participant-observer, ethnographic component.

The first aspect of this longitudinal interactional histories approach (LIHA) focuses on participants' interactions with peers, teachers, texts, and other resources while creating texts. Such an emphasis attends to the larger institutional and social factors influencing teaching and learning (Moje & Lewis, 2007), mediational tools (Lantolf, 2000b) used to write, and the identities students enact (Holland et al.,

TABLE 4.1 Writing Assignments and Data Sources

Year in school	Semester	Course	Assignment	Data sources
Grade 10, high school	Spring	Humanities (untracked)	Persuasive letter based on the novel, *Nectar in a Sieve*	Student writing (multiple drafts) Student interview Teacher interview Class observations
Freshman year, college	Spring	Fundamentals of English: Cross-Cultural Perspectives (remedial)	Expository essay based on the memoir, *Burro Genius*	Student writing (final draft) Student interview

1998) as they engage in writing and conversations with others about their writing. The second focus for a LIHA analysis is how such interactions impact students' writing. When possible, these influences can be traced textually across multiple drafts of writing, but when only a single draft is available, the texts themselves and participants' accounts can be used as the basis for this analysis. Attention to the impact of interactions emphasizes that texts are embedded in, and, I would argue, inextricable from, the contexts in which they were created (Tusting et al., 2000). In this way, texts make visible the "necessarily dialectal relationship between the individual and the social" (Lantolf, 2005). The final focus of a LIHA analysis is an emphasis on change over time in students' written texts and/or the processes through which they were created. Compton-Lilly (2007) suggests that longitudinal data provide a type of depth especially valuable for literacy research, and just as Moje and Lewis (2007) suggest with ethnographic data, the depth of understanding made possible by several years' study of a small group of individuals can help researchers make informed hypotheses about participants' motives and desires, thus allowing insightful analysis of the literacy practices in which they engage and their literacy development over time.

The Path From "I Can Write" to "I Didn't Know the Basics": A Longitudinal Interactional Histories Approach

I begin this analysis of the two writing assignments with a focus on interactions (including the institutional and social influences on interactions, the use of mediational tools during interactions, and the negotiation of identity through interactions) and the impact of these interactions for each assignment. I then turn to an analysis of changes over time in the characteristics of these interactions and their effects on Diego's texts.

Grade 10 Letter: Interactions While Creating the Text

The institutional and social contexts in which Diego completed this writing task provide an important frame in which to situate the assignment. South Sierra High School was located in an under-resourced community, and the small school's college preparatory agenda was standard for all of the students, most of whom were immigrants or children of immigrants from Latin America. Humanities courses, through which students learned both English and social studies, were centered on a philosophy of teaching challenging texts ("big books"), but there was no articulated writing curriculum for any grade level. At the time of this assignment, Mr. Smith, Diego's teacher, did not have preparation in writing instruction or in teaching multilingual students, although he did earn an ESL endorsement later in Diego's high school career. Outside of the school community, an important contextual issue relevant to Diego was his immigration status: as a U.S. citizen, he was eligible for higher education scholarships and job opportunities that many of his peers were not. In this way, persisting with schoolwork in order to attend college, earn a degree, and begin a career was potentially more rewarding for him than for many of his peers, who were undocumented immigrants and therefore had fewer future employment options.

In-class activities related to this writing task began when Diego and his peers started reading *Nectar in a Sieve*, a novel about industrialization in mid-twentieth-century India. During in-class reading time, Diego often appeared to read just a page or two while other students read several pages, and he usually relied upon peers to complete homework and in-class activities. As I explore in detail elsewhere (Kibler, 2011a), Diego seemed to have understood very little of the text, despite informal conversations about the book with his peers during small group activities. A conversation with his teacher during an early pre-writing activity makes this clear: once assigned the task of writing a persuasive essay (in letter form) based on the novel's plot and characters, Diego could not, or did not, articulate any information about the book's characters when asked by his teacher to do so.

1 Mr. Smith:	ok so what do you think you remember MOST from the	
2	book.	
3	<3>	
4 Mr. Smith:	maybe if you just had to pick a character and talk about	
5	that character/	
6	just talk to me about anybody.	
7	<1>	
8	let's just have a conversation,	
9	about what you read and what you think about that	
10	person.	
11 Daniel:	that she kills the the her daughter/	
12 Mr. Smith:	Diego [your voice changed,	
13 Jaime:	[DIEGO DIEGO,	
14	<6>	
15 Jaime:	*de cuáles de cuál te acuerdas más güey.*	
	('which ones which one do you remember the most about dude')	
16 Diego:	*de NINGUNO.*	
	('about NONE')	
17 Jaime:	NONE,	
18	he said none.	

Transcript 1 (February 14, 2008, 35:20)

(Kibler, 2011a. See also for transcription conventions.)

After this interaction, Mr. Smith gave Diego a two-page summary of the book and asked him to find key ideas from it that he could use for his letter.

From this point onward, Mr. Smith and Diego had 26 audio-recorded informal "conferences" about Diego's text, both during and outside of class. In the early drafting phase Mr. Smith initiated many interactions with Diego, using intonation, along with "directed" questions, in efforts to check Diego's comprehension and help him develop ideas for his writing. In this way, Mr. Smith helped Diego identify all of the major topics he would address in the essay. Later in the drafting process, Mr. Smith often suggested sentence-level wording of sentences for Diego, encouraging him through the use of intonational cues and rephrasing. Diego also frequently appealed to his teacher for help in transcribing these suggestions. In addition to these face-to-face interactions, Mr. Smith provided Diego with written feedback twice during the completion of this assignment. Diego made *all* teacher-suggested changes, and observations suggest that for almost all but the simplest revisions, he asked Mr. Smith and/or peers (see Kibler, 2010) for help in revising the essay according to these suggestions. As might be expected with such an intensive process, Diego did not have time to finish his essay: mid-way through the drafting process, Mr. Smith suggested Diego only incorporate two topics, rather than the three required of other students.

Diego's pattern of appealing to Mr. Smith for assistance throughout the process was one I had observed before. Even in Algebra II, a subject he knew well, Diego frequently "checked" his answers with his teacher before moving on to the next question. Data from formal and informal interviews conducted with Mr. Smith and other teachers at the schools suggest that such interactions helped Diego establish a reputation among his teachers as a hard-working and eager student, albeit one who struggled with academic subjects other than mathematics.

Grade 10 Letter: Impact of Interactions

As mentioned above, a lack of interaction between Diego and the novel was decisive in shaping the eventual written text (see Figure 4.1).

The first noticeable impact of the aforementioned interactions was that Diego did not include in his letter any details from the novel not mentioned in the summary, by his classmates, or by Mr. Smith: he relied on the teacher, peers, the summary document, and his own interpretations of the story, rather than the novel itself, to develop the content of his writing. Second, face-to-face interactions between Diego and Mr. Smith were clearly influential in that Mr. Smith suggested all of Diego's main topics, and several of Diego's written sentences were nearly identical to Mr. Smith's oral suggestions (see Kibler, 2011a for further discussion of this process). Third, written interactions also shaped the text, in that Diego made all changes—related to both content and written expression—that Mr. Smith suggested in written feedback. Likely as a result of this careful completion of his teacher's suggestions, Diego's text contains only two language patterns that would likely be seen as "typical" of multilingual writers at early stages of English language proficiency ("our village *need* this land to *reproduce* rice"), both of which occurred

April 19, 1950

Ruku
Village
India

Owners
Tannery of India Company
Rukmani's Village
India

To Whom It May Concern,

Is your daughter a prostitute? My name is Ruku and i have a daughter that is a prostitute. This has affected my family because people in the village criticize us saying that we don't educate our children well. I'm riding this letter to convince the owners of this tannery that Industrialization has caused major problems for my family and village.

When your factory came to our land you created problems not just for my family but also my village. When the factory came to our village prices became higher so people didn't have enough money to pay their rent or buy food. My daughter Ira became a prostitute because we needed more money to help Kuti my son. Me and my daughter Ira we are helping my son Kuti because hi is sick so we need the money to buy food to help Kuti. The people in the village think we didn't give our daughter a good education because of the job she has. The villagers and I feel defeated, but how can we help our families and our children?

It is not fair that you are taking me away from my home. You are taking land from our village so you can expand your tannery. You may say the factory has created new jobs, but our village need this land to reproduce rice so we can have food to stay alive.

FIGURE 4.1 Persuasive Letter Based on the Novel, *Nectar in a Sieve*

in the last sentence of his essay. Such a pattern could be expected given Mr. Smith's written and oral suggestions and the assistance Diego received from peers. The time-intensiveness of this process, however, also likely led to Diego not finishing his third paragraph or adding a conclusion.

Reflective interviews conducted after the essay was submitted and assessed suggest Mr. Smith and Diego both recognized how dramatically the teacher shaped Diego's writing. Mr. Smith mentioned that, "with Diego I felt that I was almost writing his essay at one point. I mean he's learning something I think, but I felt he was too dependent on me to complete the task." Although Diego told me in interviews that he relied upon others only to help him begin his paragraphs, audio-recorded peer interactions captured him confiding to a friend that, "*ahorita todo esto lo 'toy sacando de los maestros, me 'tan dando todas las respuestas* (now all this I'm getting it from the teachers, they're giving me all the answers)." Diego received the equivalent of a "D" for this assignment, and although data were not gathered related to how Mr. Smith calculated final grades, it does not appear that this assignment significantly influenced Diego's final semester grade, which was an "A−". Such a difference between the assignment and semester grades is surprising but likely the result of one or a combination of the following. The teacher might, for instance, have chosen to weight other assignments more heavily than the essay, which was the only one of its kind that semester. Alternatively, the relatively high semester grade could be the result of the school's nontraditional grading system, which incorporates elements such as "personal responsibility" and "social responsibility" alongside more traditional measures of academic achievement.

First-year College Essay: Interactions While Creating the Text

While aspects of Diego's writing process described below resonate strongly with those that occurred in tenth grade, the institutional setting in which Diego's college writing took place was quite different. Ocean College is a four-year institution that, in contrast to Diego's high school, placed students in a range of remedial courses rather than grouping them heterogeneously for English courses. Diego was placed in the two lowest levels of English, and the class for which this essay was written focused on grammar, sentence structure, punctuation, paragraphs, and short essays, according to the course description and assigned textbooks. It would take Diego at least two years of consecutive English classes, including one summer school course, to finally fulfill the writing requirement for his major, business finance. At the classroom level, Diego had the same English teacher in the fall, when he failed the course, and then again in the spring, when he passed it. Although it is not clear exactly how her background and preparation influenced his writing experiences, Diego spoke of her fondly and described her as a helpful teacher. In addition to support from his teachers, Diego also had a significant support network from his scholarship, including a mentor during the school year, a tutor in the summer, and funds for summer school classes to help him advance to credit-bearing courses more quickly. Despite a difficult start to his college career, Diego's U.S. citizenship continued to provide him a path toward a profession after earning his degree.

Although Diego did not share with me the written instructional materials his teacher provided for this assignment, in a retrospective interview he described the resources he drew upon in creating his essay. Diego explained that he learned in class about the importance of having an introduction, conclusion, and supporting paragraphs that are linked together. For the paragraph structure in this assignment, he said that he was taught and used a pattern just like one he learned in high school:

> The only thing that is helping me from high school is like, you start with a main idea and then the supporting, to support the idea, then the quote, then analysis, so that's how it goes . . . and that's how I ordered this one.

Observations and writing samples also support this claim; they indicate that Diego first learned and used this pattern in ninth grade.

In interviews Diego also admitted that—as in tenth grade—he did not read the book, *Burro Genius*, that students were supposed to read outside class and use to complete their essay assignment:

> Well, first because when I read the first chapter, I can't understand it at all. And so from there, I just like kind of like stopped reading it, and then like the teacher wasn't telling us anything about the book, like "how are you coming on your reading" or something . . . And so I just read the first chapter, and then it was kind of confusing, and then at the end like uh, like it was boring.

His teacher, Ms. Harwood, did not provide Diego with a summary, as Mr. Smith did, nor did Diego report having read summaries of the text available online. Instead, Diego explained that an in-class activity, in which the teacher had students share the theme from the book about which they were planning to write, was key in helping him develop ideas for the essay. Diego did not, however, decide to use any of his peers' ideas. Rather, he explained that

> [The other students] didn't got the one that teacher said. That, [s]he was like giving us an example, "oh, so I here, I have like the theme about making mistakes. He did a lot of mistakes on the, on the story and when he was little and when he was older." And so she just, she just like give us like simple quotes. And then so that came to my mind, and so I write about making mistakes. But I didn't use her quotes. I used different ones.

In addition to developing his theme of "mistakes" from his teacher's example, it also appears that Ms. Harwood provided Diego with individual assistance in locating quotations in the book that he could incorporate into his essay: "She was giving me more like pages, like 'oh, so you can use like this example of some mistake, or you can use this one or this one, but you only need like three.' So I'm like oh, okay."

Although transcripts of their interactions are not available, this recount of events suggests that Diego may have sought assistance from Ms. Harwood much as he did in high school, even though Diego reported that fewer opportunities were provided for in-class writing. These interactions, along with his story of bringing a high school paper to this teacher to re-grade, provide tentative evidence that Diego made efforts to develop and maintain a "hardworking student" identity at college as well, and the assistance that Ms. Harwood reportedly provided suggests that she responded to Diego by giving him additional tools—including specific examples from the text—as he wrote.

First-year College Essay: Impact of Interactions

Although it is impossible to know exactly how the aforementioned interactions unfolded for Diego, it appears that Ms. Harwood's individualized assistance in providing a theme and quotations formed the basis of Diego's text (see Figure 4.2).

Diego explains that after he received the quotation suggestions from his teacher,

> I needed to read like a little bit from the page from for where was the quote so I can get an idea how to start the paragraph to make it clear when I'm going to get to the quote. And then from there, the quote, I need to make it, like summarize it the quote to make it more clear, and I, I had some problems with that because I didn't read the book.

This pattern of retrieving information only from the selected quotations and the text surrounding it can be seen in the text, in which almost without exception Diego does not include details about the novel that cannot be gleaned from the quotations themselves. He did, however, closely follow the paragraph pattern he learned, first in ninth grade and then again in college.

As in tenth grade, Diego explained that he ran out of time to complete the assignment. Even though students completed most of their writing at home, rather than in class, at some point Ms. Harwood saw Diego's draft in progress and told him, "that it was okay, that [I] did not add a conclusion." As can be seen in Figure 4.2, Diego did not add a conclusion. Diego also said that he did not have time to revise his essay or get feedback before turning it in, and while interview data suggest that time management was a problem for Diego in all aspects of his college experience, his non-reading of *Burro Genius* played a key role, since he did not develop a focus for the essay until after his teacher and peers first shared their ideas.

The expectation that students complete much of their writing out of class, a pattern prominent at the college level and different from many students' high school experiences with in-class writing (Harklau, 2001), also had a noticeable impact on Diego's final text. There are multiple examples in his essay of language patterns readers might expect from multilingual writers, such as "it makes you successful of not repeat the mistakes," "If you do a mistake to one of your friends," and "Victor notice the big mistake he did," which are more frequent in the college essay than the tenth-grade letter. This pattern likely occurred because Diego reportedly wrote this text at home and did not receive feedback from his teacher or peers as he did in tenth grade.

No teacher interview was possible to determine how Ms. Harwood would

Burro Genius
Author: Victor Villasenor

You may feel Guilty because of your mistakes, but learning from your mistakes, it makes you successful of not repeat the mistakes Victor succeeds because he learned from his mistakes.

Victor was learning things from his parents by thinking ahead before the same mistake happens again. Victor made a mistake before when he was young. He realizes that if it happens again it will hurt him more than the first time. "I nodded. This was something that I really liked a lot about my mother and father. They were always thinking ahead so we didn't make the same mistake twice. Making the same mistake which I used to do when I was little could really be painful if you kept getting knocked on your ass by life." (p. 56) It's better to think ahead before you do something, otherwise someone else might get hurt. Therefore, if you think before you do something then there won't be any regrets.

If you do a mistake to one of your friends or to anyone that you are trying to make friends with. You may lose hope and respect from anyone by doing mistakes to them you will feel bad by making it and you end apologizing them, but they may not like you as they liked you before. "And to learn how to do this, you watch, mijito, think, figure, and smell. Then, also, you don't get bitter and lose hope on people when you make mistakes. Because you can bet your boots that I've made my share of mistakes in the past on this one, and that's okay. This is how we learn, by making mistakes. And big ones, too!" (p. 87) Victor learn that when he makes a mistake he realized that he done a bad thing to people and he learned that doing mistakes is not a good thing to do.

Victor learned from his big mistake by burning a lizard. Victor's dad told him that is not a good idea to burn any cane of animal just for fun because you are not showing respect to them. Victor notice the big mistake he did and makes him feel sad and guilty of what he did to an innocent lizard. "Nothing to a frog, papa, I said, beginning to cry. It was a lizard that we caught and we . . . we burnt him." (p. 139) Victor's dad thought him about this cane of mistakes of never take any life without showing respect, but he learned what is inappropriate to do to animals.

FIGURE 4.2 Expository Essay Based on the Memoir, *Burro Genius*

describe Diego's performance, but when I asked Diego in an interview how he felt about the essay he submitted, he said,

> I was still thinking that I was gonna do like, I was gonna get a bad grade because I didn't give it to no one to give me some feedback, but still I got, I got like a B plus because now I was like learning now how to do sentences and paragraphs and an essay.

When asked what specific feedback the teacher gave him on the essay, he explained that because it was a final assignment, she only provided him with a score rather than individual comments. Diego passed Ms. Harwood's course on his second try and moved to the next English composition course in the remedial English sequence the next fall.

From Grade 10 to the First Year of College: Change Over Time

The challenge of Diego's story lies in understanding how his writing can be considered "successful" and "unsuccessful" at the same time and over time, by both institutional standards and teacher guidelines or expectations. The longitudinal nature of this analysis and in-depth attention to the conditions under which the texts were created are key elements in such an endeavor, providing insight into the process of writing development for Diego, the ways in which his written texts are impacted by social and instructional settings, and his use of various strategies to cope with these writing situations.

Although the tenth-grade letter writing assignment had an element of persuasion and a fictional audience not present in the expository essay assignment in college, the tasks were, in fact, quite similar. Students were expected to read a single text assigned to the class, create a thesis based on the text, select specific details or quotations from the text to support this thesis, write body paragraphs according to a given structure, and include an introduction and conclusion.

Across these two contexts, it appears that Diego "form[ed] as well as perform[ed]" (Bartlett & Holland, 2002, p. 14) similar identities as a hardworking yet struggling student who was motivated to complete classroom assignments and sought his teachers' help to do so. These enactments of identity, which afforded Diego individualized assistance from his teachers, were clearly valuable in helping him to finish writing tasks and (eventually) pass classes, despite not having read assigned class texts. However, when Diego was placed in writing tasks—such as the high school exit exam or college placement tests—in which he could not receive assistance from others, he scored at consistently low levels.[1]

Diego developed his writing abilities to some degree over this three-year span of time. For example, his college essay uses a more consistent paragraph structure and a clearer focus for his writing than in tenth grade. His completion of the second writing task out of class, rather than in class with the almost constant assistance of his teacher and peers as occurred in tenth grade, also provides an indication of this development. Yet at neither level did Diego appear to meet reading and writing expectations for the assignment. In fact, he seemed to be moving further from this goal, since he continued to struggle with similar reading and writing tasks after three additional years in school.

Conclusions

How does a student like Diego leave high school as a successful writer but arrive in college and quickly come to believe he didn't know the "basic things"? Callahan (2005) and Harklau (1994) suggest that high school tracking could contribute to such a situation, yet Diego was not in classroom environments that were officially tracked.[2] Nonetheless, Diego left high school unable to place into college-level English writing courses. Diego's experiences suggest that, most obviously, this change occurred because classroom performance—in which he could appeal for teacher assistance—suddenly mattered less than individual performance on a standardized placement measure. Once in remedial college writing classes, the notion of not knowing the basics was reinforced by the teacher's initial evaluations of his high school writing. By the end of the second term, however, Diego was able to earn a passing score on the essay and the course overall, suggesting that classroom performance once again played a decisive role in his ability to complete writing tasks and pass courses.

Although Diego's case is necessarily unique, his experiences suggest several insights about secondary writing practices and multilingual students' transitions from high school to college, particularly as they relate to the varied conceptions of "essay writing" as a literacy practice, the multiple ways in which institutional settings shape multilingual students' interactions and opportunities to learn, and the complex manner in which students' previous experiences with writing influence their approach to writing tasks.

"Essay writing" had somewhat stable characteristics as a literacy practice (Street, 2000, 2003) in this study across high school and college settings. Although the two assignments cannot be seen as necessarily representative writing tasks for the courses as a whole, both were the primary writing assignments for the grading periods in which they occurred. They shared other important similarities across time and institutions as well. In both instances, essay writing and reading were necessarily linked in that students were expected to read a book-length text and gain information from it in order to develop ideas to write about. Teacher assistance with this process occurred during writing rather than during the reading phase for both assignments, even though problems first occurred for Diego during the reading tasks. It is possible that teachers did not "see" a lack of reading comprehension until Diego began writing, especially in college when reading was done entirely at home. In both instances, teachers and student valued production of the written text, engaging with each other and using individualized resources to do so.

As Moje and Lewis (2007) suggest, macro-level forces also shape and at times constrain students' opportunities to learn; in Diego's case it was institutional and classroom-based forces that had the most noticeable effect on his writing. At the institutional level, standardized assessments placed Diego in remedial courses that covered some material, such as Diego's paragraphing structure, he had learned before. Yet Diego was still not able to pass the course the first time he took it. As instructional settings and assignments shifted, Diego seemed unable to transfer his writing knowledge across contexts, a trend found in L2 writing research more generally (Tardy, 2006). In such a situation, re-learning appears to be a necessity, but the institutional structure provided for doing so—in this case, remedial coursework—may not have fully accomplished this goal.[3] At the classroom level, both Mr. Smith and Ms. Harwood faced the task of supporting and encouraging Diego, an eager multilingual student from a language minority background, as he completed writing assignments and persevered with schoolwork even when it appeared difficult for him due to his English language proficiency. These two teachers, embedded in different institutional cultures, may have had different expectations related to how "error-free" Diego's text should be and how much writing should be done out of class, but both provided extensive support related to the content of Diego's writing.

Diego's approach to both writing tasks provides convincing evidence that writers arrive in classrooms with a complex set of strategies and expectations for negotiating writing tasks. His interactions with texts, peers, the teacher, and other resources were shaped by his histories of participation (Rogers, 2002), or what had "worked" for him in the past. Diego employed similar coping strategies of eliciting assistance in both high school and college, with comparable results, despite institutional differences between the mainstream college-prep secondary class and the remedial college course. Although at the macro level Diego's strategies appear to mark him as someone who didn't know "the "basic things," his classroom-based approach to writing afforded him a level of success in completing classroom writing tasks and eventually passing his classes, much like the L2 writer profiled in Leki (1999), a college student who developed course survival skills that did not support the development of his critical thinking or learning.

In an earlier article, I suggested that in looking at the tenth-grade assignment alone, "it is difficult for either teacher or researcher to assess the long-term implications of the teacher–student interactions on Diego's writing development" (Kibler, 2011a, p. 54). This longitudinal analysis suggests that, although Diego has progressed through grade levels and shown a certain amount of development in his writing, his learning trajectory has been far from predictable (Lantolf & Pavlenko, 2001), and he continues to rely heavily on teacher mediation when he encounters course texts he cannot comprehend.

Implications

Adolescent multilingual writers are far from a monolithic group: they differ in relation to language and literacy backgrounds, levels of language proficiency in various contexts, past and current educational experiences and opportunities, race/ethnicity, goals, motives, and a host of other factors, all of which create unique learners with their own histories (and futures) of writing participation. With such a caveat in mind, this longitudinal interactional histories analysis suggests several directions for schools, teachers, and researchers who are concerned with these students' academic progress and writing development.

At the institutional level, students writing in their non-primary languages can clearly benefit when writing curricula are aligned from year to year through high school—and ideally, from high school to college as well—so that they are encouraged to build upon what they know and transfer writing skills across contexts and settings (e.g., Johns, 2009). In addition, creating portfolio systems can help institutions and teachers track students' progress across academic years as language proficiency develops. These portfolios would optimally include not only student work but also teacher observations about how students engage in the *process* of writing, helping teachers more effectively identify priorities for instruction and literacy needs—such as Diego's struggle with reading course texts in English—impacting writing performance. Additionally, students would benefit from clear information, particularly at the secondary level, regarding placement testing they will encounter after high school. K–12 schools invest significant time and resources into helping students pass standardized annual assessments, but relatively less attention is paid to preparing them for subsequent assessments they may encounter after high school that will fundamentally shape their post-secondary careers.

From a pedagogical perspective, Diego's story suggests the importance of recognizing the histories of participation that students bring to writing tasks. For example, students' expectations for what "essay writing" is will powerfully shape the ways in which they approach writing tasks and how they draw upon resources in their environments, including their teachers. Additionally, multilingual students' ability to comprehend written texts in their non-primary languages can be a key factor in determining how they will engage in subsequent writing tasks. In this sense, teaching and interactions before students begin drafting can be as influential on the eventual text as those during the composition process itself. Teachers of multilingual students must be both planners and responders, not only responding thoughtfully during face-to-face or written interactions with students but also planning strategically to help students comprehend source texts, understand genre features, and generate ideas for their writing.

From a research perspective, this analysis suggests that the "story" of adolescent multilingual writers' development may be occurring *off* the page for many students. Students' interactions with texts, peers, teachers, and other resources can play significant roles in how students create texts and the writing they eventually produce, which may or may not meet institutional standards for a variety of reasons. As such, writing research should attempt to recognize and trace the influence of such mediational tools—along with relevant institutional and social forces—on both students' writing and students themselves.

Notes

1 The validity of such standardized assessments for bilingual students like Diego has been questioned theoretically and empirically (Valdés & Figueroa, 1994), but regardless of such concerns, these measures had a significant impact on Diego's academic trajectory in relation to post-secondary English coursework.
2 The extent to which his experiences were truly "college prep" is a matter outside the scope of this article.
3 As has been argued elsewhere, alternative conceptualizations of academic coursework for language minority students may be necessary to facilitate their success in higher education (Kibler, Bunch, & Endris, 2011).

References

Allison, H. (2009). High school academic literacy instruction and the transition to college writing. In M. Roberge, M. Siegal, & L. Harklau (Eds.), *Generation 1.5 in college composition: Teaching academic writing to U.S.-educated learners of ESL* (pp. 75–90). New York: Routledge.

Bartlett, L., & Holland, D. (2002). Theorizing the space of literacy practices. *Ways of Knowing Journal, 2(*1), 10–22.

Barton, D., & Hamilton, M. (2000). Literacy practices. In D. Barton, M. Hamilton, & R. Ivanič (Eds.), *Situated literacies: Reading and writing in context* (pp. 7–15). London: Routledge.

Barton, D., Hamilton, M., & Ivanič, R., Eds. (2000). *Situated literacies: Reading and writing in context*. London: Routledge.

Bunch, G., & Panayotova, D. (2008). Latinos, language minority students, and the construction of ESL. *Journal of Hispanic Higher Education, 7*(1), 6–30.

Callahan, R. M. (2005). Tracking and high school English learners: Limiting opportunity to learn. *American Educational Research Journal, 42,* 305–328.

Compton-Lilly, C. (2007). *Re-reading families: The literate lives of urban children four years later*. New York: Teachers College Press.

Gee, J. (2010). *An introduction to discourse analysis: Theory and method*. New York: Routledge.

Harklau, L. (1994). Tracking and linguistic minority students: Consequences of ability grouping for second language learners. *Linguistics and Education, 6*(3), 217–244.

Harklau, L. (2000). From the "good kids" to the "worst": Representations of English language learners across educational settings. *TESOL Quarterly, 34*(1), 35–67.

Harklau, L. (2001). From high school to college: Student perspectives on literacy practice. *Journal of Literacy Research, 33*(1), 33–70.

Holland, D., Lachicotte, W., Skinner, D., & Cain, C. (1998). *Identity and agency in cultural worlds*. Cambridge, MA: Harvard University Press.

Johns, A. M. (2009). Situated invention and genres: Assisting generation 1.5 students in developing rhetorical flexibility. In M. Roberge, M. Siegal, & L. Harklau (Eds.), *Generation 1.5 in college composition: Teaching academic writing to U.S.-educated learners of ESL* (pp. 203–220). New York: Routledge.

Kibler, A. (2010). Writing through two languages: First language expertise in a language minority classroom. *Journal of Second Language Writing, 19*, 121–142.

Kibler, A. (2011a). "*Casi nomás me dicen qué escribir*/They almost just tell me what to write": A longitudinal analysis of teacher–student interactions in a linguistically diverse mainstream secondary classroom. *Journal of Education,* 191(1), 45–58.

Kibler, A. (2011b). "I write it in a way that people can read it": How teachers and adolescent L2 writers describe content area writing. *Journal of Second Language Writing, 20*, 211–226.

Kibler, A., Bunch, G., & Endris, A. (2011). Community college practices for U.S.-educated language-minority students: A resource-oriented framework. *Bilingual Research Journal, 34*, 201–222.

Lantolf, J. P. (2000a). Introducing sociocultural theory. In J. P. Lantolf (Ed.), *Sociocultural theory and second language learning* (pp. 1–26). Oxford: Oxford University Press.

Lantolf, J. P. (2000b). Second language learning as a mediated process. *Language Teaching, 33*, 79–86.

Lantolf, J. P. (2005). Sociocultural and second language learning research: An exegesis. In E. Hinkel (Ed.), *Handbook of research in second language teaching and learning* (pp. 335–354). Mahwah, NJ: Lawrence Erlbaum.

Lantolf, J. P., & Appel, G. (1994). Theoretical framework: An introduction to Vygotskian approaches to second language research. In J. P. Lantolf & G. Appel (Eds.), *Vygotskian approaches to second language research* (pp. 1–32). Norwood, NJ: Ablex.

Lantolf, J. P., & Pavlenko, A. (2001). (S)econd (L)anguage (A)ctivity: Understanding learners as people. In M. Breen (Ed.), *Learner contributions to language learning: New directions in research* (pp. 141–158). London: Pearson.

Lave, J., & Wenger, E. (1991). *Situated learning: Legitimate peripheral participation.* Cambridge, England: Cambridge University Press.

Leki, I. (1999). "Pretty much I screwed up": Ill-served needs of a permanent resident. In L. Harklau, K. Losey, & M. Siegal (Eds.), *Generation 1.5 meets college composition: Issues in the teaching of writing to U.S.-educated learners of English as a second language* (pp. 17–43). Mahwah, NJ: Lawrence Erlbaum.

Martin-Jones, M., & Jones, K. (2000). Introduction: Multilingual literacies. In M. Martin-Jones & K. Jones (Eds.), *Multilingual literacies: Reading and writing different worlds* (pp. 1–15). Amsterdam: John Benjamins.

Moje, E. B., & Lewis, C. (2007). Examining opportunities to learn literacy: The role of critical sociocultural literacy research. In C. Lewis, P. Enciso, & E. B. Moje (Eds.), *Reframing sociocultural research on literacy: Identity, agency, and power* (pp. 15–48). Mahwah, NJ: Lawrence Erlbaum.

Moore, C., & Shulock, N. (2010). *Divided we fail: Improving completion and improving racial gaps in California's community colleges.* Sacramento, CA: Institute for Higher Education Leadership and Policy, Sacramento State University.

Pardoe, S. (2000). Respect and the pursuit of "symmetry" in researching literacy and student writing. In D. Barton, M. Hamilton, & R. Ivanič (Eds.), *Situated literacies: Reading and writing in context* (pp. 149–165). London: Routledge.

Rodriguez, G. M., & Cruz, L. (2009). The transition to college of English learner and undocumented immigrant students: Resource and policy implications. *Teachers College Record, 11*(10), 2385–2418.

Rogers, R. (2002). Between contexts: A critical analysis of family literacy, discursive practices, and literate subjectivities. *Reading Research Quarterly, 37*, 248–277.

Ruiz-de-Velasco, J., & Fix, M. (2000). *Overlooked and underserved: Immigrant students in U.S. secondary schools.* Washington, DC: Urban Institute.

Street, B. (2000). Literacy events and literacy practices: Theory and practice in the new literacy studies. In M. Martin-Jones & K. Jones (Eds.), *Multilingual literacies: Reading and writing different worlds* (pp. 17–29). Amsterdam: John Benjamins.

Street, B. (2003). What's "new" in new literacy studies? Critical approaches to literacy in theory and practice. *Current Issues in Comparative Education, 5*(2), 77–91.

Tardy, C. M. (2006). Researching first and second language genre learning: A comparative review and a look ahead. *Journal of Second Language Writing, 15*, 79–101.

Tusting, K., Ivanič, R., & Wilson, A. (2000). New literacy studies at the interchange. In D. Barton, M. Hamilton, & R. Ivanič (Eds.), *Situated literacies: Reading and writing in context* (pp. 210–218). London: Routledge.

Valdés, G., & Figueroa, R. A. (1994). *Bilingualism and testing: A special case of bias.* Westport, CT: Ablex Publishing.

Van Oers, B. (1998). The fallacy of decontextualization. *Mind, Culture, and Activity, 5*(2), 135–142.

Vásquez, O. A. (2006). Cross-national explorations of sociocultural research on learning. *Review of Research in Education, 30*, 33–64.

Vygotsky, L. S. (1978). *Mind in society.* Cambridge, MA: Harvard University Press.

PART II
Academic Issues

5

PREPARING ENGLISH LANGUAGE LEARNERS FOR ARGUMENTATIVE WRITING

Alan Hirvela

As they make their way through the American school system (and perhaps other systems as well), one of the greatest challenges many English language learners (ELLs) are likely to face is learning how to write (and read) argumentatively. There are two primary reasons for this. First, as research has shown, argumentative writing is generally difficult for pre-college students (including ELLs). For instance, as reported by Perie, Grigg, and Donahue (2005), in the United States only 6 percent of twelfth-grade students can execute moves that undergird argumentative writing, such as making informed critical judgments about texts, and only 15 percent of twelfth-grade students have been evaluated at the "proficient" level with respect to writing essays in which they state and clearly support a position (the thesis-support move at the heart of argumentation). Citing a number of studies and analyses of research findings, Reznitskaya, Anderson, and Kuo (2007) note that "numerous nation-wide assessments and research studies have consistently documented the lack of proficiency in argumentation by the majority of American students" (p. 450). Compounding that situation, from the ELL perspective, is the research finding that it may take ELLs six to ten years to develop the levels of reading and writing proficiency required to perform at appropriate grade levels (Hakuta, Goto Butler, & Witt, 2000). This suggests that gaining command of a type of writing and reading as complex as argumentation will pose especially strong challenges for ELLs, and this during that six- to ten-year learning period when they are endeavoring to acquire baseline proficiency and thus may not be well equipped to engage argumentation meaningfully.

Second, ELLs, especially in the higher grades, face the added challenge of already possessing, in their native language writing and thinking, what Richard Anderson and his colleagues researching collaborative reasoning call *argument schema*: knowledge of how to organize information in order to present it for argumentative purposes. Because of differences in how people conceptualize and practice argumentation across cultures and languages, the argument schema possessed by older and more experienced ELLs may run counter to what they are expected to know and do in their American classrooms. Thus, in addition to issues pertaining to the acquisition of academic literacy skills, ELLs may have to cope as well with potential interference from different cultural norms and writing practices from those that obtain in their new learning environment.

At the same time that argumentative writing may be difficult for ELLs (and their native English-speaking peers), an added and significant new development faces them: the impending implementation (in 2014) in the United States of what are known as the *Common Core Standards* for academic achievement in various subject areas. As I will show shortly, a key component in these standards is writing (and reading) that, in one form or another, involves argumentative skills. Indeed, argumentation will take on considerably more importance in pre-college education in the United States in the coming years. There is already recognition of argument's importance, as Newell, Beach, Smith, and VanDerHeide (2011), summarizing the work of a number of scholars in this area, explain: "the ability to identify the underlying argument, and its claims, warrants, and evidence, in reading and the ability to compose a high-quality argument, and its claims, warrants, and evidence, in writing are critical skills for academic success" (p. 274). Graff (2003) makes a similar point: "For American students to do better—all of them, not just twenty percent—they need to know that summarization and making arguments is the name of the game" (p. 3). Those points are amplified when seen in conjunction with the *Common Core Standards*.

In light of these factors just cited, there is a need to look at what we already know about argumentation and what can be done to help ease ELLs' transition into this type of literate activity. That is what I will do in this chapter. The chapter is divided into two parts. In Part One, I provide context for the chapter by briefly defining argumentation. This is followed by a discussion of what relevant research has shown about second language (L2) writers and argumentation and what the field of intercultural rhetoric has revealed about this type of writing. In Part Two the focus shifts to pedagogy: first, a short summary of relevant information from the *Common Core Standards*, and then a review of what some scholars have already proposed with respect to helping students (including ELLs) to write argumentatively. The chapter concludes with a discussion of how to prepare ELLs to engage argumentation meaningfully, relative to the information presented in the chapter.

Part One: Context

Defining Argumentation

In defining argumentation, it is first necessary to distinguish it from persuasion, since the two terms may at first sight appear to mean the same thing (and not infrequently are treated as such). In their popular book, *Everything's an Argument* (2004), Lunsford and Ruszkiewicz note that

> the point of argument is to discover some version of the truth, using evidence and reasons. Argument of this sort leads audiences toward conviction, an agreement that a claim is true or reasonable or that a course of action is desirable. The aim of persuasion is to change a point of view or to move others from conviction to action. In other words, writers or speakers argue to find some truth; they persuade when they think they already know it.
>
> *(p. 7)*

Looking further at persuasion, Kinneavy and Warriner (1993) say that, "In a persuasive essay, you can select the most favorable evidence, appeal to emotions, and use style to persuade your readers. Your single purpose is to be convincing" (p. 305). According to Hillocks (2011), "Argument, on the other hand, is mainly about logical appeals and involves claims, evidence, backing, and rebuttals" (p. xvii). Fulkerson (1996) adds that argument should be seen "not as victory over an opponent but mutual dialectical interchange through which, out of opposing yet simultaneously cooperating voices, wise decisions can be reached, decisions always subject to revision as better arguments and better evidence become available" (p. ix). Persuasion, by contrast, consistently performs the function of bringing the audience into agreement with the author's point of view or desired form of action.

Ramage and Bean (1989) identify three major conceptualizations of argument generally used for classroom purposes (though, as will be seen later, there is also considerable variation). One, they say, stresses the importance of formal logic. They explain that "Typical of this approach is a classroom emphasis on the study of syllogisms, problems of valid and invalid syllogistic forms, patterns of inferences, Venn diagrams, and the traditional informal fallacies" (p. v). Another pedagogical approach revolves around a "stasis system" and "attempts to classify arguments according to types of claims and teaches typical patterns of developing each claim type" (p. vi). The third type is the one that seemingly is most commonly employed, an approach rooted in the Toulmin model, developed originally in 1958 by Stephen Toulmin and updated in 2001. This approach, which Ramage and Bean frame as operating more rhetorically than other approaches, revolves around three main components: claims, data, and warrants. As Fulkerson (1996) explains, in this model "The data are the facts cited as premises or support. The claim is the argument's conclusion, and the warrant is a general operating principle or rule of thumb allowing a bridge to be made between data and claim" (p. 18). He portrays what he calls "the core of the Toulmin model" in the following example (p. 19):

DATA: Russia has violated 50 of 52 international agreements.
CLAIM (therefore): Russia would violate a proposed ban on nuclear weapons testing.

> **WARRANT** (since): Past violations are symptomatic of probable future violations.

The Toulmin model has since been expanded to include other key components. In his well-known work on argumentative writing in middle schools and high schools, Hillocks (2011, p. xix) offers this expanded view of the Toulmin model (emphasis his):

- a *claim*
- based on *evidence* of some sort
- a *warrant* that explains *how the evidence supports the claim*
- *backing* that supports the warrants
- *qualifications* and *rebuttals* or counterarguments that refute competing claims.

The Toulmin model, or variations of it, seems to play a major role in argumentative writing instruction. As we will see shortly, it appears to be the model underlying the conceptualization of argumentation in the *Common Core Standards*. An informal scan of popular writing textbooks focusing on argument also suggests the dominance of the Toulmin model. Argumentative writing instruction, then, often involves helping students understand the key components of argument as defined by Toulmin as well as learning how to manipulate them successfully.

Because of their prior exposure to writing instruction in earlier grades, students in high school may well be familiar with the core idea of a thesis statement supported by reasons or evidence. However, good argumentative writing extends well beyond that approach, and gaining command of these other important areas of argumentative writing is an elusive matter. This highlights the need for well-designed and effectively implemented instruction that is inclusive enough to account for all of these measures of argumentation, though a challenging question is: At what point in the instructional ecology should students be exposed to these various components of argument? For instance, should all five of the components of the Toulmin model be introduced as early as ninth grade? Should the seemingly more challenging components of warranting and dealing with counterarguments be introduced later? These are just some of the pedagogical issues that must be addressed, especially for ELLs relative to their unique backgrounds and needs.

Other instructional issues must also be considered. One is selecting quality evidence or data that relate closely to the thesis. This can be especially challenging for ELLs, whose notion of evidence from their native culture may be at variance with what is considered effective evidence in the Anglophone context. Identifying suitable sources for the gathering of evidence is another potentially problematic area. Student writers, including ELLs, may also wrestle with the issue of how much evidence is necessary to argue successfully. Another issue is what comes first: the claim or the data? That is, should students generate a claim and then find data to support that claim, or should they select a topic, gather data, and then generate a thesis on the basis of what the evidence suggests?

Related Research

In this subsection I will look at relevant research from various perspectives. First is research regarding L2 writers and argumentation, including contributions from the field of contrastive/intercultural rhetoric. Then I shift to what recent research has revealed concerning ELLs and writing.

L2 Writers and Argumentation

My purpose in this subsection is not to provide an exhaustive review or to look intensively at what the research has found. Rather, I want to show how interest in argumentation has evolved in the L2 context and what, specifically, has drawn the attention of L2 writing researchers.

An important starting point for this topic from the L2 perspective is the field of contrastive (now more commonly called intercultural) rhetoric, which explores various writing-related issues across languages and cultures. The field itself started in 1966 with the publication of Robert Kaplan's famous "doodles article" in which he attempted to capture the basic direction taken by different writing systems via a series of brief sketches. Argumentation began to draw serious interest among contrastive rhetoricians in the 1980s. This is not surprising, as it is clear that argument is a form of writing that is practiced in many parts of the world, as shown, for example, in Foster and Russell's book, *Writing and Learning in Cross-National Perspective* (2002), which looks at writing instruction in several countries around the world; a special issue (1995) of the *Journal of Asian Pacific Communication* (edited by Robert Kaplan) entitled "The Teaching of Writing in the Pacific Basin"; and a book chapter by Carter (1996) that focuses specifically on argumentation in the Far East. These sources show that, both in English and in other languages, argument often figures in writing instruction. This, too, is not surprising, as argumentation itself has a very long and notable history, beginning with Aristotle's seminal book *Rhetoric*, where argument figures heavily. Along the same lines, Kadar-Fulop (1988) notes that "Classical rhetorical education knew four conventional forms of spoken or written discourse: argumentation, exposition, description, and narration" (p. 42). Then, too, argumentation has been included in a number of published typologies of major types of writing, including Moffett (1968) as well as James Kinneavy's (1971) oft-cited analysis. Of particular importance to contrastive rhetoricians was a typology developed by Werlich in 1976, as this one accounted for the influence of culture and thus looked at primary text types across different languages (including argumentative texts).

Also significant, in the 1980s, was the International Association for the Evaluation of Educational Achievement (IEA) Study of Written Composition. As Purves (1988) explains, the study intended to

> provide a way of examining a systematically drawn sample of writing in a number of rhetorical modes by an average school population writing in the language of instruction. It also examines the criteria of "good" writing used by teachers of writing in each of the countries in order to see if there are systematic differences that might help define rhetorical communities.
>
> *(p. 14)*

Argument was among the rhetorical modes included in the study, and this led to important early efforts to analyze argumentative/persuasive writing across languages and cultures (e.g., Connor, 1990; Connor & Lauer, 1985, 1988; Purves, Soter, Takala, & Vahapassi, 1984). Silva's (1993) meta-analysis of L2 writing research also provided evidence of this early interest in argumentation, especially as influenced by contrastive rhetoric.

Also important in the contrastive rhetoric literature were early attempts to look at argument/persuasion among writers from specific countries, e.g. Connor (1987), who studied students from England, Finland, Germany, and the United States, and Crismore, Markkanen, and Steffenson (1993), who compared the writing of Finnish and American university students. Such research continues to appear, such as Wu and Rubin (2000), who looked at the argumentative writing of Chinese and North American university students, and, more recently, Concha and Paratore (2011), who studied the persuasive writing of Chilean high school (twelfth-grade) students.

Argumentative writing research in the L2 context has gradually expanded its scope beyond conventional school-based coverage. For example, Bruce (2002) looked at the roles of both language and content in the teaching of legal argumentation, Coffin (2004) investigated the role of argumentation in the popular IELTS test, and Dressen (2003) explored persuasive writing strategies in the writing of geologists. More striking is the interest in the connection between argument and technology. Charles (2007) and Hyland and Tse (2005), for instance, have used corpus technology to investigate grammatical issues in argumentative writing. Bloch (2004) and Laurinen and Marttunen (2007) studied the use of argument in online chat settings; Radia and Stapleton (2008) researched undergraduate students' use of internet sources in argumentative essays; Ho, Rappa, and Chee (2009) explored the use of virtual role-playing software for argumentative purposes; and Lee, Wong, Cheung, and Lee (2009) looked at the use of a web-based critiquing system to evaluate students' argumentative essays.

What We Have Learned about ELLs as Writers

Before looking at what we know about ELLs as writers, it is important to establish the scope of the importance of the issues discussed in this chapter. For instance, recent statistics indicate that there are more than five million ELLs in public schools (National Clearinghouse for English Language Acquisition, 2011). Furthermore, as already indicated in sources such as Ortmeier-Hooper and Enright's (2011) special issue of the *Journal of Second Language Writing*, Silva's (1993) article examining L2 writing research up to that point in time, and the recent synthesis of L2 writing research for students writing in English by Leki, Cumming, and Silva (2008), ELLs clearly are writers who are different in important ways from their native English-speaking peers. However, also worth noting is Harklau's stark observation about the "sparse research literature" on these individuals (2011, p. 211).

To establish some understanding of the current picture, I will look at what two recent analyses of the literature have revealed and concluded. One, published by the Education Alliance at Brown University (Panovsky et al., 2005), offers the disturbing comment that "alarming numbers of nonnative English speaking college freshmen fail entry-level writing assessments despite their years of schooling in the mainland U.S." (p. 1). The authors of the report add that "The recent change in the SAT writing assessment and the related raising of the writing performance standard in 2005 lend greater urgency to those findings" (p. 1). To these comments can be added the recent decision (in 47 of 50 states in the U.S.) to adopt the *Common Core Standards* (discussed later), which will place added pressure on ELLs to develop at least proficient writing (and reading) skills, especially in argumentation.

Several findings and conclusions reported in the other major source, the extensive and influential *Report of the National Literacy Panel on Language-Minority Children and Youth* (August & Shanahan, 2008), are also worth noting. This report, commissioned by the Institute for Education Sciences of the U.S. Department of Education, was intended to "identify, assess, and synthesize research on the education of language-minority youth with respect to their attainment of literacy, and to produce a report evaluating and synthesizing this literature" (August & Shanahan, 2008, p. 1). In general, this analysis of the research literature, like that in the Brown Education Alliance report, shows that ELLs tend to struggle in the development of literacy skills in English, thus leading to the lack of readiness for college level writing (and reading) cited earlier. The following points relative to this chapter emerge in August and Shanahan's introduction to the report:

> certain aspects of second-language literacy development are related to performance on similar constructs in the first language. . .well-developed literacy skills in the first language can facilitate second language literacy development.
>
> *(pp. 7–8)*

> as is true for language-majority students, instruction that provides substantial coverage of key components of literacy has a positive influence on the literacy development of language-minority students.
>
> *(p. 9)*

Although second language literacy instruction should focus on the same curricular components as first language literacy development, the differences in the children's second-language proficiency make it important to adjust this instruction to effectively meet their needs. The research has provided a sketchy picture of what some of these adjustments might be.

(p. 10)

successful instructional approaches usually do not improve the literacy skills of second-language learners as much as they do for first-language learners.

(p. 10)

Language-minority students who are literate in their first language are likely to be advantaged in the acquisition of English literacy.

(p. 11)

Collectively, these results suggest that the job of preparing ELLs to learn to write and read argumentatively, especially as higher expectations for being able to do so enter the instructional picture via the *Common Core Standards*, is, and will be, a difficult one, as well as an extremely important one. Using what was reported in Part One as a backdrop, in Part Two I look at what is possible, and what can be recommended, for the instructional domain.

Part Two: Pedagogy

In this section I examine ways of teaching argumentation. My primary purpose is to show, and discuss (from the perspective of ELLs' characteristics and needs), some of the primary approaches that have emerged in recent years as a way of identifying options that could be applied to instruction with ELLs. Because the *Common Core Standards* will, for those students in the United States, shape the instructional environment in which they will engage with argumentation, I begin with a review of what those standards involve with respect to argumentation. I focus on the writing standards, though it should be noted that the reading standards also have important implications for argumentatively oriented instruction.

The Common Core Standards

As noted earlier, the *Common Core Standards*, which will constitute the exact same standards for proficiency in literacy used in 47 of the 50 states in the United States, will significantly "up the ante" where argumentation is concerned. Hence, in addressing pedagogical issues, it is important to account for what these standards will mean for ELLs in the coming years.

Now being tested in various schools, the standards will take full effect in 2014. What is interesting about them with respect to argumentation is not only the way in which they increase argumentation's profile, but also how they run across the domain of reading as well as writing, and how they extend across different grade levels. The message they convey is very clear, and is of great significance for ELLs: students from the earliest grades through high school will be expected to perform various acts of reading and writing related to argumentation and will need to demonstrate at least an adequate command of the various skills involved in such reading and writing. Furthermore, these standards apply to more than writing and reading for Language Arts (i.e. English) classes. They also apply to the use of literacy in history/social sciences, science, and technical subjects. Thus, it will be incumbent upon ELLs to understand and use argumentation as it pertains to English.

The Standards for Writing

Interestingly, the writing standards begin as early as kindergarten, where the very first expectation stated with respect to "text types and purposes" is that students should "Use a combination of drawing, dictating, and writing to compose *opinion pieces* in which they tell a reader the topic or the name of the book they are writing about and *state an opinion or preference about the topic or book*" (emphasis mine). Thus, even at this initial point in their schooling, ELLs will need, in a roundabout way, to experience the argumentative component of claim. As they move to first grade, they must "supply a reason" for the opinion they express. In the second grade they will be expected to provide "reasons," not a single reason. In grades 3–5 the same core requirement is seen, but with added conditions, such as generating appropriate organizational strategies for the presentation of their reasons as well as language appropriate for effectively linking reasons and opinions. In grades 6–8, with respect to English Language Arts, the word "argument" first appears and continues to be the first type of writing discussed, and students are expected to perform the same core act (with increasing sophistication) across these grades: "Write arguments to support claims with clear reasons and relevant evidence." Beginning in the seventh grade, they will have to "Introduce claim(s), acknowledge alternate or opposing claims, and organize reasons and evidence logically." There is also an expectation to provide "relevant evidence, using accurate, credible sources" and to show relationships between claims and evidence. In other words, as early as the seventh grade, all of the elements of the Toulmin model of argumentation will be in play. Across grades 9–12, argumentative writing is once again the first writing type discussed, with the core expectation being to "Write arguments to support claims in an analysis of substantive topics or texts using valid reasoning and relevant and sufficient evidence." Thus, at this stage the logic of the reasoning takes on greater importance, as does the quality of the evidence used.

As for writing in the other subject areas mentioned earlier, argumentation once again is the first type of writing introduced, with the same core task aligned with grades 6–12: "Write arguments focused on the discipline-specific content."

Other elements of the Toulmin model also continue to appear: claims, evidence, warrants. In addition, the quality of the evidence and the "logical reasoning" remain important.

To summarize briefly, at whatever grade levels they enter an American school, ELLs will encounter argumentation in one form or another in their English classes and will be expected to work with it in other subject areas as early as the sixth grade. This represents a very important change in pedagogical circumstances for ESL writing specialists to address and necessitates greatly increased attention to ways of teaching and researching argumentative writing.

Approaches to Argumentative Pedagogy

In this subsection I briefly review several different approaches to argumentative writing instruction. This coverage is not meant to be exhaustive. The emphasis is on (a) discussing particularly well-known and popular approaches, (b) providing a wide-ranging sampling of possible approaches, and (c) exploring approaches that show promise for work with ELLs.

The Collaborative Reasoning Approach

Developed by Richard Anderson and a large research team at the University of Illinois, this cognitively based approach has been developed and tested in a number of studies since the mid-1990s with elementary school children in the United States and, more recently, in China and Korea. As explained in Reznitskaya, Anderson, McNurlen, Nguyen-Jahiel, Archodidou, and Kim (2001), collaborative reasoning (CR) is based on the premise "that reasoning is fundamentally dialogical and, hence, the development of reasoning is best nurtured in supportive dialogical settings such as group discussion" (p. 155). After participating in a series of group discussions in response to a story they have read, students then write a short "reflective essay" in which they argue a position relative to a dilemma or a question raised in the assigned text. The belief underlying this approach is that students will transfer to their writing elements of argumentative discourse experienced during the group discussions.

This approach brings into play a few key components of argumentative writing instruction. One is "argument schema," which Reznitskaya et al. (2001) define in this way: "According to our theory, an argument schema is an abstract knowledge structure that represents extended stretches of argumentative discourse" (p. 158). Argument schema generate "argument stratagems," which are specific enactments of argumentative strategies and language, such as "one reason for this is" (Reznitskaya et al., 2007, p. 467). Another important component is the "snowball phenomenon," a term which captures the idea that, as students discuss a story, argument stratagems spread from one child to others as they are put in use (Anderson, Nguyen-Jahiel, McNurlen, Archodidou, Kim, Reznitskaya, Tillmans,

& Gilbert, 2001). This snowball effect helps develop and instantiate argument schema and equips students with an array of argument stratagems to employ. Thus, through engagement with oral (collaborative) reasoning, which entails offering opinions or making claims and then finding evidence to support them, students encounter, and rehearse, the various moves at the heart of argumentation during the creation of argument schema. As described in Reznitskaya et al. (2001),

> we hypothesize that an argument schema enables organization and retrieval of argument-relevant information, facilitates argument construction and repair, and provides the basis for anticipating objections and for finding flaws in one's own argument and the arguments of others. An important feature of an argument schema is that it is abstract and therefore enables transfer among situations.
>
> *(p. 158)*

Various studies conducted by Anderson's research team have generally shown positive results for the collaborative reasoning approach. Of particular interest for the purposes of this chapter is a recent attempt to employ CR outside the United States. Dong, Anderson, Kim, and Li (2008) report on a large CR study that took place in fourth-grade classrooms in China and Korea. They were interested in these settings because of the assumption that collaborative discussion, or reasoning, is not a typical element of the pedagogical practices in those countries. What they found was that "students made a fast and smooth adaptation to the new discussion format, were highly engaged, and for the most part were able to manage the discussions themselves" (p. 400). They also found that the "Chinese and Korean students showed a pattern of social propagation of 'argument stratagems' parallel to that of American students" (p. 400).

An important underlying feature of argument schema is strategies, in that the construction and use of an argument schema involves, in part, the use of strategies to facilitate the planning necessary for the "construction," "repair," and "anticipation of objections" cited above. Thus, while an argument schema takes shape through socially mediated learning contexts, a cognitive framework is also in place.

The Cognitive Strategies Approach

The emphasis on helping students develop argumentative strategies at the heart of collaborative reasoning brings into play the contributions that strategies can make to academic writing (and reading) and the goal-directed behavior at the heart of cognitive views of writing. According to Langer (1991),

> As children learn to engage in literate behaviors to serve the functions and reach the ends they see modeled around them, they become literate—in a

culturally appropriate way; they use certain cognitive strategies to structure their thoughts and complete their tasks, and not others.

(p. 17)

Drawing on this belief in the importance of strategies, Olson and Land (2007) offer a recent collection of such strategies that comprise what they call a "Cognitive Strategies Reader's and Writer's Tool Kit" for the use of ELLs in completing various academic literacy tasks in high school, including argumentative writing and reading. These strategies include: Planning and Goal Setting, Tapping Prior Knowledge, Asking Questions, Making Predictions, Making Connections, Constructing the Gist, Summarizing, Clarifying, Visualizing, Monitoring, Revising Meaning, Reflecting and Relating, and Evaluating.

Teachers introduce these strategies to students and help them explore their use in various interpretative reading and analytic writing tasks. Students thus learn not only about the value of strategies for academic reading and writing, but also about how to draw the appropriate strategies from the tool kit for the particular task at hand. Olson and Land (2007) and Olson, Kim, Scarcella, Kramer, Pearson, van Dyk, Collins, and Land (2012) provide detailed descriptions of applications of this tool kit and results obtained in large-scale intervention studies featuring the tool kit. They report that teachers adapt well to the use of the kit and that, with sufficient time for exposure and practice, ELLs demonstrate progress in their reading and writing, thus proving the value of a cognitive strategies approach for high school-level ELLs, including argumentative writing.

Audience-Oriented Approach

Another approach, first discussed here in the context of college-level ESL writers, is an audience-based one in which Ann Johns (1993, 1997) builds upon the idea of students researching the writing practices of a specific academic discourse community they expect to enter (and thus playing the role of ethnographers studying a specific community). In this way they must develop a clear understanding of a particular audience. In Johns (1993) she illustrates this process through a study she conducted of undergraduate ESL engineering students writing a grant proposal. By its very nature, the grant proposal is an argumentative type of document, and Johns shows how students studying the audience of grant reviewers and their likely expectations for a successful grant application learn how to write argumentatively because of the targeted nature of the activity. In other words, argumentative writing skills will develop more successfully if students are asked to study, and write for, a specific audience.

Ramage and Bean (1989), in a popular textbook called *Writing Arguments*, have also presented an audience-based approach which requires students to anticipate the type(s) of logic that will work best for specific audiences and then learn how to account for that logic in the development of their arguments. Central to their approach is the well-known "rhetorical triangle" consisting of audience, message, and writer. Ramage and Bean assert that "In composing an effective argument, writers must concern themselves with all three elements in this 'rhetorical triangle'" (p. 43) and, while doing so, must identify and control the type of logic that is consistent across all three components of the triangle. This emphasis on logic is likewise seen in Richard Fulkerson's approach as delineated in his popular (1996) book, *Teaching the Argument in Writing*. While not citing the key role of audience as overtly as Johns or Ramage and Bean, Fulkerson's approach nevertheless places audience at the heart of argumentation in his focus on what kinds of logic will work best in different settings (and thus address different audiences).

The Argument is Everywhere Approach

By all appearances, an extremely popular book among teachers of argumentation is Lunsford and Ruszkiewicz's *Everything's an Argument* (2004), which builds on the idea conveyed in the book's title: in our various locations in daily life, all of us are surrounded by argumentation in one form or another. As they explain: "In fact, it's hard to go more than a few minutes without encountering some form of argument in our culture . . . an argument can be any text—whether written, spoken, or visual—that expresses a point of view" (p. 4). This notion of the ubiquity of argument plays out in two important ways in the book. First, in demystifying the common notion of argument as something one person must win (thus defeating opponents), the authors delve into other common forms of argument: Arguments to Inform, Arguments to Convince, Arguments to Explore, Arguments to Make Decisions, and Arguments to Meditate or Pray.

Second, in explaining and illustrating these different types of argumentation, the authors draw on materials and examples from a myriad of sources appearing in daily life circumstances, thus demystifying the notion of what students must read and utilize in building arguments. In this way they connect students to argumentation as it exists and operates in real-life circumstances, thus making it more accessible and more manageable for students, who will feel empowered by the vast array of everyday resources available to them as well as the existing knowledge of argumentation they already possess by virtue of their many experiences in real-life contexts. In this way they can make use of already existing argument schema acquired in the course of living their lives. Ultimately, this approach is designed to minimize, if not eliminate, the intimidation factor many students experience upon being asked to write (and read) argumentatively for academic purposes.

The Argument as Moves Approach

The apparent popularity, among teachers, of Lunsford and Ruszkiewicz's book and approach appears to be matched by Gerald Graff and Cathy Birkenstein's book, *They Say / I Say: The Moves That Matter in Persuasive Writing* (2007). It offers a few key conceptualizations of argumentative pedagogy that are captured in the book's title. One is the "they say/I say" idea, which, in instructional terms, boils down to first identifying and then summarizing what those on the opposing side of one's claim say, and then constructing an argument that is at least in part a response to their points of view. This simple formulation of an argumentative writing structure holds great appeal to both teachers and students.

Second, much of the book consists of what the authors call "templates," that is, specific formulations for how various kinds of argumentative statements can be made. This is the "moves" portion of the book's title. For instance, in their section on how authors can express both agreement and disagreement with an opposing point of view, they note that students could use these boilerplate statements as starting points (p. 60):

- Although I agree with X up to a point, I cannot accept his overall conclusion that . . . .
- Although I disagree with much that X says, I fully endorse his final conclusion that . . . .
- Though I concede that . . . I still insist that . . . .
- While X is probably wrong when she claims that . . . she is right that. . . .

Argumentation, then, is taught as becoming familiar with a kind of tool kit (similar to the cognitive strategies tool kit discussed earlier) of possible moves for different moments or places in an argumentative essay and selecting wisely among the available moves, with the moves clustering around the "they say" and "I say" domains of argumentation.

The Problem-Solving Approach

Drawing on a combination of cognitive and social perspectives on writing and on aspects of writing presented earlier—argument schema, collaboration/dialogue, strategy use—some scholars have articulated an approach to argumentation rooted in the idea of students developing argumentative skills via various problem solving activities. This approach has been described most notably in the work of George Hillocks (1995, 1999, 2011), who refers to it as an "inquiry approach to instruction" (2011, p. 16). In his words:

> Briefly, inquiry involves a number of strategies that range from observing and attempting to construct an interpretation of the observations to imagining what could be. It includes comparing, contrasting, testing, evaluating, and hypothesizing—and interpreting the results of all these. Such a list as there is space to present here is suggestive rather than exhaustive.
>
> *(1995, pp. 91–92)*

In his most recent presentation of this approach, his 2011 book *Teaching Argument Writing, Grades 6–12*, he explains that he and his colleagues

> use the Toulmin model to help students learn to develop arguments from existing data. To do this, we begin with a specific problem—a crime that needs to be solved—that contains data about which claims can be made and for which warrants may be developed. We believe that by starting with a problem, students learn the strategies for making arguments.
>
> *(p. 16)*

This occurs through the following actions (p. 16):

* analyzing evidence critically in light of existing knowledge
* interpreting the evidence to explain what it shows
* developing warrants that show why the evidence is relevant
* using the evidence and the explanations to solve the problem.

As in the case of collaborative reasoning, students conduct these actions via class discussions, and in that respect are engaged in a process of the social construction of knowledge. However, this process also engages them in the use of various strategies in the course of completing those actions, and in this regard students are also aligned with the cognitive dimension of writing. As Hillocks (1995) sees it, "Once the impulse to write is in place, the composing process brings the writer's repertoire of knowledge and strategies into play" (p. 87).

McCann (2010) works according to similar principles, but presents an approach that revolves around works of art instead of the crime-oriented mysteries in Hillocks' most recent work. In McCann's approach, students are presented with problems such as making an argument for which of a series of paintings by an artist should be selected for display in a public place.

Klein and Rose (2010) have also presented a problem-solving approach, though in their case the emphasis is on writing to learn in various content areas in school. They present a two-phase approach in which students learn about argumentation (first phase) and then explanation (second phase), two contrasting ways in which writers use argumentative principles in the course of addressing the kinds of problems featured in different content areas (social studies, science, English, etc.). Where Hillocks illustrates the value of an inquiry-based approach to argumentation and problem solving, they emphasize connections between writing to learn and argumentation.

Discussion and Conclusion

What this chapter shows, for writing teachers who work with ELLs, is a complex configuration of factors that will need to be accounted for if ELLs are to learn to write (and read) argumentatively at an acceptable (at least) level of proficiency. First, as contrastive rhetoric shows, ELLs may well be familiar with argumentation when they encounter it in English, but not necessarily in ways which align well with argumentation as it is defined and practiced in Anglophone settings. That is, they have already developed some type of argument schema in the L1, and this schema is available for use in the L2. Whether this prior exposure will be an asset or a disadvantage will vary considerably according to such factors as students' age and prior experience, native language and culture, and reading and writing proficiency in their native language. Second, research shows that most students, including ELLs, struggle in learning how to write and read argumentatively. Third, the *Common Core Standards* will place increasing pressure on teachers and ELLs to account for argumentation, in early grades of education in the United States as well as the higher grades where argumentation has historically played a role. Collectively, these factors may appear to present a somewhat troubling picture for ELLs and argumentation, especially when the *Common Core Standards* are fully implemented.

However, I hope that this chapter has also provided some reasons for encouragement. For instance, the report edited by August and Shanahan (2008) suggests that ELLs may be able to benefit from their prior knowledge of argumentation via their native language and culture. Even with differences in cultures, and therefore ways in which argumentation is practiced, ELLs, at least at the high school level, may already possess argument schema and argument stratagems that could be adjusted and transferred to use in English-oriented argumentation. Teachers aware of this could use this information to help ELLs tap productively into their L1 argument schema and stratagems. Having ELLs discuss (and compare/contrast with English) what their native language and culture have taught them about argumentation could help in this regard. A valuable perspective to adopt here is that many ELLs do not necessarily have to *learn about* argumentation; instead, they may be relearning it. This relates to another relevant and important contribution of work discussed in this chapter: the value to teachers of understanding and embracing the notions of argument schema and argument stratagems. Building argumentative writing instruction around these constructs could prove extremely useful in leading ELLs into argumentation and inculcating in them knowledge and skills they will need for effective use of argumentation.

Second, with respect to August and Shanahan's conclusion that "instruction that provides substantial coverage of key components of literacy has a positive influence on the literacy development of language-minority students" (2008, p. 9), the specific approaches to argumentation reviewed earlier offer considerable promise. For example, collaborative reasoning could help elementary school ELLs acquire argumentative skills that would provide a foundation that might be solidified and expanded as these students pass through later grades, culminating in a possibly higher degree of readiness in high school. The "cognitive strategies kit" approach articulated by Olson and Land could have a similar effect at various grade levels.

So, too, could the templates provided by Graff and Birkenstein. Indeed, the templates may hold great appeal to ELLs who, as many teachers have found, express a fondness for "models" from which to work. These templates could be used in multiple grades as the *Common Core Standards* become standard operating procedure in schools. Linking these templates and the strategies from the cognitive strategies tool kit with the problem-solving approach discussed earlier could also be productive. That is, problem-solving scenarios could be used to help ELLs learn how to employ specific strategies and templates and thus gain greater command of them.

Third, the audience-related approaches discussed earlier could be quite useful in helping ELLs better understand the expectations of those who will read (and evaluate) their argumentative writing. Because of their perhaps very different native language and cultural backgrounds, ELLs may well struggle to decode the evaluative criteria and cultural assumptions guiding their teachers' views of their writing. Bringing audience into instruction could help teachers and ELLs deconstruct these perhaps mystifying expectations.

Fourth, the "everything is an argument" approach described earlier holds great appeal for making argumentative writing in English more accessible and manageable for ELLs. This approach would enable teachers to draw ELLs' attention to the many resources surrounding them and help them realize how much useful material they have at their disposal, including, potentially, sources from their native language and culture.

In conclusion, while the task of easing ELLs into argumentation (at any grade level) likely looks daunting, what I hope this chapter shows is that teachers have at their disposal a wide-ranging and rich supply of resources from which to draw in designing instructional approaches appropriate to the needs of ELLs and aligned with the demands embedded in the *Common Core Standards*. Valuable tools are available, and, given the widespread presence of argumentation in school and in everyday life, as well as the need to employ argumentative skills for a variety of purposes across various settings, teachers of argumentative writing are fortunate in having something to teach that ELLs, like other students, genuinely need. That in itself is an important point to build on. While the days ahead may be challenging, they also offer exciting prospects as we seek to prepare ELLs to engage argumentation as it will unfold in the *Common Core Standards*.

References

Anderson, R. C., Nguyen-Jahiel, K., McNurlen, B., Archodidou, A., Kim, S.-Y., Reznitskaya, A., Tillmans, M., & Gilbert, L. (2001). The Snowball Phenomenon: The spread of ways of talking and ways of thinking across groups of children. *Cognition and Instruction, 19,* 1–46.

August, D., & Shanahan, T. (Eds.). (2008). *Developing reading and writing in second-language learners: Lessons from the report of the National Literacy Panel on Language-Minority Children and Youth.* New York: Routledge; Newark, DE: National Reading Association: Baltimore, MD: Center for Applied Linguistics.

Bloch, J. (2004). Second language cyber rhetoric: A study of Chinese L2 writers in an online usenet group. *Language Learning and Technology, 8,* 66–82.

Bruce, N. (2002). Dovetailing language and content: Teaching balanced argument in legal problem answer writing. *English for Specific Purposes, 21,* 321–345.

Carter, R. E. (1996). The background to argument in the Far East. In P. Berrill (Ed.), *Perspectives on written argument* (pp. 205–220). Creskill, NJ: Hampton Press.

Charles, M. (2007). Reconciling top-down and bottom-up approaches to graduate writing: Using a corpus to teach rhetorical functions. *Journal of English for Academic Purposes, 6,* 289–302.

Coffin, C. (2004). Arguing about how the world is or how the world should be: The role of argument in IELTS tests. *Journal of English for Academic Purposes, 3,* 229–246.

Common Core Standards. (2010). *Common Core Standards for English Language Arts and Literacy in History/Social Studies, Science, and Technical Subjects.* Available at: http://www.corestandards.org/the-standards (last accessed November 10, 2012).

Concha, S., & Paratore, J. R. (2011). Local coherence in persuasive writing: An exploration of Chilean students' metalinguistic knowledge, writing process, and writing products. *Written Communication, 28,* 34–69.

Connor, U. (1987). Argumentative patterns in student essays: Cross-cultural differences. In U. Connor & R. B. Kaplan (Eds.), *Writing across languages: Analysis of L2 text* (pp. 57–72). Reading, MA: Addison-Wesley.

Connor, U. (1990). Linguistic/rhetorical measures for international persuasive student writing. *Research in the Teaching of English, 24,* 67–87.

Connor, U., & Lauer, J. (1985). Understanding persuasive essay writing: Linguistic/rhetorical approach. *Text, 5,* 309–326.

Connor, U., & Lauer, J. (1988). Cross-cultural variation in persuasive student writing. In A. C. Purves (Ed.), *Writing across languages and cultures: Issues in contrastive rhetoric* (pp. 138–159). Newbury Park, CA: Sage.

Crismore, A., Markkanen, R., & Steffensen, M. S. (1993). Metadiscourse in persuasive writing: A study of texts written by American and Finnish university students. *Written Communication, 10,* 39–71.

Dong, T., Anderson, R. C., Kim, I.-H., & Li, Y. (2008). Collaborative reasoning in China and Korea. *Reading Research Quarterly, 43,* 400–424.

Dressen, D. (2003). Geologists' implicit persuasive strategies and the construction of evaluative evidence. *Journal of English for Academic Purposes, 2,* 273–290.

Foster, D., & Russell, D. R. (2002). *Writing and learning in cross-national perspective: Transitions from secondary to higher education.* Mahwah, NJ: Lawrence Erlbaum; Urbana, IL: National Council of Teachers of English.

Fulkerson, R. (1996). *Teaching the argument in writing.* Urbana, IL: National Council of Teachers of English.

Graff, G. (2003). *Clueless in academe: How schooling obscures the life of the mind.* New Haven, CT: Yale University Press.

Graff, G., & Birkenstein, C. (2007). *They say/I say: The moves that matter in persuasive writing.* New York: W. W. Norton.

Hakuta, K., Goto Butler, Y., & Witt, D. (2000). *How long does it take English learners to acquire English proficiency?* University of California Linguistic Minority Research Institute. Retrieved from http://repositories.cdllib.org/lmri/pr/hakuta/

Harklau, L. (2011). Commentary: Adolescent L2 writing research as an emerging field. *Journal of Second Language Writing, 20,* 227–230.

Hillocks, G., Jr. (1995). *Teaching writing as reflective practice*. New York: Teachers College Press.

Hillocks, G., Jr. (1999). *Ways of thinking, ways of teaching*. New York: Teachers College Press.

Hillocks, G., Jr. (2011). *Teaching argument writing, grades 6–12*. Portsmouth, NH: Heinemann.

Ho, C. M. L., Rappa, N. A., & Chee, Y. S. (2009). Designing and implementing virtual enactive role-play and structured argumentation: Promises and pitfalls. *Computer Assisted Language Learning, 5,* 381–408.

Hyland, K., & Tse, P. (2005). Hooking the reader: A corpus study of evaluative *that* in abstracts. *English for Specific Purposes, 24,* 123–139.

Johns, A. M. (1993). Written argumentation for real audiences: Suggestions for teacher research and classroom practice. *TESOL Quarterly, 27,* 75–90.

Johns, A. M. (1997). *Text, role, and context: Developing academic literacies*. Cambridge: Cambridge University Press.

Kadar-Fulop, J. (1988). The problem of selection of writing tasks in cross-cultural study. In A. C. Purves (Ed.), *Writing across languages and cultures: Issues in contrastive rhetoric* (pp. 25–50). Newbury Park, CA: Sage.

Kaplan, R. B. (1966). Cultural thought patterns in inter-cultural education. *Language Learning, 16,* 1–20.

Kaplan, R. B. (Ed.). (1995). Special Issue: The teaching of writing in the Pacific Basin. *Journal of Asian Pacific Communication, 6 (1 & 2).*

Kinneavy, J. L. (1971). *A theory of discourse*. Englewood Cliffs, NJ: Prentice-Hall.

Kinneavy, J. L., & Warriner, J. E. (1993). *Elements of writing: Course 3*. New York: Harcourt School.

Klein, P. D., & Rose, M. A. (2010). Teaching argument and explanation to prepare junior students for writing to learn. *Reading Research Quarterly, 45,* 433–461.

Langer, J. A. (1991). Literacy and schooling: A sociocognitive approach. In E. H. Hiebert (Ed.), *Literacy for a diverse society: Practices and policies* (pp. 9–27). New York: Teachers College Press.

Laurinen, L. I., & Marttunen, M. (2007). Written arguments and collaborative speech acts in practising the argumentative power of language through chat debates. *Computers and Composition, 24,* 230–246.

Lee, C., Wong, K. C. K., Cheung, W. K., & Lee, F. S. L. (2009). Web-based essay critiquing system and EFL students' writing: A quantitative and qualitative investigation. *Computer Assisted Language Learning, 22,* 57–72.

Leki, I., Cumming, A., & Silva, T. (2008). *A synthesis of research on second language writing in English*. New York: Routledge.

Lunsford, A. A., & Ruszkiewicz, J. J. (2004, 3rd edition). *Everything's an argument*. Boston: Bedford/St. Martin's Press.

McCann, T. M. (2010). Gateways to writing logical arguments. *English Journal, 99(6),* 33–39.

Moffett, J. (1968). *Teaching the universe of discourse*. Boston: Houghton Mifflin.

National Clearinghouse for English Language Acquisition. (2011, February). The growing numbers of English learner students, 1998/99–2008/09. Retrieved November 20, 2012 from http://www.edweek.org/ew/issues/english-language-learners/

Newell, G. E., Beach, R., Smith, J., & VanDerHeide, J. (2011). Teaching and learning argumentative reading and writing: A review of research. *Reading Research Quarterly, 46,* 273–304.

Olson, C. B., & Land, R. (2007). A cognitive strategies approach to reading and writing instruction for English Language Learners in secondary school. *Research in the Teaching of English, 41,* 269–303.

Olson, C. B., Kim, J. S., Scarcella, R., Kramer, J., Pearson, M., van Dyk, D. A., Collins, P., & Land, R. E. (2012). Enhancing the interpretive reading and analytic writing of mainstreamed English learners in secondary school: Results from a randomized field trial using a cognitive strategies approach. *American Educational Research Journal, 49,* 323–355.

Ortmeier-Hooper, C., & Enright, K. A. (Eds.). (2011). Special issue: Adolescent L2 writing in U.S. contexts. *Journal of Second Language Writing, 20.*

Panovsky, C., Pacheco, M., Smith, S., Santos, J., Fogelman, C., Harrington, M., & Kenney, E. (2005). *Approaches to writing instruction for adolescent English language learners.* Providence, RI: The Education Alliance at Brown University.

Perie, M., Grigg, W., & Donahue, P. (2005). *The nation's report card. Reading 2005* (NCES 2006–451). Washington, DC: National Center for Education Statistics, Institute of Education Sciences, U.S. Department of Education.

Purves, A. C. (1988). Introduction. In A. C. Purves (Ed.), *Writing across languages and cultures: Issues in contrastive rhetoric* (pp. 9–21). Newbury Park, CA: Sage.

Purves, A. C., Soter, A., Takala, S., & Vahapassi, A. (1984). Towards a domain-referenced system for classifying composition assignments. *Research in the Teaching of English, 18,* 385–416.

Radia, P., & Stapleton, P. (2008). Unconventional Internet genres and their impact on second language undergraduate students' writing process. *Internet and Higher Education, 11,* 9–17.

Ramage, J. D., & Bean, J. C. (1989). *Writing arguments: A rhetoric with readings.* New York: Macmillan.

Reznitskaya, A., Anderson, R. C., & Kuo, L.-J. (2007). Teaching and learning argumentation. *The Elementary School Journal, 5,* 449–472.

Reznitskaya, A., Anderson, R. C., McNurlen, B., Nguyen-Jahiel, K., Archodidou, A., & Kim, K.-Y. (2001). Influence of oral discussion on written argument. *Discourse Processes, 32,* 155–175.

Silva, T. (1993). Toward an understanding of the distinct nature of L2 writing: The ESL research and its implications. *TESOL Quarterly, 27,* 657–677.

Toulmin, S. E. (1958). *The uses of argument.* Cambridge: Cambridge University Press.

Toulmin, S. E. (2001). *Return to reason.* Cambridge, MA: Harvard University Press.

Werlich, E. (1976). *A text grammar of English.* Heidelberg: Quelle & Meyer.

Wu, S.-Y., & Rubin, D. L. (2000). Evaluating the impact of collectivism and individualism on argumentative writing by Chinese and North American college students. *Research in the Teaching of English, 35,* 148–178.

6

THE ROLE OF SOCIAL RELATIONSHIPS IN THE WRITING OF MULTILINGUAL ADOLESCENTS

Jennifer Shade Wilson

In recent years, the field of education has recognized that students' learning and development cannot be explained only by cognitive factors and specific teaching strategies. At the same time, the fields of literacy and composition have acknowledged the social nature of reading and writing—viewing literacy as purposeful communication among human beings and recognizing that literacy practices are constructed in different ways by different societies.

Drawing inspiration from previous work on the social nature of literacy (see Figure 6.1 for additional readings), this chapter explores the *socioliterate relationships* that influence the writing activities, practices, and skills of multilingual high school students. The concept of *socioliterate relationships* is adapted from the term "socioacademic relationships" used by second language writing scholar Ilona Leki (2007) in a longitudinal study of the literacy development of multilingual, multicultural undergraduates. Leki used this term to describe social interactions between her focal students, their classmates, and faculty members "that proved to be critical to the students' sense of satisfaction with their educational work and sometimes even to the possibility of doing that work" (p. 14). Considering the widely acknowledged importance of social interactions and relationships during adolescence, the scope of this term can be further expanded: not only are *peer* and *teacher* relationships crucial to aspects of writing development and engagement for high school students, but also relationships formed within their *families* and *communities*.

There are several useful lenses to help us view the potential relevance of socioliterate relationships to the writing of multilingual teens (see Figure 6.2). In my own work I have used Ecological Systems Theory, first proposed by child psychologist Uri Bronfenbrenner (1979, 2005). This theory emphasizes the developmental importance of relationships, particularly in the physical settings where a person interacts with others; recognizes that characteristics of these

Below are some excellent texts if you are interested in reading more from literacy theorists and researchers who have been important in shaping the view of reading and writing as culturally and socially influenced.

Literacy: An Introduction to the Ecology of the Written Word, by David Barton (1994).
Barton conceived of this text as an introduction to "literacy studies." His useful summaries and descriptions of various aspects of literacy and how literacy is intertwined with all human activity make this book very accessible.

Social Linguistics and Literacies: Ideologies in Discourses, by James Gee (1990).
If you have been wondering why people in academia talk about "big D" and "little D" discourses, this book is the source. Gee's conception of how language works in concert with social practices and assumptions to create our "ways of being in the world" is an engaging read—he imagines himself walking into a biker bar as a way of illustrating his concepts.

Ways with Words: Language, Life, and Work in Communities and Classrooms, by Shirley Brice Heath (1983).
Heath went into several communities in the southeastern U.S. and gave a first-hand look at how literacy and language practices varied based on social class and race. This gripping account of these communities illustrates how deeply ingrained certain social practices and assumptions are in the American educational system.

Literacy in Theory and Practice, by Brian Street (1984).
An important contribution of this text is Street's conception (and concise discussion) of two opposing views of literacy, the "autonomous" model and the "ideological" model. He exposes flaws in the view of literacy as a neutral system that enhances intellectual development and social improvement, and he contrasts that view with a model of literacy as inseparable from the surrounding social and political context.

FIGURE 6.1 Additional Resources: The Social Nature of Literacy and Language

relationships such as emotional bonds and power relations influence how much a person can learn from others; and acknowledges that relationships are affected by the socially defined roles of the individuals in a relationship. Thus, adopting an ecological stance provides a valuable framework for considering the influence of socioliterate relationships on writing development, processes, and practices.

Why might social interactions be important in humans' writing? These theories provide possible explanations.

Sociocultural Theory (SCT)
One of the key precepts of SCT is that people need social interaction with others in order to learn. For instance, a person uses external objects and social interactions at first to help him or her carry out an intellectual activity, after which he or she is able to accomplish that same activity mentally on his or her own.

> General information: *Sociocultural Theory in Second Language Education: An Introduction through Narratives*, by Merrill Swain, Penny Kinnear, and Linda Steinman (2011).

> Use in SLW research: "'History of Theatre' Web sites: A brief history of the writing process in a high school ESL language arts class," a journal article by Parks, Huot, Hamers, and Lemonnier (2005).

Communities of Practice (CoP)
Scholars working in 'communities of practice' theory have acknowledged that "[w]riting is always the production of a community of sorts" (Wenger, 1998, p. xiv). A community of practice is formed when a group of people who are engaged in working together on a common activity or undertaking over a period of time create specific practices that are a part of their activity and often help move that activity forward.

> General information: *Communities of practice: Learning, meaning, and identity*, by Etienne Wenger (1998).

> Use in SLW research: "Identity matters: Theories that help explore adolescent multilingual writers and their identities," a book chapter by Youngjoo Yi (2010).

Identity formation
Literacy researchers who use identity to frame their work generally believe that the social interactions in a writer's past and present help to mold his or her literate identity/ies, which in turn affects the writer's writing process, practices, and products.

> General information: *Writing and identity: The discoursal construction of identity in academic writing*, by Roz Ivanič (1998).

> Use in SLW research: "The shifting nature of identity: Social identity, L2 writers, and high school," a book chapter by Christina Ortmeier-Hooper (2010).

FIGURE 6.2 Additional Resources: Theoretical Intersections of Writing and Social Interaction

What the Research Shows

What does empirical research tell us about the social relationships implicated in the writing of multilingual teenagers? With whom do they write and why? And what influences do social relationships appear to have on adolescents' writing activities/practices/development? Guided by Ecological Systems Theory, this review focuses on three physical contexts—home, school, neighborhood—in which adolescents seem most likely to participate in relationships containing writing activities.

Home

Interactions

One frequently reported interaction is that of students receiving help on their language arts or English homework from their parents (see Fairbanks & Ariail, 2006; McKay & Wong, 1996; Wilson, 2012a). However, it is important to note that parents of immigrant teenagers do not always have the linguistic—or cultural—knowledge to help their children with homework (see Gaztambide-Fernández & Guerrero, 2011; Valdés, 1998; Wilson, 2012a).

Siblings also can be sources of academically oriented social writing. Older siblings may give homework support to multilingual adolescents, such as the daily help provided by Hassan's older sister who was enrolled in college (al-Alawi, 2012), or teens may be helping younger siblings with their homework, as in the case of a sister in eleventh grade helping her brother in seventh grade write down his story ideas for English class (Fu, 1995).

Finally, several studies uncovered multilingual adolescents writing with a family member for purposes that were not academic in nature. To acquire their heritage languages, Franky wrote with his grandmother in Pashto, and Acer learned Chinese characters with his parents (Wilson, 2012a). Soohee wrote letters and emails to relatives in Korea that her mother dictated, and June corresponded via email with her father who was living in Korea (Yi, 2005). Miguel helped his mother translate court documents (Rubenstein-Ávila, 2003). Chile learned 'gangsta' literacy (such as how to write certain letters and phrases) from her older sisters in order to occupy a gangsta-related identity in her family and community (Moje, 2000a).

Influences

Parental encouragement and assistance can lead adolescents to complete homework assignments, especially assignments they would have found difficult to complete on their own, as in the example of Isabel (Fairbanks & Ariail, 2006); such assistance may also be available from older siblings. On the other hand, family influence can be negative—for example, Ning was afraid to ask her father for help with her homework because he got angry when she did not know how to do it (Wilson, 2012b).

Multilingual teens' identities as knowledgeable users of written language may be reinforced when family members need assistance, especially if the assistance is due in part to a lack of English knowledge; the teens may see themselves as 'literacy brokers' of sorts (for example, in Yi, 2010; see also the concept of 'language broker' in Orellana, Reynolds, Dorner, & Meza, 2003). But, again, adolescents' identities can be negatively influenced if family members view them as deficient in language and literacy skills, as when Lala's younger brother teased Lala about being better than her at reading and writing in English (Wilson, 2012a).

Studies that report socioliterate interactions with siblings generally do not investigate the results of these interactions, and this topic recently has been labeled "under-researched" (Sokal & Piotrowski, 2011, p. 1). Despite the lack of research investigating the effects of older–younger sibling literacy interactions, interesting parallels can be drawn from the positive outcomes found in the research on cross-age tutoring (when high school students tutor elementary students in reading)—generally, findings show an improvement in literacy skills and practices not only for the tutees, but also for the tutors themselves (see Jacobson et al., 2001; Kohls & Wilson, 2012; Paterson & Elliott, 2006). Thus, one likely assumption is that writing with both older and younger siblings has a positive effect on multiple cognitive aspects of adolescents' literacy, such as motivation, strategy use, and self-efficacy. As the above example of Lala makes clear, however, emotional influences from siblings may not always be positive.

School

Interactions

Socioliterate interactions in the ecological context of a school include both those with teachers and those with peers. While adolescents have more opportunities than younger students to make friends and same-age acquaintances outside of school, many of their friendships are still based around going to the same school (e.g., Urberg, Değirmencioğlu, Tolson, & Halliday-Scher, 1995).

Through the shared reading and writing of a wide variety of print genres, such as writing on the board, assignment sheets, homework, feedback, journals, and report cards, teachers and adolescents have multiple literate interactions every day. These interactions, however, are different from most other socioliterate interactions described in this chapter, since those initiated by a teacher are rarely focused on a specific student as an individual but are part of the teacher's general pedagogical strategy.

Although the focus in this chapter is on one-to-one literate interactions occurring in an overtly social manner, it is not possible to sustain that focus when looking at research on teacher–student socioliterate interactions for two reasons:

first, there appears to be almost no research that has explicitly investigated the socioliterate aspect of teacher–student relationships (see Moje, 1996), and, second, any socioliterate interactions that may occur do so within the overall social context the teacher has created in the classroom and cannot be separated from that context—for instance, if a student seeks out extra help from a teacher on an essay or enjoys literary discussions with a teacher at lunch, the student may feel comfortable doing so due to the classroom atmosphere the teacher has created.[1] Thus, instead of reviewing literature describing such interactions, below I will focus on "how relationships and interactions among teachers and students shape the [literacy] decisions . . . students make" (Moje, 1996, p. 177).

Peers interact through literacy in many ways, perhaps even increasing with the spread of technology. Some of these interactions are academic in nature: several researchers have found students using tools such as MSN and MySpace to tell each other about resources for projects, share written assignments, and give feedback on essays (see Yi, 2005; Greenhow & Robelia, 2009). Such interactions do not have to be electronic, as other studies have documented a bilingual high school student, who was working on a senior research project, getting both oral feedback and published sources from a friend (Villalva, 2006) and a study group that formed between friends who shared not only an ESL class but also similar orientations to their use of Spanish and the same hometown in Mexico (Valenzuela, 1999).

Beyond the school curriculum, literacy researchers have investigated multi-lingual adolescents engaging jointly in recreational writing activities such as note-writing, co-authoring stories and poems, instant messaging and online chat, and online web communities (see Figure 6.3). These interactions often took place with close friends but also could occur between classmates who were more acquain-tances than friends.

One issue regarding socioliterate interactions with peers that has come to light in research on multilingual adolescents is that these students may have fewer opportunities in the US for such interactions than teens whose first language is English. There are multiple reports of L2 adolescents feeling socially isolated across language backgrounds, gender, and age (all in high school unless otherwise noted): the four Laotian refugees profiled by Fu (1995), the Chinese immigrants Zhu and Ping (Lay et al., 1999), the Polish immigrant Jan (Leki, 1999), five immigrant students from Latin America, Taiwan, and Nigeria followed by Ortmeier-Hooper (2007), all four Latin American immigrant middle school students in Valdés (2001), and the Korean immigrant student Soohee (Yi, 2005). Many of these students talked to the various researchers about experiencing racism and ridicule directed at them by native English-speaking peers, as well as not knowing the social conventions for approaching or interacting with those peers. Moreover, several of them also felt they had little in common with other L2 students in their ESL classes, particularly feeling a gulf between themselves and newly arrived students with whom they were often enrolled in the same ESL courses or program even after spending several years in US schools. Thus, it is probable that adolescents who feel

Some of the most interesting research conducted with multicultural and/or multilingual adolescents has investigated how they interact with their peers through reading and writing. Below are a few articles you might enjoy reading to gain insights into your students' out-of-school literacy practices; the titles give a fairly good sense of the topics.

Ek, L. D. (2009). Language and literacy in the Pentecostal church and the public high school: A case study of a Mexican ESL student. *The High School Journal, 92*(2), 1–13.

Greenhow, C., & Robelia, B. (2009). Old communication, new literacies: Social network sites as social learning resources. *Journal of Computer-Mediated Communication, 14*, 1130–1161.

Lam, W. S. E. (2000). L2 literacy and the design of the self: A case study of a teenager writing on the Internet. *TESOL Quarterly, 34*(3), 457–482.

Moje, E. B. (2000). "To be part of the story": The literacy practices of gangsta adolescents. *Teachers College Record, 102*(3), 651–690.

Moje, E. B., Oversby, M., Tysvaer, N., & Morris, K. (2008). The complex world of adolescent literacy: Myths, motivations, and mysteries. *Harvard Educational Review, 78*(1), 107–154.

Yi, Y. (2007). Engaging literacy: A biliterate student's composing practices beyond school. *Journal of Second Language Writing, 16*, 23–39.

FIGURE 6.3 Additional Resources: Socioliterate Interactions with Peers

socially isolated are not experiencing many opportunities to write (and read) with a supportive peer network, certainly not in English and possibly not at all.

Influences

Teacher influences on literacy can be quite positive. Miguel, an eighth-grade ELL student, attributed his renewed interest in school to the caring and support of his two core teachers. One of the teachers allowed him to read books in Spanish (his L1) and write the book reports in English, a process that allowed him to be successful on those assignments. Miguel said, "Sometimes I wanna flunk [eighth grade], 'cause I know it won't be the same without them [in high school]. Like, [Ms. Molina and Ms. Domingo] *make me* do my work . . . .. They watch out for me. I'm gonna miss them" (Rubinstein-Ávila, 2003, p. 296, italics in original). At a more general level, a noteworthy report on best practices in middle and high school literacy programs—linguistically and culturally diverse—across three major US cities, identified caring and supportive teachers as a characteristic of effective literacy pedagogy (Langer, 2002). The teachers observed for this report built these relationships in various ways: by actively working to be viewed as a resource and mentor; by knowing "[students'] lives, their interests, their strengths and weaknesses as students of English and as young adults growing up in a troubled inner city" (p. 70); by taking on a "persona . . . of an older, wiser friend whom students know is doing everything she can to help them do well, but more than that, who is trying to bring them to truly come to love literary life as she does" (p. 71); and by allowing and engaging in personal 'chit-chat' as an English language teaching strategy. The literacy scholar Elizabeth Moje provided an explanation for why such teaching practices show up in highly effective literacy programs: "My research indicates that when kids feel cared for—when they believe they are working in a relationship with a teacher—they tend to be more willing to try different literacy practices and strategies that the teacher offers" (2000b, p. 69).

Unfortunately, these influences can be negative as well. In direct contrast to the teachers described in Langer's report, yet still drawing on the theoretical concept of *caring*, the sociologist Angela Valenzuela documented how a perceived lack of caring on the part of teachers at a Texas high school with a high Hispanic population fractured "scholastic support networks" (1999, p. 28) and created an atmosphere like the one she observed in a ninth-grade English classroom, in which the teacher publicly stated that many of his students would drop out by the end of the year—not surprisingly, the students "challeng[ed] his ability to make them learn under abusive conditions" (p. 65) by doing no work on their writing assignment during this class period. After providing multiple similar examples, Valenzuela concluded "a dearth of authentic relations with teachers subtracts, or minimizes, opportunities youth have to develop and enjoy a sense of competence and mastery of the curriculum" (p. 71). Wisdom, a ninth-grade refugee from Nigeria, had a similar story: his rapidly disintegrating relationship with his English teacher led him to stop doing his English homework and created a feeling that "she does not want to see me succeed, to do better in that class" (Ortmeier-Hooper, 2007, p. 133; see also Chapter 2 above). Wisdom blamed these problems on the fact that "she just doesn't know who I am" (p. 132), and he sought the assistance of his former middle school ESL teacher who "has been like a mother to me" (p. 134).

Even positive teacher–student relationships can have negative academic or literate influences. Jan, a teenaged immigrant from Poland, resisted engagement in his high school ESL class despite—or perhaps because of—his teacher's caring attitude that seemed to resonate with other students in the class: "And the professor was just so sweet . . . I was like, just shut up and teach. I just hate like people just being so sweet in class" (Leki, 1999, pp. 23–24). (During his first year in college, Jan was placed in a remedial composition course at university, which he failed, a possible result of his disengagement from his high school ESL class.) Why did Jan object to his teacher's attitude? Perhaps it was a personal preference, or perhaps it was due to a culturally based expectation: in a study of a California middle school beginning to implement an ESL program, Guadalupe Valdés found that "Latino children, who were used to teachers who are strict and who demand both silence and respect, had trouble reading the signals of those teachers who seemed nice, who wanted to be liked, and who wanted to make learning fun" (1998, p. 7).[2]

Shifting the focus back to peers, one particular way that these socioliterate interactions can influence adolescents is through their construction of literate identities,[3] which can have both positive and negative outcomes on literacy behavior and beliefs. Lam (2000) hypothesized that online communication (via writing) allowed his teenaged Chinese-American participant to create a "textual self," which helped him feel more connected to global users of English and appeared to improve his attitude toward and fluency in written English. The Korean-American adolescent Joan constructed identities as a poet and a knowledgeable user of technology through her written interactions in a local teen-focused web community (Yi, 2007). On the other hand, the ELL students Ken, Paul, and Wisdom felt they had to hide their enthusiasm for school from their peers in order to be 'cool' and learned from their peers to choose the assignments that required the least writing (Ortmeier-Hooper, 2010).

Literate interactions with peers may also influence students' writing simply through promoting motivation to engage in activities that require writing. One hypothesis is that motivation is the mediating factor between literate experiences and literacy development (Guthrie & Wigfield, 2000). If this is the case, then the high motivation of multilingual teens to write with and to their peers, illustrated in multiple studies, should have some positive influence on the development of their writing skills.[4]

Neighborhood

Interactions

In the limited literature related to socioliterate interactions at the neighborhood level, the most frequently discussed community setting is an organized, after-school-type program (see Figure 6.4). In these programs, students are generally taking part in academic-type literacy events and practices, with adults as tutors or teachers; however, several programs that have been described or studied by researchers have more novel designs. For example, Rubinstein-Ávila (2007) highlighted Latino youth who are writing public service announcements through Youth Radio in California; low-income high school students documenting (often in both English and Spanish) local community issues through Voices Inc. in Arizona; and African American and Latino adolescents composing multimodal personal stories through the Digital Underground Storytelling for Youth (DUSTY) in California. These programs are noteworthy for three particular reasons: the end products are not only *not* traditional academic texts but also have personal relevance to the participants, adults involved are generally seen as mentors instead of tutors, and participants appear to be working together to acquire these new literacy skills. Another program in this vein is STRUGGLE, a literacy and

Programs beyond the regular school day exist in many different forms and offer a variety of opportunities and types of assistance to multilingual adolescent writers. The studies listed below provide in-depth descriptions of several such programs.

Alvermann, D. E., Young, J.P., Green, C., & Wisenbaker, J.P. (1999). Adolescents' perceptions and negotiations of literacy practices in after-school read and talk clubs. *American Educational Research Journal, 36*(2), 221–264.

Babbitt, S., & Byrne, M. (1999). Finding the keys to educational progress in urban youth: Three case studies. *Journal of Adolescent and Adult Literacy, 43*(4), 368–378.

Ball, A., & Heath, S. B. (1993). Dances of identity: Finding an ethnic self in the arts. In S. B. Heath & M. W. McLaughlin (Eds.), *Identity and inner-city youth: Beyond ethnicity and gender* (pp. 69–93). New York: Teachers College Press.

Cumming, A. (Ed.) (2012). *Adolescent literacies in a multicultural context.* New York: Routledge.

Long, E., Peck, W. C., & Baskins, J. A. (2002). STRUGGLE: A literate practice supporting life-project planning. In G. Hull & K. Schultz (Eds.), *School's out! Bridging out-of-school literacies with classroom practice* (pp. 131–161). New York: Teachers College Press.

Rubinstein-Ávila, E. (2003). Conversing with Miguel: An adolescent English language learner struggling with later literacy development. *Journal of Adolescent and Adult Literacy, 47*(4), 290–301.

Rubinstein-Ávila, E. (2007). In their words, sounds, and images: After-school literacy programs for urban youth. In B. Guzzetti (Ed.), *Literacy for the new millennium: Vol 4. Adolescent literacy* (pp. 239–250). Westport, CT: Praeger.

FIGURE 6.4 Additional Resources: Extracurricular Literacy Programs

mentoring program offered to local adolescents through an urban community center in inner-city Pittsburgh (Long, Peck, & Baskins, 2002). The goals of STRUGGLE were more than literacy improvement or development: the program was "designed to support teens in challenging adults' naïve or reductive impressions of who they are and what they are up to in life" (p. 132), and a cornerstone of the program was supportive collaboration between a local adult and teen as each attempted to write about important aspects of their lives.

Another, much less studied, neighborhood setting for socioliterate interactions is organized religious activities. Ek (2009) approached church-based literacy through the longitudinal case study of Edgar, a 15-year-old immigrant from Mexico. Although she only documented reading activities, these occurred frequently and in a social setting. Kelly's (2001) case study of an African American teen illustrates how writing also can be part of church-based socioliterate inter-actions: through Saturday School activities, this young man took notes, wrote letters, conducted research, and wrote and edited an historical report.

Influences

These neighborhood-based socioliterate interactions have been shown to influence multilingual adolescents' literacy in several ways. First, similar to the discussion in the previous section on caring teachers, Babbitt and Byrne (1999) claimed that a relationship with a caring adult was the primary reason at-risk, inner-city youth attended an after-school tutoring program. Thus, simply by using supportive local adults as mentors and tutors, many of the after-school-type programs may exert a positive literate influence, particularly when students attend over a long period of time. Rubinstein-Ávila (2007) acknowledged that the informal nature of these programs may enhance the relationship-building process. Long, Peck, and Baskins (2002) reported more specific literacy outcomes: STRUGGLE participants were able to generate more text and more introspective compositions with the assistance of their adult mentor than when writing on their own. Likewise, Edgar was exposed to higher-quality language and literacy experiences at church than at school, experiences which supported his use of his L1 as well as statewide standards such as textual analysis and evaluation (Ek, 2009). In the community-based pro-grams that encourage critical perspectives (such as those described in Rubinstein-Ávila, 2007), adolescents see mentors engaged in writing activities that are making meaningful changes in the world and are able to join that 'community of practice.' Many of these programs, particularly those with less emphasis on traditional academic content or teaching methods, may offer safer or less threatening environ-ments in which students can engage in writing practices and practice writing skills. Moreover, those programs or sites that give teens a place to take up writing in informal ways with groups of their peers allow participants to experience writing as fun yet meaningful at the same time. Finally, identity is a relevant construct in this context also—as Kelly noted,

> All of [the literate experiences in the African-American church] contributed to the development of a sense of self for Anthony that was highly literate in multiple ways. His sense of self exists, not in isolation, but in a complexly communal and historical sense.
>
> *(p. 257)*

Also, very importantly, this new "sense of self" based in his cultural community "guided his uses of school-sanctioned written literacy" (p. 257).

One caveat about organized community programs is that they often experience high rates of staff or volunteer turn-over, due to low or non-existent pay or other benefits, making it less likely that participants can develop the long-term relationships that appear to be so meaningful as a basis for adolescents to take up and enjoy literacy events and practices. Also, there may be little to no training for the tutors or program leaders, which may lessen the effectiveness of the interactions in a program oriented to supporting academic writing practices and skills.

Implications and Conclusions

As Ortmeier-Hooper and Enright (2011) recently stated, multilingual adolescents' settings, tasks, and choices for writing "are imbued with strong social cues and consequences" (p. 172). In many cases, these social "cues and consequences" are provided by the individuals with whom the teens are directly interacting through reading and writing—the *socioliterate interactions* described in this chapter.

So, what can we learn from the varied studies on adolescent multilingual writers reviewed here? I believe there are three important conclusions. First, *socially supportive spaces for reading and writing*—in any language—are key, particularly when organized in an intrinsically interesting way. Second, we need to recognize the social aspect of *writing engagement*. Third, *identity* may be a critical concept to consider when thinking about multilingual teens' writing practices and skills.

In practice, what do socially supportive spaces look like? They may resemble after-school programs like DUSTY and Voices, Inc., where young people are apprenticed into literacy events with real-world applications, often guided by other young people who look and speak like them. They may be classrooms with an established system of teacher–student writing conferences (as in Sperling, 1991), collaborative writing (as in Rish & Caton, 2011), journal writing (see Fu, 1995), or other teacher practices that build a general sense of trust, such as creating safe spaces for students to perform their spoken word poetry (Kirsh, 2011) or simply getting to know students' lives outside the classroom. I give examples above of the various ways religious institutions can be supportive spaces for socioliterate interactions; such a safe 'space' could be located in cyber-space as well, like the local social site Welcome to Buckeye City, used by Korean teens in a midwestern US city to write texts such as comics, poems, and reviews (Yi, 2007), or more global networking sites like MySpace (Greenhow & Robelia, 2009).

A socially supportive space also is one in which multilingual writers are not allowed to 'fall between the cracks,' as illustrated by the case of Elisa, a quiet, well-behaved ESL student whose teacher "took her for granted" (Valdés, 2001, p. 87); Elisa's model behavior actually worked against her in that the teacher did not spend much time with her and had no sense of how Elisa's language skills were or were not progressing. This 'falling through the cracks' occurs when a student could benefit from direct assistance yet does not seek it out or make her needs known in any way or is not visibly at the top or bottom of the class—teachers may actually praise these students for behaving in class, although this silence more often renders the student invisible to the teacher or to other adult sources of support.

On the other hand, in a recent study I conducted with multilingual adolescents in a large city in Canada (Wilson, 2012c), students found supportive socioliterate relationships primarily with teachers and tutors who reached out to them. A Jamaican-Canadian tenth-grader who resembled students I had seen in my teaching career who were 'falling through the cracks' developed a strong relationship with his English teacher as an eleventh-grader, which contributed to a renewed interest in writing and school:

> If [this teacher] understands there's an issue, [he says] "Come to me after this class, I need to talk to you" or something. That simple. Like, there's not a lot of teachers that do that. And when I catch those, that's why I get so involved. [...] They just talk to me like I'm a human being.

Ning, a recent immigrant from China, was able to get much-needed assistance on her Canadian history homework because her ESL teacher offered to help her at lunch. Angel, an Angolan refugee, had a tutor at an after-school program who did not give up on her despite her sullen demeanor and lack of effort—in the end, with this tutor's guidance, Angel wrote several drafts of a letter to a popular singer about the serious topic of physical abuse and began to take pride in her writing.

From these specific examples, we see that socioliterate interactions appear to influence the 'writing engagement' of multilingual adolescent writers, which I define as taking up a writing activity in a positive, effortful, goal-directed manner (see Wilson, 2012c). The traditional conception of literacy engagement is that students are 'engaged' either when they are actually doing a literacy activity and/or are using strategies to complete an activity (for example, see Guthrie, Alao, & Rinehart, 1997). However, as teachers we recognize that the mere act of putting words down on paper does not necessarily signal true *engagement* in writing. Nor is strategy use an adequate measure for writing engagement, as a student can go through the motions of using a prewriting strategy, yet not give the assignment her full energy or be able to progress to composing a text. Yet a supportive socioliterate relationship can provide interesting activities that are attractive to students, new strategies to use when the going gets tough, or motivation to complete the activity. In fact, for teens, *emotional* engagement may be as important as *behavioral* engagement (e.g., just doing the writing) and *cognitive* engagement (e.g., using writing strategies). This review supports that position by illustrating the emotional dimensions of many writing activities: an enjoyment of interpersonal communication, a goal to have one's writing read by others, a desire to help family members or to take part in religious or cultural practices. Moreover, all the examples of emotional engagement in this review stem from social relationships. Thus, classroom teachers should consider how the relationships that they build with their students and that their students have in other dimensions of their lives can be tapped into to enhance multilingual adolescents' emotional engagement with writing.

Finally, as writers ourselves, we recognize that every act of writing requires us to take on a role that we have created in conjunction with social influences—how much more complicated must that creation of writerly identity/ies be for teenagers who are living within more than one culture and more than one language? The studies reviewed above uncovered a variety of socioliterate interactions—with family, friends, and educators—that framed the ways the participants felt about themselves as writers, with both positive and negative ramifications. In fact, it is possible that the most influential outcome of socioliterate interactions is the impact these have in students' identity construction. For example, all three strands of engagement (behavioral, cognitive, and emotional) described in the previous paragraph can be linked to how an individual views herself as a writer. Any pedagogy that does not adequately take into account (1) the fluid *and* social nature of identity and (2) the ways in which writing products and processes affect and are affected by a writer's identity/ies ultimately may be missing a crucial element in helping us effectively teach adolescent multilingual writers.

Notes

1 One case in which 'extracurricular' socioliterate interactions were organized by a teacher is documented in Harklau (1994).
2 Another issue with a pedagogy of caring in relation to multilingual writers in ESL and bilingual programs is the difficulty of focusing on individual students' needs in programs that are underfunded and understaffed and in which teachers often are not trained to work with ESL students (see Valdés, 1998, 2001).
3 Adopting the view of identity/ies as "locally understood and constantly remade in social relationships" (Harklau, 2000, p. 37).
4 But the little research-based evidence in this area is "highly contested" (Moje, 2009, p. 357), in particular about the influence of electronic media use on teens' literacy development.

References

Al-Alawi, M. (2012). Hassan: An independent learner with future goals. In A. Cumming (Ed.), *Adolescent literacies in a multicultural context* (pp. 159–166). New York: Routledge.
Alvermann, D.E., Young, J.P., Green, C., & Wisenbaker, J.P. (1999). Adolescents' perceptions and negotiations of literacy practices in after-school read and talk clubs. *American Educational Research Journal, 36*(2), 221–264.
Babbitt, S., & Byrne, M. (1999). Finding the keys to educational progress in urban youth: Three case studies. *Journal of Adolescent and Adult Literacy, 43*(4), 368–378.
Ball, A., & Heath, S.B. (1993). Dances of identity: Finding an ethnic self in the arts. In S.B. Heath & M.W. McLaughlin (Eds.), *Identity and inner-city youth: Beyond ethnicity and gender* (pp. 69–93). New York: Teachers College Press.
Barton, D. (1994). *Literacy: An introduction to the ecology of written language.* Cambridge, MA: Blackwell.
Bronfenbrenner, U. (1979). *The ecology of human development: Experiments by nature and design.* Cambridge, MA: Harvard University Press.

Bronfenbrenner, U. (2005). Ecological systems theory. In U. Bronfenbrenner (Ed.), *Making human beings human: Bioecological perspectives on human development* (pp. 106–173). Thousand Oaks, CA: Sage Publications. (Reprinted from *Six theories of child development: Revised formulations and current issues*, pp. 187–249, by R. Vasta, Ed., 1992, London: Jessica Kingsley.)

Cumming, A. (Ed.) (2012). *Adolescent literacies in a multicultural context.* New York: Routledge.

Ek, L.D. (2009). Language and literacy in the Pentecostal church and the public high school: A case study of a Mexican ESL student. *The High School Journal, 92*(2), 1–13.

Fairbanks, C.M., & Ariail, M. (2006). The role of social and cultural resources in literacy and schooling: Three contrasting cases. *Research in the Teaching of English, 40*, 310–354.

Fu, D. (1995). *"My trouble is my English": Asian students and the American dream.* Portsmouth, NH: Boynton/Cook.

Gaztambide-Fernández, R.A., & Guerrero, C. (2011). *Proyecto Latino: Year 1—exploratory research.* Report to the Toronto District School Board. Retrieved January 16, 2011, from http://www.oise.utoronto.ca/oise/UserFiles/File/ProyectoLatinoReportJan2011.pdf

Gee, J.P. (2012). *Social linguistics and literacies: Ideology in discourses* (4th ed.). New York: Routledge.

Greenhow, C., & Robelia, B. (2009). Old communication, new literacies: Social network sites as social learning resources. *Journal of Computer-Mediated Communication, 14*, 1130–1161. doi:10.1111/j.1083-6101.2009.01484.x

Guthrie, J.T., & Wigfield, A. (2000). Engagement and motivation in reading. In M.L. Kamil, P.B. Mosenthal, P.D. Pearson, & R. Barr (Eds.), *Handbook of reading research: Volume III* (pp. 403–422). New York: Erlbaum.

Guthrie, J.T., Alao, S., & Rinehart, J. M. (1997). Literacy issues in focus: Engagement in reading for young adolescents. *Journal of Adolescent and Adult Literacy, 40*(6), 438–446.

Harklau, L. (1994). ESL vs. mainstream classes: Contrasting L2 learning environments. *TESOL Quarterly, 28*(2), 241–272.

Harklau, L. (2000). From the "good kids" to the "worst": Representations of English language learners across educational settings. *TESOL Quarterly, 34*(1), 35–67.

Heath, S.B. (1983). *Ways with words: Language, life, and work in communities and classrooms.* New York: Cambridge University Press.

Ivanič, R. (1998). *Writing and identity: The discoursal construction of identity in academic writing.* Amsterdam: John Benjamins.

Jacobson, J., Thorpe, L., Fisher, D., Lapp, D., Frey, N., & Flood, J. (2001). Cross-age tutoring: A literacy improvement approach for struggling adolescent readers. *Journal of Adolescent and Adult Literacy, 44*, 528–536.

Kelly, M.M. (2001). The education of African-American youth: Literacy practices and identity representation in church and school. In E.B. Moje & D.G. O'Brien (Eds.), *Constructions of literacy: Studies of teaching and learning in and out of secondary schools* (pp. 239–259). Mahwah, NJ: Erlbaum.

Kirsh, C.F. (2011). Stories to yell: Using spoken-word poetry in the literacy classroom. *Journal of Classroom Research in Literacy, 4*, 50–61. Retrieved February 6, 2012, from http://jcrl.library.utoronto.ca/index.php/jcrl/article/view/14729

Kohls, R., & Wilson, J.S. (2012). Tutoring adolescents in literacy: A thematic synthesis of published literature. In A. Cumming (Ed.), *Adolescent literacies in a multicultural context* (pp. 23–35). New York: Routledge.

Lam, W.S.E. (2000). L2 literacy and the design of the self: A case study of a teenager writing on the Internet. *TESOL Quarterly, 34*(3), 457–482.

Langer, J.A. (2002). *Effective literacy instruction: Building successful reading and writing programs.* Urbana, IL: NCTE.

Lay, N.D.S., Carro, G., Tien, S., Niemann, T.C., & Leong, S. (1999). Connections: High school to college. In L. Harklau, K.M. Losey, & M. Siegal (Eds.), *Generation 1.5 meets college composition: Issues in the teaching of writing to U.S.-educated learners of ESL* (pp. 175–190). Mahwah, NJ: Erlbaum.

Leki, I. (1999). "Pretty much I screwed up": Ill-served needs of a permanent resident. In L. Harklau, K.M. Losey, & M. Siegal (Eds.), *Generation 1.5 meets college composition: Issues in the teaching of writing to U.S.-educated learners of ESL* (pp. 17–43). Mahwah, NJ: Erlbaum.

Leki, I. (2007). *Undergraduates in a second language: Challenges and complexities of academic literacy development.* New York: Erlbaum.

Long, E., Peck, W.C., & Baskins, J.A. (2002). STRUGGLE: A literate practice supporting life-project planning. In G. Hull & K. Schultz (Eds.), *School's out! Bridging out-of-school literacies with classroom practice* (pp. 131–161). New York: Teachers College Press.

McKay, S.L., & Wong, S.C. (1996). Multiple discourses, multiple identities: Investment and agency in second language learning among Chinese adolescent immigrant students. *Harvard Educational Review, 66*(3), 577–608.

Moje, E.B. (1996). "I teach students, not subjects": Teacher–student relationships as contexts for secondary literacy. *Reading Research Quarterly, 31*(2), 172–195.

Moje, E.B. (2000a). "To be part of the story": The literacy practices of gangsta adolescents. *Teachers College Record, 102*(3), 651–690.

Moje, E.B. (2000b). *"All the stories that we have": Adolescents' insights about literacy and learning in secondary schools.* Newark, DE: International Reading Association.

Moje, E.B. (2009). A call for new research on new and multi-literacies. *Research in the Teaching of English, 43*(4), 348–362.

Moje, E.B., Oversby, M., Tysvaer, N., & Morris, K. (2008). The complex world of adolescent literacy: Myths, motivations, and mysteries. *Harvard Educational Review, 78*(1), 107–154.

Orellana, M.F., Reynolds, J., Dorner, L., & Meza, M. (2003). In other words: Translating or "para-phrasing" as a family literacy practice in immigrant households. *Reading Research Quarterly, 38*(1), 12–34.

Ortmeier-Hooper, C. (2007). Beyond "English language learner": Second language writers, academic identity, and issues of identity in the US high school. *Dissertation Abstracts International, 68* (08) (UMI No. 3277145).

Ortmeier-Hooper, C. (2010). The shifting nature of identity: Social identity, L2 writers, and high school. In M. Cox, J. Jordan, C. Ortmeier-Hooper, and G.G. Schwartz (Eds.), *Reinventing identities in second language writing* (pp. 5–28). Urbana, IL: NCTE.

Ortmeier-Hooper, C., & Enright, K.A. (2011). Mapping new territory: Toward an understanding of adolescent L2 writers and writing in US contexts. *Journal of Second Language Writing, 20,* 167–181.

Parks, S., Huot, D., Hamers, J., & Lemonnier, F.H. (2005). "History of Theatre" web sites: A brief history of the writing process in a high school ESL language arts class. *Journal of Second Language Writing, 14,* 233–258.

Paterson, P.O., & Elliott, L.N. (2006). Struggling reader to struggling reader: High school students' responses to a cross-age tutoring program. *Journal of Adolescent and Adult Literacy, 49,* 378–389.

Rish, R.M., & Caton, J. (2011). Building fantasy worlds together with collaborative writing: Creative, social, and pedagogic challenges. *English Journal, 100*(5), 21–28.

Rubinstein-Ávila, E. (2003). Conversing with Miguel: An adolescent English language learner struggling with later literacy development. *Journal of Adolescent and Adult Literacy, 47*(4), 290–301.

Rubinstein-Ávila, E. (2007). In their words, sounds, and images: After-school literacy programs for urban youth. In B. Guzzetti (Ed.), *Literacy for the new millennium: Vol 4. Adolescent literacy* (pp. 239–250). Westport, CT: Praeger.

Sokal, L., & Piotrowski, C. (2011). My brother's teacher? Siblings and literacy development in the home. *Education Research International.* doi:10.1155/2011/253896

Sperling, M. (1991). Dialogues of deliberation: Conversation in the teacher–student writing conference. *Written Communication, 8*(2), 131–162.

Street, B.V. (1984). *Literacy in theory and practice.* Cambridge: Cambridge University Press.

Swain, M., Kinnear, P., & Steinman, L. (2011). *Sociocultural theory in second language education: An introduction through narratives.* Bristol: Multilingual Matters.

Urberg, K.A., Değirmencioğlu, S.M., Tolson, J.M., & Halliday-Scher, K. (1995). The structure of adolescent peer networks. *Developmental Psychology, 31*(4), 540–547.

Valdés, G. (1998). The world outside and inside schools: Language and immigrant children. *Educational Researcher, 27*(6), 4–18.

Valdés, G. (2001). *Learning and not learning English: Latino students in American schools.* New York: Teachers College Press.

Valenzuela, A. (1999). *Subtractive schooling: U.S.-Mexican youth and the politics of caring.* Albany, NY: SUNY Press.

Villalva, K.E. (2006). Hidden literacies and inquiry approaches of bilingual high school writers. *Written Communication, 23*(1), 91–129.

Wenger, E. (1998). *Communities of practice: Learning, meaning, and identity.* Cambridge: Cambridge University Press.

Wilson, J.S. (2012a). Students and their social networks for literacy. In A. Cumming (Ed.), *Adolescent literacies in a multicultural context* (pp. 56–65). New York: Routledge.

Wilson, J.S. (2012b). Ning: A recent immigrant student. In A. Cumming (Ed.), *Adolescent literacies in a multicultural context* (pp. 191–196). New York: Routledge.

Wilson, J.S. (2012c). Social support networks for literacy engagement among culturally diverse urban adolescents. Unpublished doctoral dissertation, University of Toronto.

Yi, Y. (2005). Immigrant students' out-of-school literacy practices: A qualitative study of Korean students' experiences. *Dissertation Abstracts International, 66* (06) (UMI No. 3177154).

Yi, Y. (2007). Engaging literacy: A biliterate student's composing practices beyond school. *Journal of Second Language Writing, 16,* 23–39.

Yi, Y. (2010). Identity matters: Theories that help explore adolescent multilingual writers and their identities. In M. Cox, J. Jordan, C. Ortmeier-Hooper, & G.G. Schwartz (Eds.), *Reinventing identities in second language writing* (pp. 303–323). Urbana, IL: NCTE.

7

EMERGING LITERACIES IN DIGITAL MEDIA AND L2 SECONDARY WRITING

Melissa Niiya, Mark Warschauer, and Binbin Zheng

Over the last half-century, the development and diffusion of information and communication technologies have dramatically transformed the way people write. On the one hand, written interaction, for example via email or text messages, has both supplemented and supplanted forms of communication previously conducted orally. On the other hand, blogs, wikis, and social media have given many more people the means to experience authorship and publication than ever before in human history. In addition, word processing software and the Internet provide tools for conducting and authoring academic research that previous generations could only imagine.

In this chapter, we consider the role of digital media for second language writing, in particular for adolescent English language learners (ELLs) in the US. Although most research regarding digital media and ELLs focuses on college or elementary school students, many of the lessons learned from these studies can be applied or adapted to ELLs in secondary schools. Adolescent ELLs have three main challenges in writing. First, their *language skills* naturally lag those of English native speakers, a lag that can limit their ability to write effective sentences. Second, ELLs often have trouble with *academic writing*, due to poor research skills, unfamiliarity with academic genres, or over-attention to discrete language matters at the expense of broader issues of content and organization. Third, ELLs often suffer a conflict of *identity* in second language literacy activities, as difficulties with academic language spur them to disengage from the classroom. Our chapter is organized around each of these three issues and the ways that digital media use can reshape them.

Language Skills

For English learners, academic language proficiency poses a major challenge. While ELL students may develop conversational English with ease, it takes years of exposure to and practice with academic language to develop the skills of a scholarly writer. For ELLs, this transition can be especially difficult as they have to acquire an understanding of both mechanics, such as the phonetics of specialist words, and social contexts, such as the sociolinguistic practices appropriate to academic English (Scarcella, 2003). Without these skills, adolescent ELLs struggle to find success. Worse, the difficulties they face in secondary school are compounded when they pursue a college education (Scarcella, 2003).

Digital writing and computer-mediated communication can assist in the development of these language skills. Research concerning adolescent ELLs and language skill development is sparse. Results from the analysis of adult and elementary school student technology use can feasibly be applied to adolescents. Computer-mediated communication (CMC) such as blogging and chatting can help students use more complex language. These same types of communication can also increase language learners' ability to notice and emulate new language. Perhaps the most basic way digital media can facilitate language skill development is by increasing the time ELLs spend writing.

Practice and Participation

Academic writing requires practice. Access to technology may improve student engagement, thereby increasing time spent on task. In their study of a secondary school one-to-one laptop program, McMillan and Honey (1993) report students "fitting the laptops smoothly into life" and feeling able to write more on their laptops (p. 17). More frequent access to writing tools may be helpful both for engaging students (Silvernail & Lane, 2004, p. 20) and for increasing the amount of writing that students do in the classroom (Warschauer, 2009, p. 104).

While technology access via laptops and other devices can have positive effects on the amount of time that students practice writing, specific modes of computer-mediated communication—either synchronous forms, such as instant messaging or asynchronous forms such as email or discussion forums—can also help increase student participation in writing. For adolescent students, many of whom already engage in online writing (Ito et al., 2009), these types of communication may be a less foreign space in which to write. In a study of adult ELLs, students who participated little in face-to-face discussions took part in synchronous CMC discussions at nearly the same rates as their more talkative classmates (Warschauer, 1996). Bloch (2008) suggests that blogs, in particular, can benefit ELLs, as they require "little background in technology to share their ideas about whatever topics they think are important" (p. 165). The asynchronous nature of blogs can be less interactive, but this quality also tends to result in posts with more formal language than synchronous conversation (p. 153). Able to engage in discourse with their peers, students could use blogs to practice English in addition to their formal classroom writing. In addition to increasing the quantity of ELL writing practice, CMC can also increase the complexity of language used in writing, thus promoting the use of more academic language.

Language Complexity

While an increased amount of writing can help ELLs, the types of language practiced in this writing can also affect English learning. The syntactic and lexical qualities of academic language are quite different from those adolescent ELLs encounter in conversational English (Scarcella, 2003). The very nature of CMC may encourage complex language use. When compared with face-to-face discussion, students' language use tends to be more lexically and syntactically complex in online discussions (Chun, 1994; Kern, 1995; Warschauer, 1996; Zheng & Warschauer, 2012). For example, Chun's (1994) study regarding first-year German college students suggests that students produce more complex sentences than simple sentences after spending a semester communicating via CMC. Kern (1995), in his study comparing college student learning in electronic discussion with oral discussion, found students produced more complex structures in electronic discussions. Similar findings were shown in Warschauer's (1996) study comparing face-to-face discussion with electronic discussion in a college-level English as a second language class; the results suggest that electronic discussions fostered the use of more complex and formal language. While the majority of similar research has been conducted with college students, a recent study suggests that blogging could foster complex language use in fifth-graders (Zheng & Warschauer, 2012). Additionally, Chun (1994) argues that because electronic discussions force students to compose the "types of sentences . . . [that] would be said in a spoken conversation" in text, these discussions can potentially help students bridge between their written skills and speaking skills (p. 29). These traits could be especially beneficial for ELLs, since the spoken language in their home environment is usually disconnected from their written language in school contexts.

In addition to language complexity, student vocabulary could also be enhanced by CMC (Abrams, 2001; Blake, 2000; Swain, 1995, 1998; Warschauer, 1999). Blake (2000) claimed that since CMC requires students to produce texts, this *forced output* could be used to provide a favorable language learning environment. Furthermore, information exchange among students could increase vocabulary as well as facilitate students' reflection on their individual and peers' vocabulary use (Swain, 1998). In a study of college students in a second language class, Abrams (2001) found that students adopted different and more varied roles in CMC than in written collaboration. In his case study, Warschauer (1999) additionally noted that CMC permitted students to write in different genres, from multimedia web pages to emails. That CMC may enable second language students to write in more diverse roles and genres suggests that ELLs may be able to develop a wider range of vocabulary through CMC. In these studies, the electronic discussions were used primarily in college classrooms; however, the benefits of CMC appear to exist also in secondary schools (e.g., Beach, Anson, Breuch, & Swiss, 2009, pp. 55–58).

Noticing and Adopting

For ELLs, appropriating the style and vocabulary of academic language can be problematic. Students may not always *notice* words they do not recognize (Swain & Lapkin, 1995). ELLs learn to use new language by noticing words and phrases they do not yet understand, "triggering mental processes that lead to modified output" (pp. 372–373). CMC can assist ELLs in noticing and subsequently adopting academic language in writing.

Computer-mediated communication appears to increase language noticing in English learners (Lai & Zhao, 2006; Smith & Gorsuch, 2004). In a study of adult ELLs, Lai and Zhao (2006) found that synchronous CMC allowed for "more processing time" for composing and reading responses during and after sessions, enabling participants to more frequently notice unfamiliar words (p. 112). One student noted that "[i]n online chatting, I'm more concerned about my typing mistake and grammar," suggesting that the social qualities of CMC might also contribute to increased noticing (p. 112). Additionally, Smith and Gorsuch's (2004) study of college ELLs and their use of chat suggests that CMC increases the students' "attention to form," which Smith and Gorsuch argue increases student usage of new words (pp. 568–569). Whereas CMC out of school may expose adolescent ELLs to informal language, CMC used in the classroom has the potential to help them identify the gaps in their understanding of academic language.

As suggested by Smith and Gorsuch's (2004) study, CMC may also assist English learners by scaffolding the appropriation of new language. Language learners grasp new words through the *assimilation* of the language of others (Bakhtin, 1986). CMC can support this assimilation. In examining online communication of Chinese-English bilingual students, Huang (2009) found that this writing had many instances of *code-switching*, where participants swapped languages during communication. Huang (2009) argues that the informal, text-based nature of CMC enables this frequent code-switching and allows for increased language adoption. Although research into K–12 CMC is more limited, Zheng and Warschauer's (2012) study of blogging in fifth-graders suggests that CMC can facilitate both teacher and peer scaffolding. While students emulated teacher models of mentorship and phrasing, they also imitated peers in their citation of sources and sharing of hyperlinks (Zheng & Warschauer, 2012).

CMC can provide new opportunities for ELLs to practice complex syntax and language, to notice and adopt new forms of academic language, and to simply have more time to practice writing. Digital communication can empower students to adopt new roles and language in written exchanges (Zheng & Warschauer, 2012; Abrams, 2001). In adolescent English learners, assuming the role and language of an academic is complicated by questions of identity.

Identity

For English language learners, problems with language and writing often intersect with issues of identity. Identity conflicts typically arise in early school years, when classroom language and interaction patterns are far different from the home language and interaction patterns of immigrant children (Gonzalez, Moll, & Amanti, 2005). In spite of these conflicts, the literacy achievements of immigrant children in lower elementary grades has improved in recent years, due to more focused phonics instruction (Cummins, Brown, & Sayers, 2007, p. 25). However, in upper elementary grades, as students transition from "learning to read" (through decoding of simple decontextualized language) to "reading to learn" (accessing more complex texts for content), the limited academic vocabulary and syntax of English language learners come more strongly into play (Chall, 1996). When students fall behind in the kinds of academic reading and writing that take place in upper elementary grades, they often begin a mutually reinforcing downward cycle of poor performance leading to low motivation. Simply put, the eager kindergarten student becomes an adolescent who "doesn't do school" and who views school and writing as being for a different type of youth.

For many immigrant youth, the use of digital media for writing provides an effective way to help break this cycle. Digital media use can support several learning processes that help strengthen students' positive identities as English language writers.

Peer Feedback

The writing experience, especially for ELLs, can intimidate and dishearten. In Lam's (2000) case study, a Chinese immigrant student, Almon, knows that this inability to achieve will impact his success as an adult: "It's like this place isn't my world, I don't belong here. . . . And I have a feeling that my English won't be that good even in 10 years" (p. 467). Alienated from English learning, students like Almon need to view writing not as a decontextualized class assignment but as a medium they can master. Sharing writing with peers is one way students may be able to reengage with writing. While opportunities for this type of sharing are not always present in the classroom, online writing communities present possibilities for English learners to practice language in ways that relate to them.

Youth flock to *interest-driven* online communities where they can relate to others, display their expertise, and practice skills (Ito et al., 2009). Many publishing sites have functions for writers to give and receive feedback from fellow authors. The authority and information in such groups is dispersed, collective, and diverse;

such *affinity spaces* (see Gee, 2004) can create the sense of belonging and ownership that many ELL youth do not find in the classroom.

One online stomping ground where youth practice peer feedback is fanfiction. These communities allow users to post, review, and collaborate in writing stories based on fictional texts. Fanfiction reviewers typically "focus on function rather than form" and give ample praise and encouragement (Black, 2005, p. 127). Community conventions such as these can create a positive climate where ELL writers can concentrate on expression and meaning. Peer feedback in these writing sites can be a way for ELLs to grow more comfortable with writing—and, moreover, to view writing as a tool and art that is within their grasp.

Fanfiction sites may also empower users to contribute to community knowledge. In her study of three adolescent ELL authors, Black (2009) finds the youths imparting their knowledge of cultural practices and non-English words (p. 692). That these students feel secure enough to fully participate in this writing community suggests that web-facilitated peer criticism could be a way to reengage ELL interest in writing. Black's work on fanfiction also illuminates another aspect of voluntary writing: youth who participate in these fan-based affinity spaces often create works that incorporate digital media, including images, movies, and music. ELL youth are using these multiple modalities to express themselves and to write their identities.

Multiple Modalities

That English language learners often supplement their writing with other media is no surprise. Bolter (1991) argues that visual imagery is more accessible to ELLs than text; images embody and transmit *natural signs* that cross cultural and language barriers, whereas the meaning of text is arbitrarily defined. Web authoring tools allow even users with limited technical experience to create collages of images, sound, and text. The ability for authors to dwell at once in a textual and a visual space has potential both as a motivating factor and as a way for English learners to practice their communication skills.

Numerous investigations have found multimedia use to be potentially motivating for young writers. Using software to compose and illustrate their stories, students may write more and experience "less fatigue" than with pen and paper (Warschauer, 2008, p. 60). Able to supplement their texts and convey meaning, English learners can express themselves in sophisticated ways while adopting new vocabulary. Lam's (2000) study of Almon illustrates an instance of a young person driven to improve his second language and digital media skills as he fashions his online self. In teaching himself to create a website and maintain communication with his website visitors, Almon becomes more positive about learning a second language: "I wasn't doing well at it, and so I used hating it as a way to deal with the problem. But I think it's easier for me to write out something now" (p. 468). Through the creation of their online identities, students like Almon might discover new incentives to master writing. The integration of media may help ELL youth define their digital selves as they learn to write.

The caveat to embracing these multiple modes of expression, however, is that simply adopting them in school contexts is not enough. An encounter with one implementation illustrates the effect of a multimodal science assignment with dubious academic goals: "It appeared that the purpose of this assignment and grading rubric . . . was not to teach students to develop an effective presentation but rather to check off that they had mastered the various features of the PowerPoint software program" (Warschauer, Knobel, & Stone, 2004, p. 576). While students might have benefited from using multimedia to share their research, their focus was instead the *use* of multimedia, to the detriment of the project content. Used to supplant rather than support text, digital media becomes yet another decontextualized tool that is irrelevant to the student and less likely to help struggling ELL writers.

Writing the Word and the World

Students value writing when they write about what they value. The opinions expressed by the students in Chandler-Olcott and Mahar's study, "that their personal writing [is] more important to them and higher in quality than the work they completed for class," is not rare (2003, p. 561). An aspiring businessperson, one youth uses software to create a "professional-looking flyer" with sophisticated marketing language despite maintaining: "I'm like my dad. I'm not a pencil man" (Knobel, 1999, p. 104 as cited in Hull & Schultz, 2002). The examples discussed above suggest the potential motivation that students can gain when writing with digital media about topics that interest them; however, these examples originate largely in out-of-classroom situations. These acts of writing all share qualities that Cummins (2008) would suggest make them *identity texts*, that is, texts that help students define themselves. Cummins (2008) suggests that leveraging digital media as well as student sociocultural knowledge is essential to promoting the creation of identity texts in the classroom.

One way of bringing sociocultural contexts and knowledge into the classroom is to encourage the cultural literacies students already carry into the classroom (Hull & Schultz, 2002). In Project FRESA, students—mostly children of immigrant strawberry workers—began with a premise relevant to their lives: strawberries (Cummins et al., 2007). Motivated by the project's relationship to their communities, students used digital tools to conduct research, write, and publish their work online. The tools were means for students to achieve academic goals and to construct their identities, as their teacher describes: "It made a world of difference having something the students could connect to and relate to" (as cited in Cummins et al., 2007). While Project FRESA served third graders, similar multimodal, community-centric projects are finding success in secondary schools (e.g., Crandall, 2009). The potential positive impact for similar writing projects on at-risk secondary students is also seen in efforts such as the "Freedom Writers" project, where teacher Erin Gruwell focused her curriculum on drawing parallels between literature, her students' lives, and their journaling (Gruwell, 1999).

There is much more to becoming a good writer than developing a positive identity. However, without a positive identity toward writing, little can be achieved. Ample evidence from out-of-school activities suggests that use of digital media can strengthen ELL students' identity as English language writers. Examples such as Project FRESA show how these lessons can be carried into schools as well.

Academic Writing

As the ability to write well has steadily gained importance in the knowledge economy (National Commission on Writing, 2003, 2004), academic writing has taken on increasing importance in schools. Essay writing is now included in many states' high school exit exams, and writing ability is considered a key component to a successful transition to college. ELLs face particular challenges in developing academic writing skills. They may have insufficient background knowledge and research skills. Due to gaps between norms of informal and academic communication, they may have trouble finding their voice in academic writing. They may also receive insufficient feedback on their writing and may revise their writing in limited ways.

Writing as Research

If a student knows little about a topic, it is difficult to write well about it. ELLs, many of whom come from low-income immigrant families (Batalova, Fix, & Murray, 2007), may have less background knowledge on academic topics than their counterparts (Gonzalez et al., 2005). Good research skills are thus especially critical for ELLs. While web research tools can be starting points for academic inquiry, these tools require both access to the Internet and technical competence. As with issues of language and identity, digital media are not an end but a means of supporting academic writing.

One way schools tackle the need for technology access is through one-to-one laptop programs. One-to-one laptop deployments have attempted to address issues of access and research skill development with varying degrees of success. In Warschauer's (2007) investigation, positive effects of such programs include improvements in students' ability to perform basic research, learn on their own, and conduct research (p. 2516). With a diverse population, including a high proportion of low socioeconomic status and immigrant ELL students, King Middle School implemented a laptop program to supplement their eight- to twelve-week research project curriculum (Warschauer, 2007, p. 2532). All students contribute to a collaborative product that includes essays and other multimedia (p. 2535). At King, research is allied with the expression of that research through writing and multimodal communication. Laptops and digital media provide the means and medium for that research and writing. Whereas research at King engages students and produces meaningful projects and writing, laptop and research programs at other schools are not always successful. At Plum Middle School, for example, students received no digital literacy training and gave PowerPoint recitals of information gathered from questionable sources (p. 2531). Lacking guidance in research techniques and without the support of an overarching research goal, these students engaged in little writing or research.

Across multiple studies, the value of bringing laptops and research technologies into the classroom appears to be dependent on execution. While one-to-one laptop research involving secondary schools is limited, the lessons learned from successful middle and elementary school implementations can be applied to secondary schools. Information literacy and inquiry-based curricula cannot be overlooked when using technology for research and academic writing.

Academic Voice

Though ELLs can benefit from research projects, they often lack the types of language necessary to write on academic topics. Gee (2004) suggests that students who do not bring the "prototypes of academic language" into the classroom will not make this transition without practice (p. 19). While native speakers may have seen academic English as young children, adolescent ELLs must acquire academic language without prior prototyping. Learning to master academic language can involve using a combination of academic and colloquial language (p. 25); digital media can provide ELLs a way to practice this mixing.

Online writing offers opportunities for ELLs to *apprentice* into academic discourse by combining casual and formal language. In his ELL blogging class on plagiarism, Bloch (2007) describes how the blog served to gather academic writing, as exemplified by one student, Abdullah: "Many classmates thought academic plagiarism must be punished, but I thought the punishment like expulsion is not the best way for academic life of students" (p. 135). Less formal than an academic essay, blogging allows Abdullah to practice critical writing while allowing him to use the more conversational language he already knows.

The fusion of informal writing style and academic content in online writing also takes place in comments. Allison (2009) encourages student bloggers to participate in online communities by citing other blogs and writing feedback for other bloggers. To assist students in forming their responses, Allison gives students a framework for a focused analysis of a blog post, suggesting they quote sentences and specify reasons for their opinions (pp. 82–83). This fill-in-the-blank framework for commenting, framed as a letter addressed to the blog author, permits students to use a personal voice as they express academic ideas. The act of providing comments and feedback to classmates can be a valuable experience in itself. Digital media can assist ELLs in the process of revision and rewriting.

Iterative Writing

The academic writing process demands revision, and digital tools simplify this process. Not only are iterations simpler in a word processor; receiving and giving feedback can be expedited. Edits are instantaneous. Grammar and spelling checks are on the fly. Merely having access to a laptop and a word processor appears to affect the quantity of student writing, as noted by a teacher in a one-to-one laptop program: "They are writing more, it's better quality, it's produced faster. I think the laptops facilitate the writing because there is less fatigue involved than with cursive or print" (as cited in Warschauer, 2009, p. 104). Word processing has the potential to make the writing process faster and less intimidating for ELL students.

The same tools with which students write can enable teachers to provide more timely and in-depth feedback. Teachers in Warschauer's (2009) study of one-to-one laptop programs report that they read and comment on their students' typed essays more quickly in digital or print format than on handwritten work (p. 106). With automated writing evaluation (AWE) software, students can receive immediate feedback on structure as well as mechanical issues such as grammar (Grimes & Warschauer, 2010). While the automatic feedback is not always accurate, students tend to write more and make more revisions, though these revisions are often limited to issues such as spelling and grammar (p. 27). While AWE has limitations, its use may free teachers to "focus on higher-level concerns instead of writing mechanics" (p. 34). When used not to lessen teacher load but to shift it from mechanics to content and structure, AWE may benefit ELL students.

Digital media can also provide ways for students to obtain feedback from peers. Critiquing can be awkward, especially for ELLs who may not feel their mastery of English writing is sufficient to critique others' work. In his ELL blogging classroom, Bloch (2008) suggests that the large amount of critique he saw in students' blog comments was the result of "the distance between reader and writer" (p. 162). Able to read and comment at their own pace and not face to face, ELL youth may be more willing to give peer feedback. With access to online resources, the depth of discussion about paper revisions can also increase. Upon receiving criticism from her peer, one ELL college student blogger (Sun & Chang, 2012) defended her word choice, citing its similar use in publications; she also documents her online search for examples of the word (p. 56). This type of dialogue—of criticism, refuting, and sharing—may help English learners develop their revision skills. The studies discussed focus primarily on middle school classrooms, but the positive effects of online writing and peer feedback on post-secondary students suggest that benefits may accrue across age groups.

Writing in a digital medium does not guarantee that ELL students will develop better revision and rewriting skills, but there is considerable potential for technology to support them in learning academic writing. Research projects can be misguided or sophisticated depending on their implementation. Faced with similar caveats, automatic writing evaluation has potential as one feedback tool.

Meanwhile, online writing platforms such as blogs offer a social space for ELLs to exchange feedback with peers and to develop their academic voices.

Conclusion

Adolescent English language learners face many challenges when learning how to write. Digital media can play a role in helping ELLs confront these challenges, but the success of these technologies relies on implementation and teacher support. Without basic language instruction and inquiry-based goals, multimodal academic writing assignments can be as irrelevant and inaccessible as those written with pencil and paper. Syntax and vocabulary instruction via computer-mediated communication will not help student writing if students have no motivation to use what they have learned. Moreover, writing technologies alone cannot span the gulf between in- and out-of-classroom sociocultural contexts and language. In cases of successful integration of digital media into the ELL classroom, curriculum and teacher support factor into that success. With this support, digital media have the potential to assist ELLs in developing a foundation of syntax and vocabulary, the ability to write in academic language, and the desire to write. Tools such as web search and word processors can make possible more in-depth academic writing and research. CMC can help lay the groundwork for this academic writing by enabling ELLs to learn new words and sentence structures. With the majority of adolescents already participating in digital media and online communication, these technologies also have the potential to engage and motivate students to participate in academic discourse.

References

Abrams, Z. I. (2001). Computer-mediated communication and group journals: Expanding the repertoire of participant roles. *System, 29*(4), 489–503. doi: 10.1016/S0346-251X(01)00041-0

Allison, Paul. (2009). Be a blogger: Social networking in the classroom. In A. Herrington, K. Hodgson, & C. Moran (Eds.), *Teaching the new writing: Technology, change and assessment in the 21st century classroom* (pp. 75–91). New York: Teachers College Press.

Bakhtin, M. M. (1986). *Speech genres and other late essays.* C. Emerson & M. Holquist (Eds.). (V. W. McGee, Trans.). Austin: University of Texas Press.

Batalova, J., Fix, M., and Murray, J. (2007). *Measures of change: The demography and literacy of adolescent English learners—A report to the Carnegie Corporation of New York.* Washington, DC: Migration Policy Institute. Retrieved November 12, 2012 from http://www.migrationpolicy.org/pubs/Measures_of_Change.pdf

Beach, R., Anson, C., Breuch, L., & Swiss, T. (2009). *Teaching writing using blogs, wikis, and other digital tools.* Norwood, MA: Christopher-Gordon Publishers.

Black, R. W. (2005). Access and affiliation: The literacy and composition practices of English-language learners in an online fanfiction community. *Journal of Adolescent and Adult Literacy, 49*(2), 118–128.

Black, R. W. (2009). English-language learners, fan communities, and 21st-century skills. *Journal of Adolescent and Adult Literacy, 52*(8), 688–697.

Blake, R. (2000). Computer-mediated communication: A window on L2 Spanish interlanguage. *Language Learning and Technology, 4*(1), 120–136.

Bloch, Joel. (2007). Abdullah's blogging: A generation 1.5 student enters the blogosphere. *Language Learning and Technology, 11*(2), 128–141.

Bloch, Joel. (2008). *Technologies in the second language composition classroom.* Ann Arbor, MI: University of Michigan Press.

Bolter, J. D. (1991). *Writing space: The computer, hypertext, and the history of writing.* Hillsdale, NJ: Lawrence Erlbaum Associates.

Chall, J. S. (1996). *Stages of reading development (2nd Edition).* Fort Worth, TX: Harcourt Brace College Publishers.

Chandler-Olcott, K., & Mahar, D. (2003). Adolescents' anime-inspired "fanfictions": An exploration of multiliteracies. *Journal of Adolescent Literacy, 46*, 556–566.

Chun, D. (1994). Using computer networking to facilitate the acquisition of interactive competence. *System, 22*(1), 17–31. doi: 10.1016/0346-251X(94)90037-X

Crandall, B. R. (2009). Senior boards: Multimedia presentations from year-long research and community-based culminating projects. In A. Herrington, K. Hodgson, & C. Moran (Eds.), *Teaching the new writing: Technology, change and assessment in the 21st century classroom* (pp. 107–123). New York: Teachers College Press.

Cummins, J. (2008). Technology, literacy, and young second language learners: Designing educational futures. In L. L. Parker (Ed.), *Technology-mediated learning environments for young English learners: Connections in and out of school* (pp. 61–98). New York: Lawrence Erlbaum Associates.

Cummins, J., Brown, K., & Sayers, D. (2007). *Literacy, technology, and diversity: Teaching for success in changing times.* Boston, MA: Allyn and Bacon.

Gee, J. P. (2004). *Situated language and learning: A critique of traditional schooling.* New York: Routledge.

Gonzalez, N., Moll, L., & Amanti, C. (Eds.) (2005). *Funds of knowledge: Theorizing practices in households and classrooms.* Mahwah, NJ: Lawrence Erlbaum and Associates.

Grimes, D., & Warschauer, M. (2010). Utility in a fallible tool: A multi-site case study of automated writing evaluation. *Journal of Technology, Learning, and Assessment, 8*(6). Retrieved from http://www.jtla.org/

Gruwell, E. (1999). *The freedom writers' diary: How a teacher and 150 teens used writing to change themselves and the world around them.* New York: Broadway Books.

Huang, D. L. (2009). Language use in asynchronous computer-mediated communication in Taiwan. *Australian Review of Applied Linguistics, 32*(2), 12.1–12.22. doi: 10.2104/aral0912.

Hull, G., & Schultz, K. (2002). Connecting schools with out-of-school worlds: Insights from recent research on literacy in non-school settings. In G. Hull & K. Schultz (Eds.), *School's out!: Bridging out-of-school literacies with classroom practice.* New York: Teachers College Press.

Ito, M., *et al.* (2009). *Hanging out, messing around, geeking out: Living and learning with new media.* Cambridge, MA: MIT Press.

Kern, R. (1995). Restructuring classroom interaction with networked computers: Effects on quantity and characteristics of language production. *The Modern Language Journal, 79*(4), 457–476. doi: 10.1111/j.1540-4781.1995.tb05445.x

Knobel, M. (1999). *Everyday literacies. Students, discourse and social practice.* New York: Peter Lang.

Lai, C., & Zhao, Y. (2006). Noticing and text-based chat. *Language Learning and Technology, 10*(3), 102–120.

Lam, W. S. E. (2000). L2 literacy and the design of the self: A case study of a teenager writing on the internet. *TESOL Quarterly, 34*(3), 457–482.

McMillan, K., & Honey, M. (1993). *Year one of project pulse: Pupils using laptops in science and English* (Tech. Rep. 26). New York: Center for Technology in Education.

National Commission on Writing. (2003). *The neglected "R": The need for a writing revolution.* Available at http://www.collegeboard.com

National Commission on Writing. (2004). *Writing: A ticket to work . . . or a ticket out: A survey of business leaders.* Available at http://www.collegeboard.com

Scarcella, R. (2003). *Academic English: A conceptual framework.* Los Angeles: University of California Language Minority Research Institute.

Silvernail, D. L., & Lane, D. M. M. (2004). *The impact of Maine's one-to-one laptop program on middle school teachers and students: Research report no. 1.* Portland, ME: Maine Education Policy Research Institute, University of Southern Maine.

Smith, B., & Gorsuch, G. (2004). Synchronous computer mediated communication captured by usability lab technologies: New interpretations. *System, 32,* 553–575.

Sun, Y., & Chang, Y. (2012). Blogging to learn: Becoming EFL academic writers through collaborative dialogues. *Language Learning and Technology, 16*(1), 43–61.

Swain, M. (1995). Three functions of output in second language learning. In G. Cook & B. Seidlhofer (Eds.), *Principle and practice in applied linguistics: Studies in honor of H. G. Widdowson* (pp. 125–144). Oxford: Oxford University Press.

Swain, M. (1998). Focus on form through conscious reflection. In C. Doughty & J. Williams (Eds.), *Focus on form in classroom second language acquisition* (pp. 64–81). Cambridge: Cambridge University Press.

Swain, M., & Lapkin, S. (1995). Problems in output and the cognitive processes they generate: A step towards second language learning. *Applied Linguistics, 16*(3), 371–391.

Warschauer, M. (1996). Comparing face-to-face and electronic discussion in the second language classroom. *CALICO Journal, 13*(2), 7–26.

Warschauer, M. (1999). *Electronic literacies. Language, culture and power in online education.* Mahwah, NJ: Lawrence Erlbaum Associates.

Warschauer, M. (2007). Information literacy in the laptop classroom. *Teachers College Record, 109*(11), 2511–2540.

Warschauer, M. (2008). Laptops and literacy: A multi-site case study. *Pedagogies: An International Journal, 3,* 52–67.

Warschauer, M. (2009). Learning to write in the laptop classroom. *Writing and Pedagogy, 1,* 101–112.

Warschauer, M., Knobel, M., & Stone, L. (2004). Technology and equity in schooling: Deconstructing the digital divide. *Educational Policy, 18,* 562–588.

Zheng, B., & Warschauer, M. (2012). *Blogging to learn: Participation and literacy among linguistically diverse fifth-grade students.* Paper presented at the 2012 American Educational Research Association Annual Meeting. Vancouver, British Columbia, Canada.

PART III
Teacher Education

8

FOCUS ON PRE-SERVICE PREPARATION FOR ESL WRITING INSTRUCTION

Secondary Teacher Perspectives

Ditlev Larsen

Writing may be referred to as "the last language skill" (after listening, speaking, and reading), but the reality is that ESL teachers at all educational levels must increasingly deal with the diverse writing abilities of their students. On the secondary level alone, the variety of writing skills that teachers encounter in their mostly immigrant ESL population can be overwhelming, and the question is what teacher educators or teacher education programs need to do in order to optimally prepare ESL teachers for the challenges they face when teaching writing to this fascinating and complex population.

Given the surge of interest in and acknowledgment of the importance of specific attention to writing in ESL classrooms, it would be reasonable to assume that ESL teacher preparation programs in the U.S. commonly require coursework specifically focusing on L2 writing theory and pedagogy. However, the fact is that this is rarely the case. Crusan (2009) conducted an informal survey of TESOL teacher education programs on the graduate level and found that only 9 percent required a course on teaching ESL writing—an additional 14 percent required it as a combined reading/writing pedagogy class—which led her to conclude that there is a dearth of teacher training in second language writing.

But to what extent is knowledge of L2 writing theory and pedagogy needed by teachers at different grade levels? How important and widespread are writing and writing instruction in the ESL classroom? The people best equipped to answer that question are likely to be currently practicing teachers. Consequently, the study presented in this chapter is aimed at investigating exactly how well prepared secondary ESL teachers found themselves after completing their teacher education programs.

Although it is not surprising that different TESOL teacher education programs diverge in their curriculum as a result of a number of contextual and institutional factors (see Ramanathan, Davies & Schleppegrel, 2001), it is surprising to see the apparently consistent omission of L2 writing theory and pedagogy, especially since the discussion of a general lack of appropriate emphasis on writing in ESL teacher preparation is not new. For example, more than 20 years ago, Grosse's (1991) examination of TESOL methods courses at more than 100 U.S. institutions revealed that writing took a relatively prominent role among topics to be covered in the course; however, because of the sheer number of topics to cover in a general methods course, the total amount of time spent on writing was limited.

Around this same time, L2 writing had started to grow into a full-fledged separate field as evidenced, among other things, by the emergence of the *Journal of Second Language Writing* in 1992. As the field developed there may have been somewhat of a struggle, as illustrated by both Santos (1992), in an article in the very first issue of that same journal, and Silva (1993), to find a distinct identity for L2/ESL writing somewhere around the intersection between Second Language Acquisition (SLA) theory, language teaching pedagogy, and L1 writing theory and pedagogy. Since then numerous book-length treatments of ESL writer charac-teristics and L2 writing pedagogy, including edited volumes addressing different aspects of ESL writing, have been published, which illustrates that scholars and professionals in the field recognized the need for providing future teachers with the appropriate background knowledge (e.g. Leki, 1992; Reid, 1993, Ferris & Hedgcock, 1998 (second edition 2005); Harklau, Losey, & Siegal, 1999; Silva & Matsuda, 2001; Ferris, 2002; Hyland, 2003; Kroll, 2003; Roberge, Siegal & Harklau, 2009). Why, then, has a writing-specific theory and pedagogy course not attracted more interest and become universal, or at the very least common, in TESOL teacher preparation programs?

It is true to a large extent that beyond a few of the works mentioned above that could be considered explicitly pedagogical textbooks for teacher education programs, most research on ESL writing has been dedicated to a focus on learner needs and challenges or how we identify or recognize such needs and challenges (Hirvela & Belcher, 2007; Lee, 2010). Unfortunately, only a small fraction of the total scholarship on ESL writers has focused on the adolescent age group that teachers encounter at the secondary level of K–12 schools (Matsuda & DePew, 2002; Leki, Cumming & Silva, 2008). However, it is encouraging to note that a scan of scholarship on secondary ESL writers seems to indicate that such work has become increasingly frequent over the last ten to twelve years. Evidence of this trend can be seen in Valdés (1999), Harklau (2000), Reynolds (2002, 2005), Bunch (2006), Villalva (2006), Ortmeier-Hooper (2010), Yi (2010), Enright and Gilliland (2011), and Kibler (2011), who all address various aspects of the concerns and challenges that this secondary school-age ESL student population face.

Still, it seems important that we also pay more attention to the preparation of the teachers of these adolescent ESL writers. Hirvela and Belcher (2007) offer a likely explanation as to why L2 writing pedagogy may not have become as prominent as we might want and need it to be. They explain that second language writing scholars tend to focus on the ESL learners in their own classrooms and their own research interests, and consequently, their identity as "*teachers of teachers of writing*" (in addition to their writing teacher and writing researcher identities) has been neglected (p. 125, emphasis in original). Therefore, Hirvela and Belcher call for more attention to what happens in teacher education programs in terms of preparing pre-service teachers for the reality of working with student writing in their future classrooms. Likewise, it is important, as Lee (2010) points out, to gain insight into what new in-service teachers might do to continue their development.

It should be mentioned, also, that another reason for the relatively infrequent offering of an ESL writing pedagogy course in teacher preparation programs might be a result of the fact that, in many instances, K–12 state standards and requirements for teacher licensure do not include specific references to *writing* pedagogy but mostly just to pedagogy in general. As mentioned above, Grosse (1991) reported that L2 writing theory and pedagogy have traditionally been included in a general ESL methods class, and the problem with that, as Harklau (2002) asserts, is that throughout history in the field of applied linguistics there has always been an emphasis, albeit implicit, on the spoken language.

With this background in mind, this study will try to determine how common student writing is in the daily work of secondary ESL teachers and examine to what extent those teachers consider themselves prepared to teach writing to their ESL students after having completed their teacher education programs. Additionally, the study will explore what kind of additional development and training they may undertake to be successful in working with their students.

The Study

Data Collection and Participants

An on-line questionnaire (see appendix) was sent to approximately 500 teachers in the upper Midwest, representing all educational levels including K–12, college, and adult education. Of the 155 teachers who responded to the survey, 54 identified themselves as secondary teachers and given this book's focus on secondary education, only those will be reported on here. However, I also found it very interesting to notice that even the elementary teachers responding to the survey identified student writing as something they deal with on an almost daily basis.

The study addresses three main research questions:

1. What are typical requirements of ESL teacher education programs in terms of ESL/L2 writing pedagogy?
2. How often do practicing ESL secondary teachers work with their students' writing?
3. To what extent do practicing ESL secondary teachers feel that their teacher education programs prepared them to deal with students' writing?

The questionnaire included mostly multiple-choice items and a few open-ended questions for teachers to provide details of different aspects of their teacher education program, their own preparedness after finishing their program, and any subsequent training and development they may have completed. The data analysis procedure first focused on the multiple choice items of the questionnaire in order to quantify the answers to the three research questions. For the first research question, this involved item 5 on the questionnaire; for the second research question, items 6 and 10; and for the third research question, item 7 (see appendix). However, a more in-depth investigation of the third research question seemed to require more details, which is what items 8 and 9 on the questionnaire were designed to provide. These open-ended responses from the participants allowed for insight into these teachers' perceptions and opinions of their pre-service training as well observations of their professional development as practicing teachers. In the analysis of these responses the focus was on detecting trends or commonalities rather than isolated or individual commentary.

Findings

The first few questions of the survey focused on background information about the teachers and their students, which helps in interpreting the responses more accurately. Essentially all respondents, not surprisingly, reported that the majority of their students are immigrant ESL learners who fall into the diverse category identified as Generation 1.5 (see e.g. Harklau, Losey, & Siegal, 1999 for a description of this population).

The hope was to have many recently educated teachers respond to the survey in order to get as current information as possible about the curricular requirements in terms of L2 writing pedagogy in teacher education programs. Of the respondents, 27 percent had finished their programs within the last five years, 68 percent in the last ten years and 80 percent in the last 15 years. Less than 14 percent finished their programs more than 20 years ago. These numbers indicate that the vast majority of the respondents went through ESL teacher education programs after L2 writing had gained prominence as a separate field of study and pedagogy. More than one in four finished in 2005 or later. Their degrees range from BS TESOL (K–12 licensure/certification) to MA/MS TESOL (K–12 licensure/certification) to a variety of other undergraduate/graduate education degrees with added ESL certification. Most of them (over 70 percent) fall into the MA/MS group.

The second research question addresses how often secondary teachers work with writing, and two questions on the survey questionnaire addressed this issue. Figure 8.1 clearly indicates that writing is a major component of the teachers' daily work.

A total of 76 percent of the teachers indicated that they respond to/comment on student work from two or three times a week to every day. Partly in order to verify the accuracy of the responses on "responding to" and "commenting on"

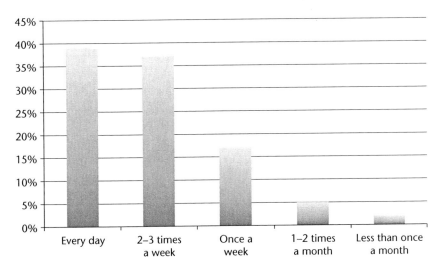

FIGURE 8.1 Distribution of Responses to Question 10: "I respond to, or I comment on, ESL students' written work . . ."

written work and partly to get a wider range of reactions to working with student writing, a second question was added at a different point on the questionnaire, asking the teachers to indicate to what extent they work with their students' writing ("How often do you deal with your ESL learners' writing?"). The term "deal with" was deliberately chosen to recognize that the teaching of writing involves more than just commenting or responding. This question revealed an even more pronounced picture of the omnipresence of writing in ESL teaching: 98 percent chose the response "all the time" (70 percent) or "often" (28 percent). Only one of the teachers chose one of the other three options ("sometimes," "rarely," or "never").

It is clear that student writing occupies a significant part of the regular work of these ESL secondary teachers, but to what extent do they report their ESL teacher education programs as requiring or offering a course specifically focusing on L2 writing theory and pedagogy (first research question)? The responses to that question are shown in Figure 8.2.

So these teachers are faced with extensive work on student writing in their daily work, but, unfortunately, 60 percent of them did not have a chance to take a course preparing them specifically for that purpose. As we shall see next, it is not surprising that one of the results is that the majority of the teachers do not feel adequately prepared for teaching writing.

Figure 8.3 shows that more than half, 54 percent to be exact, of the responding secondary teachers reported that they felt either marginally or not at all prepared to teach writing. Only 11 percent answered "very much so" to this question. The teachers clearly recognized the need for more emphasis on writing in TESOL programs, most likely as a result of the daily realities in their teaching situations.

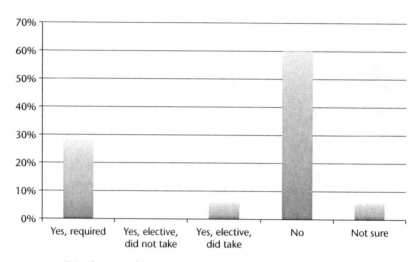

FIGURE 8.2 Distribution of Responses to Question 5: "Did your teacher education program offer a separate course focusing specifically on ESL/L2 writing theory and pedagogy?"

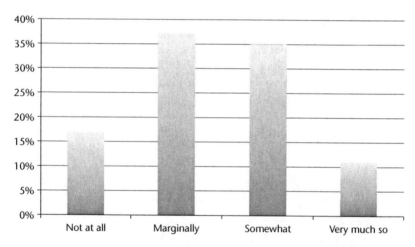

FIGURE 8.3 Distribution of Responses to Question 7: "Do you feel that your teacher education program adequately prepared you for dealing with the written work of ESL learners in your classes?"

Discussion

The Teacher Education Program Curriculum and Teacher Preparedness

The findings reveal some problematic issues that should be a cause of concern for teacher educators. Most troublesome is probably the fact that only about one out of ten of the teachers considered themselves well prepared to teach ESL writing. That is not good enough. It is likely that a large part of this non-preparedness is a result of the lack of an L2 writing theory and pedagogy class. Although this study shows slightly better numbers in terms of requiring such a course than Crusan's (2009)[1] survey, we can see that it is still not a common part of TESOL program curricula and certainly nowhere near as universal as could be argued that it should be—only 34 percent of the teachers being required to take it or having it as an elective option. To put it another way, it is rather discouraging that as many as six out of ten of the secondary teachers in this study did not get to take a course preparing them specifically for the writing of their ESL students, especially considering the amount of time they reported spending on writing in the classes they are teaching.

It is interesting, however, to note the relationship between an L2 writing course and the teachers' responses to preparedness. Every single one of the secondary teachers in the study who considered themselves well prepared had taken such a course. Out of those who were either required to take it or had taken it as an elective, 30 percent considered themselves well prepared and not a single one responded that they were not prepared at all. In contrast, of the teachers who reported not having taken the course, not a single one considered him/herself well prepared, whereas 31 percent found themselves not prepared at all. In other words, none of the teachers who said they were not prepared at all had taken an L2 writing pedagogy course.

Although the teachers who did take the L2 writing course do not universally report being well prepared, these numbers clearly indicate that the course can go a long way to improve teacher preparedness to teach ESL writing. As Grosse (1991) reported, ESL writing pedagogy has traditionally been addressed in the general TESOL methods course that is the cornerstone of nearly all teacher preparation programs, but because of the extensive amount of material to cover in such a course, it can only superficially address an area as vast as ESL writing, which should include both the complexity of writing in a second language (what the learner does), and how to teach writing in a second language (what the teacher does). As we shall see below, some teacher commentary reflected that very same problem.

Teacher Commentary: What Was Missing

The teachers had an opportunity to explain what they felt was missing from their teacher education programs if they considered themselves less than well prepared for teaching writing. Their comments illustrate the need for addressing several different issues of theory and pedagogy in ESL writing, but they could be divided into two broad categories: general attention and focus on ESL student writing in their programs, and specific strategies for providing effective feedback, error correction, and assessment. It appears that the teachers acknowledge that a separate L2 writing class would be able to provide this focus as they mention time being an issue in other classes. A few of them reflected on a (non-ESL) "literacy" class they had, which supposedly was to address writing, but the class did not have time for the necessary depth. Others saw the very brief and limited overview of writing in their general TESOL methods class as inadequate. These complaints are illustrated by the following list of teacher comments, which also point out that much more specific and explicit instruction in how to teach writing to ESL learners is needed:

> We did have a brief module in our literacy course focusing on writing and ELLs, but it would have been great to go deeper.

> The topic of writing was covered only on the surface in a "literacy" class.

> I had a literacy course, but the focus was reading. I would have benefited from some writing pedagogy materials.

> "Literacy"—as my class was called—focused on reading and comprehension.

> [Writing] was only a small unit in a class on teaching methods. We didn't work on it extensively.

> I remember mostly learning about how organization of writing differed between cultures in my methods class; very little, if any, direction on how to actually teach writing—or how writing skills are acquired differently by ELLs.

As ineffective as it may be, it appears that either a literacy class or a general TESOL methods course is relied upon, implicitly, in the various teacher preparation programs to supply pre-service teachers with L2 writing knowledge and pedagogical skills.

The teachers also expressed a desire to learn more about the uniqueness of acquiring L2 writing skills, as opposed to L1, and which skills to address or prioritize at which proficiency levels. One statement can serve as a representation of what seemed to be a general frustration the teachers felt about being unprepared to teach writing after completing their teacher education programs: "Everything [was missing]. There was not much at all offered in the areas [sic] of actually working on writing with ELLs."

Among the more specific issues which the teachers overwhelmingly seemed to agree were lacking in their programs were training in effective feedback strategies and error treatment as well as grading/assessment. They simply felt that they left their programs with a lack of knowledge or experience in regard to responding to student writing. As we have seen, there did not seem to be enough time to address such specific issues of writing in their general pedagogy or methods classes. A snapshot of the teachers' reactions as to what they felt they needed in terms of these issues is captured in the following comments: "How to give feedback on student writing so students learn from their mistakes, and how to grade them," "which errors to address when and where," "how to respond to writing without discouraging the student," "the details, when or how to correct errors," "specific instructions or suggestions for how to grade essays," "it can be tricky to figure out which errors to focus on, rather than just marking up the whole paper."

Responding to writing, grading, and assessment obviously often are, if not parts of the same process, then at least very closely related, and therefore solid preparation in all should be ensured in teacher education programs. However, Ferris (2007) has noted that "[t]eacher educators preparing current and future teachers to respond to student writing face an uphill battle," since it is extraordinarily challenging to provide really beneficial response to student writing (p. 179). Real confidence and competency in providing successful feedback will likely only come through years of repeated practice and experience. Consequently, novice teachers will most likely always feel the anxiety and frustration expressed in the teachers' comments shown above; however, that must not cause teacher educators to neglect specific preparation in this area of ESL writing pedagogy, for, as Ferris (2007) concludes, "[e]xperience alone will not make a teacher an effective responder, but solid principles, useful techniques, and thoughtful reflection and evaluation probably will" (p. 179). It is those principles and techniques that the teacher education program should provide—the tools for eventually gaining the proper experience.

Weigle (2007) has lamented the lack of attention to assessment of student writing in TESOL graduate teacher education programs. The commentary provided by the teachers in this study certainly appears to corroborate the need for more explicit attention to ESL writing assessment. Weigle further asserts that programs tend to lack courses in assessment. Add to that the fact that courses in ESL writing pedagogy and theory are not that common either, and it is easy to see why ESL teachers find themselves unprepared for grading and other forms of assessment.

Teacher Commentary: Remedies

Finally, the teacher respondents were asked to reflect on what they have done to train themselves to deal with the writing of their ESL students, if they indicated that they did not feel prepared after completing their teacher education programs. Many of those responses, not surprisingly, focused on *trial and error* and *self-study*: "Talking with colleagues, looking at books, experimenting, experience," "trial and error, reading and studying on my own," "read textbooks on writing; learn by experience," "trial and error, discussion with other ELL teachers." It is probably too optimistic to think that by providing a course in L2 writing theory and pedagogy, covering everything from L2 writer characteristics to sound strategies for providing feedback, we will eliminate the need for novice teachers to resort to self-study, trial and error, and on-the-job learning. However, it could allow us to provide appropriate background and supply the solid principles (Ferris, 2007) for conducting truly beneficial self-study.

Weigle (2007) pointed out that even though many new teachers step into the classroom unprepared for assessment, as well as for other issues of L2 writing, there are resources available through regional and national associations and conferences that could help teachers to take charge of their professional development. Fortunately, many of the secondary teachers in this study have done exactly that. They reported taking full advantage of conferences and workshops: "I have had a lot of training through workshops, through local TESOL conferences," "reading TESOL journals and publications, attending sessions about writing at MinneTESOL and TESOL." It is indeed encouraging to see the resourcefulness that the teachers have shown in remedying the apparent lack of preparation for teaching ESL writing provided by their programs. However, it may be a disservice to leave it up to the teachers themselves to gain the appropriate knowledge base through self-study, for, as Lee (2010) concluded in her study of EFL teachers, the trajectory of teachers' professional development is likely to be influenced by their teacher education program.

A final comment from one of the teachers in this study can serve as a reminder of the importance of providing, at the very least, the knowledge base to get started: "I have not done anything yet . . . I am a first year ESL teacher and am very much struggling to survive." This is telling and somewhat disheartening. New teachers, who are most in need of assistance, do not have time to seek out remedies to make up for a lack of pre-service preparation.

Conclusion

In their introductory editorial to the special issue of the *Journal of Second Language Writing* ("Adolescent L2 Writing in U.S. Contexts"), Ortmeier-Hooper and Enright (2011) express concern that the second language writing field, with its close ties to college-level ESL writing and mainstream composition, has appeared indifferent when it comes to issues regarding the specific sub-population of ESL writers that could be categorized as adolescents—the group represented in secondary education. This is a valid concern, but so is the concern that the field may have been neglecting the *teachers* of that population (Hirvela & Belcher, 2007). It may be time for more attention to be paid to both.

This investigation of the challenges that the teachers experienced shows that teacher preparation programs may need to do a more thorough job of training new secondary ESL teachers for teaching writing. We saw that the teachers fairly overwhelmingly responded that they did not feel they initially had been prepared adequately to deal with their students' writing—a main reason they provided was that their programs had offered no specific instruction in pedagogy and best practices of teaching writing to ESL learners in terms of such issues as the uniqueness of ESL writers, how to provide appropriate feedback, how and when to respond to errors, and how to grade students' written work.

However, many of the teachers displayed great resourcefulness by educating themselves on the job and taking advantage of various opportunities for professional development, but they also agreed that a lot of frustration could have been avoided with better pre-service preparation. The teachers' qualitative responses offer important insight into what they perceived was missing in terms of helping them gain better pre-service knowledge of L2 writing theory and recognizing practical applications of such knowledge. The limitations of written responses may have affected the depth of the commentary, and it would have been interesting to have had the opportunity to probe further into the comments by interviewing some of these teachers about their experiences.

In closing, based on the findings of this study, I would like to offer four statements that I believe are worthy of the attention of ESL teacher educators when making curricular decisions about how to most effectively prepare teachers for the realities of their future ESL teaching in the secondary school context:

- Writing might in some contexts be considered the "last language skill," but its importance in the teaching of ESL in secondary schools appears evident.
- Secondary teachers are expected to teach and respond to their ESL students' writing more or less on a daily basis, which means that thorough training in L2 writing theory and pedagogy is essential.
- Teachers should be given the opportunity to gain in-depth knowledge of ESL writing before they leave their teacher education programs.
- Providing a course specifically addressing L2 writing theory and pedagogy, covering issues such as ESL writer characteristics, effective feedback, and error correction, as well as appropriate grading and assessment strategies, seems to be the most effective way of ensuring that teacher education programs provide successful pre-service training for teachers.

Appendix

1. **Which of the following best describes your teaching situation?**
   ___ Elementary school
   ___ Middle school
   ___ High school
   ___ Adult education
   ___ College

2. **How long have you been teaching ESL at this level?**
   ___ 5 years or less
   ___ 6–10 years
   ___ 11–15 years
   ___ 16–20 years
   ___ More than 20 years

3. **Have you taught ESL at other levels? If so, at what level and how long?**

4. **Which of the following best describes your degree(s)?**
   ___ B.S. TESOL (K–12 License)
   ___ M.A. or M.S. TESOL (including K–12 License)
   ___ M.A. TESOL (no K–12 License)
   ___ Other. Please specify: _____

5. **Did your teacher education program offer a course focusing specifically on ESL writing or second language writing theory and pedagogy?**
   ___ Yes, it was required
   ___ Yes, as an elective, but I did not take it
   ___ Yes, as an elective, and I did take it
   ___ No
   ___ Not sure

6. **How often do you deal with your ESL learners' writing?**
   Never   Rarely   Sometimes   Often   All the time

7. **Do you feel that your teacher education program adequately prepared you for dealing with the written work of ESL learners in your classes?**
   ___ Very much so
   ___ Somewhat
   ___ Only marginally
   ___ Not at all

8. **If your answer to question 7 above was anything other than "very much so," can you specify what was missing?**

9. **If your answer to question 7 above was anything other than "very much so," what have you done to train yourself in dealing with the writing of your ESL learners?**

10. **I respond to, or I comment on, ESL students' written work**
    ___ Every day
    ___ 2–3 times a week
    ___ Once a week
    ___ Once or twice a month
    ___ Less than once a month

Note

1   Crusan's data were collected in 2007 by reviewing all MA programs listed in the TESOL organization publication *Directory of Teacher Education Programs in TESOL in the United States and Canada*, and it is possible that the higher number in the programs offering/requiring an L2 writing theory/pedagogy course is an indication of the beginning of increased awareness of the importance of specific teacher preparation in this area.

References

Bunch, G. C. (2006). "Academic English" in the 7th grade: Broadening the lens, expanding access. *Journal of English for Academic Purposes, 5,* 284–301.

Crusan, D. (2009, March). Preparing teachers to be effective assessors of writing. Paper presented at the 43rd Annual TESOL Convention, Denver, CO.

Enright, K. A., & Gilliland, B. (2011). Multilingual writing in an age of accountability: From policy to practice in U.S. high school classrooms. *Journal of Second Language Writing, 20,* 182–195.

Ferris, D. (2002). *Treatment of error in second language student writing.* Ann Arbor, MI: University of Michigan Press.

Ferris, D. (2007). Preparing teachers to respond to student writing. *Journal of Second Language Writing, 16,* 165–193.

Ferris, D., & Hedgcock, J. (1998). *Teaching ESL composition: Purpose, process and practice.* Mahwah, NJ: Erlbaum.

Ferris, D., & Hedgcock, J. (2005). *Teaching ESL composition: Purpose, process and practice* (2nd ed.). Mahwah, NJ: Erlbaum.

Grosse, C. U. (1991). The TESOL methods course. *TESOL Quarterly, 25,* 29–49.

Harklau, L. (2000). From the "Good Kids" to the "Worst": Representations of English language learners across educational settings. *TESOL Quarterly, 34,* 35–67.

Harklau, L. (2002). The role of writing in classroom second language acquisition. *Journal of Second Language Writing, 11,* 329–350.

Harklau, L., Losey, K. M., & Siegal, M. (Eds.). (1999). *Generation 1.5 meets college composition.* Mahwah, NJ: Erlbaum.

Hirvela, A., & Belcher, D. (2007). Writing scholars as teacher educators: Exploring writing teacher education. *Journal of Second Language Writing, 16,* 125–128.

Hyland, K. (2003). *Second language writing.* New York: Cambridge University Press.

Kibler, A. (2011). "I write it in a way that people can read it": How teachers and adolescent L2 writers describe content area writing. *Journal of Second Language Writing, 20,* 211–226.

Kroll, B. (Ed.). (2003). *Exploring the dynamics of second language writing.* New York: Cambridge University Press.

Lee, I. (2010). Writing teacher education and teacher learning: Testimonies of four EFL teachers. *Journal of Second Language Writing, 19,* 143–157.

Leki, I. (1992). *Understanding ESL writers: A guide for teachers.* Portsmouth, NH: Boynton/Cook.

Leki, I., Cumming, A., & Silva, T. (2008). *A synthesis of research on L2 writing in English.* Mahwah, NJ: Erlbaum.

Matsuda, P. K., & DePew, K. E. (2002). Early second language writing: An introduction. *Journal of Second Language Writing, 11,* 261–268.

Ortmeier-Hooper, C. (2010). The shifting nature of identity: Social identity, L2 writers, and high school. In M. Cox, J. Jordan, C. Ortmeier-Hooper, & G. Gray Schwartz (Eds.), *Reinventing identities in second language writing* (pp. 5–28). Urbana, IL: NCTE.

Ortmeier-Hooper, C., & Enright, K. A. (2011). Mapping new territory: Toward an understanding of adolescent L2 writers and writing in U.S. contexts. *Journal of Second Language Writing, 20,* 167–181.

Ramanathan, V., Davies, C. E., & Schleppegrel, M. J. (2001). A naturalistic inquiry into the cultures of two divergent MA–TESOL programs: Implications for TESOL. *TESOL Quarterly, 35,* 279–305.

Reid, J. M. (1993). *Teaching ESL writing*. New York: Longman.

Reynolds, D. W. (2002). Learning to make things happen in different ways: Causality in the writing of middle-grade English language learners. *Journal of Second Language Writing, 11,* 311–328.

Reynolds, D. W. (2005). Linguistic correlates of second language literacy development: Evidence from middle-grade learner essays. *Journal of Second Language Writing, 14,* 311–328.

Roberge, M., Siegal, M., & Harklau, L. (Eds.). (2009). *Generation 1.5 in college composition: Teaching academic writing to U.S. educated learners of ESL*. New York: Routledge.

Santos, T. (1992). Ideology in composition: L1 and ESL. *Journal of Second Language Writing, 1,* 1–15.

Silva, T. (1993). Toward an understanding of the distinct nature of L2 writing: The ESL research and its complications. *TESOL Quarterly, 27,* 657–677.

Silva, T., & Matsuda, P. K. (Eds.). (2001). *On second language writing*. Mahwah, NJ: Erlbaum.

Valdés, G. (1999). Incipient bilingualism and the development of English language writing abilities in secondary school. In C. J. Faltis & P. M. Wolfe (Eds.), *So much to say: Adolescents, bilingualism, and ESL in the secondary school* (pp. 138–175). New York: Teachers College Press.

Villalva, K. E. (2006). Hidden literacies and inquiry approaches of bilingual high school writers. *Written Communication, 23,* 91–129.

Weigle, S. C. (2007). Teaching writing teachers about assessment. *Journal of Second Language Writing, 16,* 194–209.

Yi, Y. (2010). Adolescent multilingual writers' transitions across in- and out-of-school writing contexts. *Journal of Second Language Writing, 19,* 17–32.

9

ESOL TEACHERS AS WRITING TEACHERS

From the Voices of High School Pre-Service Teachers

Youngjoo Yi

With recent changes in standardized testing and policies in K–12 schools in the United States, writing has been weighted more than ever. For instance, in the State of Georgia, students in grades three, five, eight, and eleven take performance-based writing assessments. In particular, high school students must pass the eleventh-grade writing assessment that is also called Georgia High School Writing Testing in order to earn a regular high school diploma. They have to produce a response to one on-demand persuasive writing prompt within 100 minutes. Further, the Gwinnett County public schools, the largest school system in Georgia, assess student learning in the areas of language arts, science, and social studies through a writing test called the High School Gateway in which students write essays on science and social studies topics. Students in the Gwinnett County public schools must pass the Georgia High School Graduation Tests, and the Georgia High School Writing Test, as well as the High School Gateway writing test, in order to earn a regular high school diploma. These policies in which writing is heavily weighted appear to have influenced writing instruction and practice in the classroom as well as generating implications for writing research.

On a positive note, such an emphasis on writing may draw attention to writing pedagogy and research in K–12 settings. Yet it "might serve as a gatekeeper" for many immigrant students and English language learners (ELLs) and "might produce an even greater number of high school dropouts" (Valdés, 2001, p. 2). In addition to such a political concern, classroom teachers and researchers have raised pedagogical concerns. For instance, classroom teachers are likely pressured to conduct writing instruction for or to the standardized writing assessments; additionally, such standardized testing "often narrowed the focus of instruction" (Reid, 2011, p. 696). Further, teachers may often not feel that they are prepared to teach writing as it has received relatively less attention than other skills (e.g. reading, speaking). This reality of lack of teacher preparation for writing instruction has been sharply pointed out along with the lack of attention to the teaching of writing pedagogy in teacher education programs (Coker & Lewis, 2008; Hirvela & Belcher, 2007). For instance, in a recent review on adolescent writing development and instruction, Coker and Lewis (2008) noted:

> Much of the research on writing is produced by scholars in research-intensive colleges and universities, and little of it is conducted by scholars in teacher-preparation programs. As a result, students preparing to be teachers may not be reading and discussing the most current literature on writing instruction. When teachers complete their training and enter the classroom, they may begin teaching without the breadth and depth of understanding needed to carry out effective writing instruction.
>
> *(p. 243)*

More specifically, very few addressed "writing as a component of teacher education directly" (Grisham & Wolsey, 2011, p. 348), and little is known about how in-service and pre-service teachers learn to teach writing in K–12 settings (Hall & Grisham-Brown, 2011).

Similarly, second language (L2) writing teacher education has not been adequately addressed in the field of English language teaching. For instance, Hirvela and Belcher (2007) pointed out the lack of attention to "what actually takes place in teacher education programs with respect to how writing, and the preparation of writing teachers, is treated" (p. 125). In other words, the notion of English to Speakers of Other Languages (ESOL) teachers as writing teachers has been overlooked even though student writing development is likely ultimately influenced by how ESOL teachers teach writing in the classroom. Given the significance of and relative lack of attention to L2 writing in K–12 settings and L2 writing teacher education, it is important to investigate ESOL teachers' experience with the learning of L2 writing pedagogy and their writing instruction.

This chapter reports findings from research that investigated two pre-service ESOL teachers' sense of preparedness to teach L2 writing in Pre-K–12 settings, their perceived challenges for L2 writing instruction, and their negotiation of L2 writing teacher identity, if any, during their internship that took place at the end of a pre-service ESOL teacher education program. This research aims to obtain better understandings of pre-service ESOL teachers and simultaneously serves as a critical and reflective process of looking into my own practice as a teacher educator. The report from this reflective exploration will offer ESOL teacher educators some valuable insights into what can and should be done to enhance ESOL teachers' writing pedagogies. In the next section, I will review the most relevant research on L2 writing teacher education.

Review of the Literature

Attention to writing pedagogy education has recently emerged from discussions across several fields and national organizations. In the context of L1 writing pedagogy, Reid (2011) tried to bring more professional attention to writing teacher preparation within composition and English studies while proposing a collaborative endeavor for writing pedagogy education between the National Council of Teachers of English (NCTE) and the Conference on College Composition and Communication (CCCC). In her piece, "Preparing writing teachers: A case study in constructing a more connected future for CCCC and NCTE," she argues that writing pedagogy education should be an emerging scholarly (sub)field on its own. As such, L1 researchers have engaged in discussing ways of cultivating an emerging scholarly field for writing pedagogy education and called for more data-driven, longitudinal research.

In the field of L2 writing, discussions of issues around writing pedagogy education have been invisible. One of the early conversations of L2 writing teacher education was initiated from a special issue of the *Journal of Second Language Writing* on "Writing scholars as teacher educators" by Hirvela and Belcher (2007). The special issue tried to draw attention to the "teacher education realm of the L2 writing field" (p. 126) while several L2 writing scholars as teacher educators addressed four key areas of L2 writing pedagogies where writing teacher education is especially needed, such as (a) writing teachers' exploration into academic language to better teach the vocabulary and grammar of academic prose (Coxhead & Byrd, 2007), (b) genre-based writing pedagogies that focus on the identification and analysis of text features (Hyland, 2007), (c) the use of the "approach/response/follow-up" model for writing teachers to respond to student writing (Ferris, 2007), and (d) teachers' assessment of students' written performance (Weigle, 2007). This special issue seems to have raised L2 writing scholars' attention to or awareness of the urgent needs of educating about writing pedagogies for teachers in K–12 and post-secondary contexts.

While taking up Hirvela and Belcher's call for attention to L2 writing scholars as "teachers of teachers of writing," several L2 writing scholars presented their US-based research in a colloquium, "Building bridges between second language writing and teacher development and education" at the *Symposium on Second Language Writing* (e.g. Ortmeier-Hooper, Yi, & Cox, 2009). For instance, Ortmeier-Hooper proposed a collaborative model of in-service teachers and teacher education faculty while stressing the important role of L2 writing pedagogy in the teacher training of content-area teachers at a secondary level. Another panelist, Yi, examined pre-service ESOL teachers' experience and education about the teaching of writing. Drawing upon the concept of "pedagogical content knowledge" (Shulman, 1987), Yi revealed that four pre-service teachers felt quite prepared to teach L2 writing thanks to their course work and their internship experiences in an ESOL teacher education program, and yet, notably, these pre-service teachers' own writing experiences, preferences, and view of writing turned out to have greatly influenced their L2 writing instruction during internship. As such, these two public forums of discussions about the L2 writing teacher education provided a platform to further explore writing pedagogy education; yet little is known about L2 writing teacher education and teacher practice of L2 writing pedagogy in the secondary education context in the United States.

Lee's studies (2010, 2011), while conducted in Hong Kong, are worth attention here given their relevance to the research reported in this chapter. While teaching a writing teacher preparation course, "Reading and Writing: Teaching and Learning," Lee conducted research in her classroom on EFL teachers' perspectives on their growth as writing teachers. Lee (2011) found that a research participant, Iris (a Cantonese-speaking secondary school English teacher with six years of teaching experience) thought of herself as "a language teacher but not a writing teacher" (p. 35). In addition, in-service teachers' view of writing instruction is quite intriguing. For instance, for Iris, the teaching of writing meant to assign writing topics to students; another participant, Betty (with 15 years of teaching experience), considered the teaching of writing primarily the teaching of grammar and vocabulary. However, engaging in a class research project and reading research literature on writing pedagogy helped them broaden their view of writing. Most importantly, two in-service teachers, Iris and Cindy, who had six and five years of teaching experience respectively, "felt a strong sense of empowerment as writing teachers" (p. 154) after taking this class. The excerpt from an interview with Iris (Lee, 2011, p. 35) illustrates her forging a new identity as a writing teacher as follows:

> In the past, I didn't consider myself as a writing teacher. Now I like this name a lot. I'm a writing teacher. I'm not a robot. I'm not asking my students, "Okay, you do Set A, Set B, Okay. You do this, and do that," and I mark, I mean, I'm really teaching them how to think, how to organize ideas, how to write creatively. I'm introducing different genres.

As such, the writing teacher education course helped these in-service teachers change their perspectives of writing and writing pedagogy as well as develop their professional knowledge and skills, thereby better preparing them to teach writing and construct a writing teacher identity.

Another significant finding from Lee's research (2011) is that even though these in-service teachers expanded their knowledge and view of the nature of writing and writing instruction, they encountered *tensions* between what they learned from the writing teacher preparation class and what they learned informally from their own classrooms. In other words, the in-service teachers were pressured to follow their school policy with respect to writing instruction (e.g. textbook-bound, grammar-focused, and error-focused writing instruction), but the focus of writing instruction was not congruent with what they learned in the writing teacher preparation course (e.g. recognizing a localized, situated practice of teaching writing). Eventually, negotiating the tensions arising from such a contradiction turned out to be one of the greatest challenges for them in teaching L2 writing.

Methodology

In order to examine pre-service ESOL teachers' sense of preparedness to teach writing, their perceived challenges for L2 writing instruction, and their negotiation of L2 writing teacher identity, I employed a multiple case study approach, following van Lier's (2005, p. 203) argument that the case study approach can be very useful in teacher education research.

Context, Participants, and the Researcher

Two participants, whom I call Adele and Molly (pseudonyms), were pre-service teachers in an ESOL initial teacher education program in a southeastern city in the United States. Students who successfully complete the program obtain a teaching certificate in ESOL for Pre-K–12, a master's degree in ESOL, and a reading endorsement. Given that three courses required for a reading endorsement are embedded in the program of the study, the ESOL program has strong emphasis on teaching about reading instruction.

I purposely selected Adele and Molly mainly because of their strong orientation toward writing and writing instruction. Based on my observations of them in the program and their performance in my graduate class, Applied Linguistics for ESOL and Bilingual Teachers, both expressed strong interest in writing and writing instruction. Adele had taught immigrant and refugee students and families in Chicago for five years prior to the program. Molly was a former reporter and journalist who wanted to change her career to be a teacher. In addition, I was privileged to supervise them during their internship at a local high school where I conducted a larger study, and thus I was able to observe their teaching in the classroom.

For their internship, both were placed in the same classroom to work with their mentor teacher, Dr. Larson (pseudonym), with Molly taking the lead on the first block, "Reading and Listening Content-ESOL," Adele on the second block, "9th Grade Sheltered Literature," and both co-teaching the third block, "ESOL-IV." Even though the name of each 90-minute block was different, the mentor teacher decided to cover almost the same content across the three blocks. This situation allowed Adele and Molly to collaborate to design and teach lessons and share their materials.

I was very mindful of the multiple layers of a power relationship between research participants and me. They were my research participants and simultaneously my students in the program. From the beginning of the study, I was very explicit about possible tensions between us, and they were constantly reminded that they should share with me any concerns regarding the participation in this research.

Data Collection and Analysis

I gathered several different kinds of data. For instance, four individual and three group interviews were digitally audio-recorded and transcribed. I also observed their instruction at least three times for each participant. Further, I collected artifacts, such as all the teaching materials that they created before and during their internship, all the assignments that they completed for the internship course, and their exit portfolios.

The data were analyzed inductively and recursively following the procedures of qualitative data analysis (see Bogdan & Biklen, 1998; Miles & Huberman, 1994). Initially I repeatedly read interview transcripts, field notes, and all the artifacts, engaged in memoing, and used open coding to record topics that came up frequently. I then reviewed codes to eliminate the less useful and combine smaller categories into larger ones. At this point of focused coding, I saw repeating ideas and began organizing codes into larger themes that connected different codes. I captured the major themes and recorded verbatim quotations as well as considered contradictions. In both open and focused coding, I organized and analyzed the data by question and by case and later compared and contrasted within and across the case. I identified themes or patterns and organized them into coherent categories. As I did so, I began to see patterns and connections both within and between the categories. My analysis and written interpretation of findings were influenced by member-checks. For member-checks, I asked Adele and Molly separately what they thought of my interpretation of particular incidents and major findings, and they commented on the preliminary data analysis and an initial draft of this chapter in order to establish the validity of the interpretations.

Findings and Discussion

This section focuses on three major findings about pre-service teachers' writing pedagogy: (a) their sense of preparedness to teach L2 writing, (b) their perceived challenges and concerns about L2 writing instruction, and (c) their negotiation of L2 writing teacher identity.

Sense of Preparedness to Teach Writing

Pre-service teachers' sense of preparedness to teach L2 writing was found from their planning and delivery of writing instruction as well as their knowledge of and belief in writing and L2 writing pedagogy. Thus, this section focuses on writing tasks and activities that Adele and Molly designed and delivered for teaching the unit *Elements of Drama: Romeo and Juliet* as well as their knowledge of writing and L2 writing pedagogy.

Writing Tasks and Activities in the Classroom

Three major writing tasks that Adele and Molly implemented in their lessons included (a) *Testimonial Tuesday* writing activity, (b) script writing, and (c) a Facebook character project. Ways in which they designed and implemented these tasks and activities demonstrate the extent to which they were prepared to teach writing to ESOL students in the high school classroom.

First, *Testimonial Tuesday* writing activity is part of *Daily Sparks* (see Appendix), a daily bell ringer activity. Each day the activity has a different focus. For instance, on Mondays, students are asked to edit a paragraph that has many grammatical or spelling mistakes, which is called a *Mastery Monday* activity. On Tuesday, students engage in *Testimonial Tuesday* activity in which they respond to a writing prompt. *Daily Sparks* was originally created by their mentor teacher, and *Testimonial Tuesday* writing prompts were usually unrelated to what students learned during the week. Adele and Molly were not happy about the lack of continuity and contextualization of Tuesday writing activities and began to design writing prompts that were directly related to the then current unit. For instance, one Tuesday writing prompt for the *Romeo and Juliet* unit was "Imagine you work at a newspaper and people write letters to you asking for advice to help them solve their problems. You receive a letter from Romeo and Juliet, who want to get married, but don't know what to do about their feuding families. What advice would you give the couple? Respond in a letter that begins with 'Dear Romeo and Juliet . . .'" (see Appendix for another prompt). These writing prompts that require a clear sense of audience and purpose turned out to be very engaging and extremely well received by their students.

Two of the most innovative writing tasks that Adele and Molly created included script writing and a Facebook character project. Initially, the students were given an adapted narrative version of *Romeo and Juliet* to read. Soon Adele and Molly recognized the limit of teaching drama by reading a narrative text and decided to include 'script writing' as part of the readers' theater (which is a performance activity in which an individual or group reads directly from scripts with expressions and emotions, but does not memorize their lines and does not need sets, costumes, or other props to perform). Students worked in different-leveled groups to write a script for one assigned scene in *Romeo and Juliet* by using a narrative version as a resource. After assigning roles, highlighting dialogue, and doing a read-through of the script, students filmed their scene. All scenes were compiled into a movie that the entire class watched together. While Adele and Molly considered differentiated instruction, advanced students were required to turn a short narrative into a script, and the intermediate and newcomer students were required to identify characters, stage directions, and dialogue in a pre-written script given by Adele and Molly. Adele proudly stated about script writing and the readers' theater that "they [students] loved it. It really gave them a chance to actually see and do writing with a reason" (interview, May 3, 2011).

The last intriguing writing task that they designed was a Facebook character project where small groups of students constructed a Facebook profile page of the main characters in *Romeo and Juliet*. Since students were not allowed to access Facebook on school computers, Molly and Adele created a paper-based Facebook template based on what the students see on the website to help them understand what information they would need to fill out and display for their characters (e.g. profile picture, bio information, friends, likes/interests, status updates, and wall posts).

Thus, Adele and Molly modified and designed the writing tasks and activities to be meaningful and engaging while attempting to help students develop a clear sense of audience and purpose for writing. Further, the tasks and activities were differentiated based on students' language proficiency, and they integrated a multimodal aspect of writing by requiring students to encompass both texts and non-linguistic modes (visual, sound, and movement).

However, one striking finding that I uncovered is that writing was extensively used to *evaluate* student learning. In other words, Adele and Molly used writing to check student understanding of the materials, and their students had relatively limited opportunities for "writing to learn about writing" and "writing to learn" (Langer & Applebee, 1987; Newell, 2006). For instance, Adele stated in her unit plan that the Facebook project "is designed as the main way of assessing students' understanding of the reading," and Molly similarly stated in her unit plan that

> The Facebook project relates to instructional goals because it assesses the students' ability to use textual evidence to support inferences and to demonstrate comprehension in writing. Creating a Facebook profile also demonstrates the students' ability to read, discuss, and put texts in context.

In particular, Molly's unit assessment plans included many writing activities, and thus I verified her use of writing for assessment purposes with her during a member-check session. She elaborated:

> Even in the class I do now, the writing I ask my students to do is more for writing for me to learn about them or for them to learn about themselves, but *not writing to learn about writing*, not writing for grammar . . . . I don't think that I have a concept of *writing to learn*. (March 23, 2012)

This finding is corroborated by what Grisham and Wolsey (2011) found: "more writing instruction appears to occur in the service of writing for assessment purposes" (p. 361).

Teacher Knowledge of and Beliefs in Writing and Writing Pedagogy

Along with writing tasks and activities implemented, Adele and Molly's knowledge of and belief in writing and L2 writing pedagogy demonstrate their preparedness to teach writing to ELLs in the high school classroom. Though both co-constructed the lesson and unit plans, slightly different aspects of L2 writing were stressed in their reflection narratives. For Molly, the sense of "authenticity" and "audience" was very important, as seen in her reflection and self-evaluation narrative:

> Since this [reader's theater] was a group project that involved reading, writing, listening, and speaking, all students who had different strengths and interests were engaged in the process and excited about the end product. This was an *authentic learning task with an authentic audience*. Diaz–Rico (2008 p. 193) states "if students know they will be sharing their writing with their classmates, their investment increases."

Perhaps Molly's journalist background influenced her teaching students a clear sense of audience in writing. For Adele, tapping into students' prior knowledge and L1 language and literacy for writing was very important, and this must be related to her experience in teaching adult immigrants and refugees who already had some prior schooling experience and world knowledge, as well as L1 literacy. (A cautionary note here is that though each seemed to stress slightly different aspects of writing in their reflection narratives, both of them understood and addressed the importance of various aspects of L2 writing.)

Another notable aspect of creating writing tasks and activities is that they seemed to believe in *collaborative writing*, and almost all writing activities, except writing for individual assessment, required students to produce in pairs or in a small group. One of the learning goals in the unit was to "collaborate to write a Readers' Theater presentation based on a dramatic selection." What they believe in and know of writing pedagogy appears to influence their decision on what to emphasize in writing instruction.

Despite their significant knowledge of writing and L2 writing pedagogy, both lacked an understanding of how their students viewed writing. When I asked Adele and Molly if they knew how writing was perceived by their students, neither seemed to have thought deeply about how adolescent ELLs think about writing for academic and other purposes. Molly added during the member-check that "I think we didn't perceive how students felt about writing because writing really was not used in Dr. Larson's classroom . . . . I think I was more concerned with how Dr. Larson perceived writing in her classroom" (March 23, 2012). Clearly, Molly's lack of knowledge about how writing is perceived by her students is related to challenges that she faced for student teaching in someone else's classroom.

Challenges and Concerns for L2 Writing Pedagogy

In the interviews, neither teacher mentioned challenges for planning writing lessons or implementing writing instruction in their teaching of the unit. Instead, both immediately pointed out the lack of writing instruction in the classroom, and I asked them directly to elaborate this point, as seen below:

Adele: I didn't really feel like there was any writing instruction.

Molly: Beyond that essay that

Adele: There were *opportunities* for the students to write, a few, but some.

Molly: But writing instruction was not present. The most writing instruction I had heard was that the essay has five paragraphs, a paragraph has five sentences. That was the writing instruction that I had heard. Kids were saying to you, but then that was the most writing instruction.

(We talked about something else and we came back to this topic.)

Adele: But in terms of how to set up writing, how to set up essays or something like, ones who were able to do it already knew, and ones who didn't know didn't learn . . . . They know how to copy. They really gotta copy.

Discussing less presence of writing instruction, both wished that they had had more opportunities to observe mentor teachers teach writing in the classrooms that Adele and Molly had observed throughout their field experiences and full-time internship. Lack of observation of writing instruction turned out to be one of the challenges for them to learn more about writing pedagogy.

Another very interesting concern about writing pedagogy was brought up by Molly. She described an incident when writing was used as "punishment." When students made up the vocabulary homework that they missed, they had to use the ten new words for the week and write an essay using them all. Molly described the situation by saying that "It's like 'You didn't do your homework, so here is an even harder task, good luck.' . . . It was the way that I would've taken it as a student, the way I feel Adam definitely took it." Molly thought that the make-up work was nearly impossible for Adam (pseudonym) to accomplish given his language proficiency.

Finally, as an emerging concern about writing pedagogy, both pointed out students' lack of *library skills*, which they believe challenges their writing instruction. When Molly helped students write a technical essay (i.e., a student career essay), she found that almost all the students sat down at the computer in the library and did not know the icon that was the library catalog. When Molly reported that it was a very enlightening experience to see how little the students knew about their library, Adele also shared a similar experience with adult immigrants and refugees whom she had taught. Both called for more systematic and better library sessions specific for ELLs so that those sessions could help students' writing practices.

Negotiating Teacher Identities

In the end-of-the-semester interview, neither Adele nor Molly could say that they actually had developed an identity as a writing teacher. Perhaps I simply assumed that both Adele and Molly might have constructed or negotiated a writing teacher identity given that Adele was very interested in issues of error correction, Molly was a journalist, and both successfully integrated writing into their teaching. When I asked them if they thought they had developed a sense of themselves as a writing teacher, they immediately answered "No," and I asked the same question twice. When both reported that they hadn't necessarily developed a writing teacher identity, I specifically asked Molly about her negotiation of a writing teacher identity. Her response below seems to sum up several issues that have been addressed in this chapter:

> No, I don't feel like [I am developing a writing teacher identity], I feel like any advances that I made in that were my own efforts to incorporate writing in our lesson planning. I was not able to witness much writing instruction from any of my mentor teachers. . . . Any of the lesson plans that I have created or tried to implement have been writing-focused ones. (Then she explained about her writing-focused lessons in other settings.) So I tried to make an effort to practice that because it's something I'm interested in doing, but I didn't witness a lot of writing instruction, which was unfortunate 'cause that was something I was hoping. *I know how to write, but I don't know how to teach writing.* I'm learning, but trying at myself, but I haven't seen it implemented by other teachers who have been teaching for a while. (May 3, 2011)

It seems that Molly had been passionate about teaching writing; however, she explicitly stated that "I know how to write, but I don't know how to teach writing." Similarly, Adele wrote about her desire to improve her writing pedagogy in her professional learning goal statement as seen below:

> My experience with the Readers' Theater projects made me think a lot about my desire to incorporate more opportunities for students to engage in collaboration for and about writing. I am interested in incorporating "Writers' Workshops" into my ESOL classes. I hope to be able to attend formal training on using Writers' Workshop techniques with English language learners, or, at a minimum, discussing these techniques and how I might apply them with more experienced colleagues.

As such, both reported that they did not construct or perform a writing teacher identity during their internship, but wished to learn more about how to teach writing. When both of them immediately reported that they had not developed any writing teacher identity, I was a bit puzzled and further probed their negotiation of teacher identities. They shared their struggles to prove themselves and construct a teacher identity, not necessarily a writing teacher identity, which will be detailed in the next section.

Struggling to Prove Themselves

One of the striking findings in this study is that both Adele and Molly struggled and invested in proving themselves though each had a slightly different aspect of proving themselves and constructing a teacher identity. For Adele, who had previously taught for five years, one of the constant struggles throughout the teacher education program was to negotiate her already constructed "teacher" identity with her new "student teacher" identity. The following interview excerpt shows her struggle and negotiation:

> I just felt constantly like I had to prove myself, like constantly . . . . I guess because I wasn't starting it at nothing, I felt like there was a lot that I had to learn, but there was also a lot that I already knew how to do it, and I had a really hard time when those things were not recognized by her [mentor teacher] and by anyone . . . . I think, well, I've identified as a teacher for the last five years. I think with a return to school and an enforced identity as a student teacher, that was actually one of the hardest things about this program. I anticipated that that would happen. Not only that I like to be identified as a teacher when I live in Chicago, like teaching was my *life*. I mean my identity as a teacher was probably among my strongest, the strongest things that I identified with. I mean it shaped my whole life . . . . I just can't be just a student. I'm not a student, I'm a teacher (chuckled). (May 3, 2011)

Apparently, Adele negotiated her teacher identity with her enforced identity as a student teacher while trying to reaffirm her teacher identity. As Adele strongly expressed above, the negotiation between a strong teacher identity already developed from her "past" teaching experience and her "new" student teacher identity that was imposed on her was a real, constant struggle for her. This suggests that identities are multiple, changing and a site of struggle (Norton, 1997).

Molly's effort to prove herself seems to be slightly different from Adele's. While Adele negotiated between her past and current identities, Molly struggled to construct her teacher identity for the first time and to prove herself, as noted in the interview (May 3, 2011):

> I felt like I did prove myself, but *I had to prove that I proved myself.* I would give you a specific example. Towards the end [of the internship], . . . Dr. Larson alluded to the fact that she wasn't sure if *I hid behind Adele this*

semester. That was really offensive to me. It was hard to hear because I felt that I proved myself at that point . . . . I felt like even after this long semester where I felt like I had accomplished so much and was very proud of the work that I did, for that to be the final word was really very difficult for me to hear.

One significant point to mention here is that Dr. Larson's comment that Molly seemed to "hide behind Adele" greatly influenced Molly's construction of a teacher identity. Unlike Adele who struggled to negotiate multiple identities, Molly greatly struggled to construct her new identity while proving to her mentor teacher (and herself) that she was capable of teaching. Until Molly received that comment, she believed that she had formed her teacher identity; however, Dr. Larson's doubtful comment hurt Molly's confidence as a student teacher, and Molly further doubted herself as a teacher for a while.

However, while Molly went through some struggles to prove herself as a student teacher during her internship, she showed a strong sense of preparedness to teach toward the end of internship by noting that "I feel like I'm a first year teacher, I do feel like I'm a teacher. I definitely feel like I found that identity this semester in particular." Molly's sense of being a first-year teacher and her teacher identity can be an important indication of her improvement and of coming into herself as a teacher.

Overall, it seems clear that both Adele and Molly invested in constructing a classroom teacher identity to a great extent. Adele, who already had a strong teacher identity, struggled to hold on to it while simultaneously negotiating her student teacher identity during internship. Thus, she might have been busy proving to others that she was not a novice student teacher, but a confident teacher. Slightly differently, Molly, who had not had a classroom teacher identity, made great efforts to construct her "new" identity as an ESOL classroom teacher. Given their efforts and struggles to negotiate their teacher identities, I speculate that perhaps they were not able to afford to pursue or explore their *writing* teacher identity. Instead, they might have focused on constructing and (re)confirming their identity as an ESOL classroom teacher. Further, Adele added another point in her member-check that "student teachers are pretty bound by the confines of their mentor teacher's classroom. I think that the classroom we taught in was not a 'writing classroom,' which gave us little opportunity to develop an identity as a 'writing teacher'" (May 2, 2012).

Discussion and Implications

Findings from this study show that despite emerging writing testing and policies in US schools, there is a huge gap between academic demands for writing assessments and actual writing instruction and practice in the classroom. In addition, pre-service teachers' opportunity to observe writing instruction was minimal, which seems to influence them not having any models or ideas of "what good writing instruction looks like" (Grisham & Wolsey, 2011, p. 362). Overall, the two pre-service teachers demonstrated their knowledge of several significant issues of L2 writing pedagogy, such as a clear sense of purpose and audience; the importance of L1 and prior knowledge for writing; and collaborative and multimodal aspects of writing. Yet writing tasks and activities that they designed were extensively used for *assessment purposes*, which is also similarly found in the research on pre-service teachers' learning of writing instruction across a three-course sequence of literacy methods (Grisham & Wolsey, 2011). With the use of writing for assessment purposes, there were relatively limited opportunities for "writing to learn about writing" and "writing to learn."

In Lee's (2010, 2011) studies on EFL teachers learning to teach writing, the in-service ESOL teachers in Hong Kong demonstrated their growth as *writing teachers*; however, my participants did not construct a writing teacher identity, instead, they focused more on constructing or reaffirming an ESOL classroom teacher identity. This difference between Lee's findings and mine is understandable in that perhaps many in-service teachers in Lee's studies already had a strong teacher identity and struggled to add a new identity as a writing teacher; yet, for Adele and Molly, establishing a teacher identity might be their priority. This particular finding calls for future research on how in-service teachers, especially those who already have a strong teacher identity, learn to teach writing and construct a writing teacher identity.

With respect to limitations of the study, I cannot help but consider Reid's (2011) recent call for research. Reid (2011) called for more writing pedagogy education studies that are "data-driven, longitudinal, or inclusive of more than one program" (p. 692). Given her call, the research reported here is rather limited in that I examined only two pre-service teachers who were placed in the same classroom during their internship. For future research, it would be beneficial if teacher educators and researchers examine both pre- and in-service teachers with respect to how to learn to teach L2 writing, how and to what extent writing instruction takes place in the classroom, and how pre-service teachers change their perspectives of writing instruction when they make transitions from pre-service to in-service teaching. Equally important, it is worth exploring what it takes to construct a writing teacher identity and what it takes to make writing pedagogy education an emerging scholarly subfield of inquiry in its own right.

Appendix

Daily Sparks

MASTERY MONDAY

Edit the below text then rewrite on a separate sheet of paper. Use a highlighter to indicate 10 mistakes in the paragraph.

Romeo and Juliet is a trajedy about two young star-crossed lovers written early in the career of playwrite William Shakespeare. It's plot is based on an Italian tail called *The Tragical History of Romeus and Juliet*. Shakespeare uses a variety of poetic forms throughout the play. Most of it is, however, written in blank verse. *Romeo and Juliet* ranks with Hamlet as one of Shakespeares most performed plays. Its many adaptations have make it one of his most enduring and famous stories. *Romeo and Juliet* is one of the first Shakespearean plays to have been performed outside england. It has been adapted numerous times for stage, film, musical and opera.

TESTIMONIAL TUESDAY

Prompt: Most of the characters in *Romeo and Juliet* fall into one of two generations. How do the opinions, values, and actions of one generation impact the other? Using a personal example, write a 3- to 5-paragraph essay that answers this question on a separate sheet of paper.

WORDY WEDNESDAY

In the following script excerpt from a modern version of **Romeo and Juliet***, circle the characters, underline the stage directions and highlight the dialogue.*

JULIET: Oh, Romeo, Romeo. I can't sleep because all I can do is think about you. Where are you now? You're the enemy of my family, a Montague, but how can I hate you? I fancy you so much. Who cares that your name starts with a 'm' sound? *(Enter ROMEO hiding beside the well)*

ROMEO: *(Addressing audience)* This is beyond my wildest hopes: she loves me too!

JULIET: I would leave my family and change my name if I could be with you, Romeo. If only I could see you again! *(Romeo stands up and waves.)*

THROW-DOWN THURSDAY

On the back of this paper, complete a comic strip based on one scene from **Romeo and Juliet** *You should have at least three pictures with a caption for each picture.*

FREESTYLE FRIDAY

See how many words you can make using the letters from the following word: **Elizabethan**

References

Bogdan, R. C., & Biklen, S. K. (1998). *Qualitative research for education: An introduction to theory and methods* (3rd ed.). Boston: Allyn and Bacon.

Coker, D., & Lewis, W. E. (2008). Beyond writing next: A discussion of writing research and instructional uncertainty. *Harvard Educational Review, 78*(1), 231–278.

Coxhead, A., & Byrd, P. (2007). Preparing writing teachers to teach the vocabulary and grammar of academic prose. *Journal of Second Language Writing, 16*(3), 129–147.

Diaz-Rico, L. (2008). *Strategies for teaching English learners* (2nd ed.). Boston: Allyn & Bacon.

Ferris, D. (2007). Preparing teachers to respond to student writing. *Journal of Second Language Writing, 16*(3), 165–193.

Grisham, D. L., & Wolsey, T. D. (2011). Writing instruction for teacher candidates: Strengthening a weak curricular area. *Literacy Research and Instruction, 50*, 348–364.

Hall, A. H., & Grisham-Brown, J. (2011). Writing development over time: Examining preservice teachers' attitudes and beliefs about writing. *Journal of Early Childhood Teacher Education, 32*, 148–158.

Hirvela, A., & Belcher, D. (2007). Writing scholars as teacher educators: Exploring writing teacher education. *Journal of Second Language Writing, 16*(3), 125–128.

Hyland, K. (2007). Genre pedagogy: Language, literacy and L2 writing instruction. *Journal of Second Language Writing, 16*(3), 148–164.

Langer, J., & Applebee, A. (1987). *How writing shapes thinking: A study of teaching and learning*. Urbana, IL: National Council of Teachers of English.

Lee, I. (2010). Writing teacher education and teacher learning: Testimonies of four EFL teachers. *Journal of Second Language Writing, 19*(3), 143–157.

Lee, I. (2011). L2 writing teacher education for in-service teachers: Opportunities and challenges. *English in Australia, 46*(1), 31–39.

Miles, M. B., & Huberman, A. M. (1994). *Qualitative data analysis*. Thousand Oaks, CA: Sage.

Newell, G. E. (2006). Write to learn: How alternative theories of school writing account for student performance. In C. A. MacArthur, S. Graham, & J. Fitzgerald (Eds.), *Handbook of writing research* (pp. 235–247). New York: Guilford Press.

Norton, B. (1997). Language, identity, and the ownership of English. *TESOL Quarterly, 31*(3), 409–429.

Ortmeier-Hooper, C., Yi, Y., & Cox, M. (2009, November). Building bridges between second language writing and teacher development and education. Colloquium session presented at the Symposium on Second Language Writing, Tempe, AZ.

Reid, E. S. (2011). Preparing writing teachers: A case study in constructing a more connected future for CCCC and NCTE. *College Composition and Communication, 62*(4), 687–703.

Shulman, L. (1987). Knowledge and teaching: Foundations of the new reform. *Harvard Educational Review, 57*(1), 1–22.

Valdés, G. (2001). *Learning and not learning English: Latino students in American schools*. New York: Teachers College Press.

van Lier, L. (2005). Case study. In E. Hinkel (Ed.), *Handbook of research in second language teaching and learning* (pp. 195–208). Mahwah, NJ: Erlbaum.

Weigle, S. C. (2007). Teaching writing teachers about assessment. *Journal of Second Language Writing, 16*(3), 194–209.

10

RESPONSIVE TEACHER INQUIRY FOR LEARNING ABOUT ADOLESCENT ENGLISH LEARNERS AS DEVELOPING WRITERS

Steven Z. Athanases, Lisa H. Bennett, and Juliet Michelsen Wahleithner

> Any knowledge gained about English learner students is a huge benefit. I think that inquiry can really support and allow a teacher to understand the needs of his/her EL students. Knowledge I have about my students, how they learn, what activities and support structures work, can come from analyzing student data and work.
>
> *(Marina, pre-service English teacher)*

A Latina with an undergraduate degree in Classics, Marina was a week away from earning her English teaching credential from a post-baccalaureate program when she wrote a reflection on her first teacher inquiry experiences. In the excerpt above, Marina reflects on values of inquiry. Among these are several focused on learning about EL students as learners: *understanding the needs of EL students*, knowledge I have *about my students*, knowledge about *how they learn*. Marina highlights a central theme from a program of research we conducted. Over a seven-year period, we analyzed product and process data in the teacher inquiry work of Marina and others from her teacher education program—96 secondary pre-service teachers of English language arts (ELA). A key finding of this work was that inquiry focused teachers' attention on the learning of culturally and linguistically diverse learners in their classes.

This finding articulates how inquiry can disrupt a common developmental trajectory of new teachers. That trajectory has been described as a focus first on self and teacher performance, classroom management, curriculum, and resources— and, after several years, on students and their learning (Fuller, 1969; Kagan, 1992). This developmental model has been critiqued, but much of the pattern continues to play out. Teacher inquiry, however, can help focus teachers on learners' curricular needs, as early as during pre-service. For writing, the content focus of this chapter, the need for close attention to individual ELs' learning processes and development is crucial. Variation in adolescent ELs' writing is complex, due to the diverse ways students produce language and the nuanced and complex ways they articulate what they know and mean. Additional challenges include understanding ways in which ELs learn and engage written language functions, academic language, genre conventions, and disciplinary grammars (Schleppegrell, 2004). Teacher education needs to foster this close student focus early in teachers' careers. In this chapter, we draw upon our research to describe elements of teacher inquiry that focused pre-service teachers in one teacher education program on adolescent English learners and their development as writers.

Background

While consensus has been building about the kinds of classroom activities that may support adolescent ELs' learning and development (e.g. Faltis, Arias, & Ramirez-Marin, 2010), less is known about the kinds of preparation that may help teachers guide the learning of ELs effectively. Teachers have reported inadequate pre-service and in-service development to teach ELs (Darling-Hammond, Chung, & Frelow, 2002; Gándara, Maxwell-Jolly, & Driscoll, 2005). Research is needed in all areas of teacher preparation for ELs (Lucas, 2011; Lucas & Grinberg, 2008).

Programs have documented relevant innovations. These include courses focused on ELs and linguistic concerns (Lucas & Grinberg, 2008), methods courses with EL attention embedded (de Oliveira & Shoffner, 2009), and programmatic infusion of attention to ELs (Athanases & de Oliveira, 2011; Coady, Harper, & de Jong, 2011). Efforts also include contact with ELs through tutoring (Walker & Stone, 2011), performance assessments to guide focus on linguistically sensitive pedagogy (Bunch, Aguirre, & Tellez, 2009), and fostering advocacy for equitable learning opportunities for ELs in and beyond classrooms (de Oliveira & Athanases, 2007).

For a narrower focus of preparing teachers to teach writing to adolescent ELs, the research base is much smaller. A larger view on the status of writing instruction in general provides some perspective. In a recent study, actual writing instruction was infrequent and narrowly conceived; 43 percent of ELA teachers reported inadequate preparation from their teacher education (TE) programs to teach writing (Kiuhara, Graham, & Hawken, 2009). Perhaps from lack of preparation, teachers may approach writing in prescriptive and limited ways, and those teaching ELs provide few authentic opportunities to try out genres and experiment with writing (Ortmeier-Hooper & Enright, 2011; Valdés, 1999). Lack of preparation to teach writing to adolescent ELs is especially problematic, given added challenges. These include managing ELs' varied academic and linguistic needs (Gándara et al., 2005), linking academic language to content (Schleppegrell, 2004), and balancing high challenge with high support (Hammond, 2006). These challenges are compounded by a larger policy context in which testing and accountability shape writing curriculum and instruction. For example, teachers of

ELs frequently feel compelled to teach writing as controlled composition, losing sight of its purposes (Valdés, 1999). Accountability pressures can lead teachers to emphasize display over development of ideas and compliance with structures over communication (Enright & Gilliland, 2011). Pressures of coverage and standardized tests also minimize teachers' capacity to diversify instruction for varied ELs' needs (de Oliveira & Athanases, 2007).

Teacher development can help guide the teaching of writing for ELs. Prior work described uses of scaffolding to help ELs work beyond current abilities (Pawan, 2008; Walqui, 2011), systemic functional linguistics as a guide to learning how language functions to shape meaning (Brisk & Zisselsberger, 2011), and modeling linguistically responsive actions to gain familiarity with students' varied linguistic and academic backgrounds (Lucas, Villegas, & Freedson-Gonzalez, 2008). We need to know more about ways to prepare teachers to learn about and meet the needs of ELs in writing. Our chapter explores contributions of teacher inquiry for this work.

The Potential of Teacher Inquiry for Learning about English Learners as Writers

Educators worldwide have used teacher inquiry in pre-service and in-service contexts. In preparing teachers to teach writing to ELs, inquiry holds promise through asking student learning questions, guided by intentional, systematic work (Cochran-Smith & Lytle, 2009). Such questioning may help student teachers (STs) move past an overreliance on methods in teaching bilingual students, which reduces capacity for in-the-moment responses to student needs (Bartolomé, 1994). Through inquiry, STs may learn patterns of English learners' writing and respond effectively. Inquiry can promote understanding of diverse EL writing needs and the pedagogy needed to address them (Lew, 1999; Sowa, 2009). Inquiry elements, including data gathering, analysis, and reflection, can help STs understand and serve the linguistic and academic needs of ELs, including ELs with academic difficulties (Dresser, 2007). By focusing inquiry on specific students, pre-service teachers can learn to capitalize on ELs' interpersonal skills and interactions as writing resources (Dana, Yendol-Hoppey, & Snow-Gerono, 2006). Also, an inquiry community can help teachers learn about ELs' development, supported by tools, peers, and mentors (Merino & Ambrose, 2009) and, in some cases, can transform teachers (Nevarez-LaTorre, 2010). Our program of research on pre-service teacher inquiry adds new insights to this developing body of work, and we focus here on those related to learning about ELs and their writing.

The Context and Model for Inquiry

The focal program for our research was a ten-month post-baccalaureate program at a research university in northern California, linked with an optional second year for the completion of an MA. Our chapter focuses on a credential-year course site for a first ten-week inquiry.

Programmatic Attention to English Learners

In addition to earning a teaching credential, candidates earned a cross-cultural language and academic development credential, essential in a state with rich cultural and linguistic diversity. The program had a history of attention to preparing teachers to advocate for equitable learning opportunities for diverse youth, through curriculum and supervision (Athanases & Martin, 2006), and graduates reported engaging in such activity in and beyond classrooms (Athanases & de Oliveira, 2008). The program infused attention to ELs through a coherent framework and goals supported by activities in coursework, field placements, and records of practice for learning to teach ELs and with activities shared by various players that supported learning to teach ELs (Athanases & de Oliveira, 2011). Graduates highlighted ways they internalized preparation for work with ELs and engaged in advocacy for ELs in classrooms and school sites (de Oliveira & Athanases, 2007). The program developed teacher inquiry courses (two in the credential year and several in the optional second year) to help teachers support their advocacy with tools of inquiry.

Placements in Diverse Settings

Central to the program's mission was developing and sustaining placements to enable pre-service teachers to work immediately with the highly diverse California student population. Most school placements were urban, some rural, and a few suburban. For ELA placements, schools overall had majority students of color, and were racially and ethnically diverse, high EL, and high poverty (Athanases, Wahleithner, & Bennett, 2012a). First languages for ELs were richly varied, with Spanish the dominant home language. At one middle school, a site for several inquiries, for example, 25 percent of students were ELs, with five home languages comprising 87 percent of the EL population: Spanish (40 percent), Hmong (31 percent), Vietnamese (8 percent), Cantonese (5 percent), and Mien (Yao) (3 percent), with 15 other languages comprising the bulk of the remaining home languages.

In secondary English, the focus of our chapter, teachers had two placements per year, typically one in a middle school and one in a high school. Also, at least one class generally had a high percentage of ELs; many of these classes were designed for ELs at various levels of English language proficiency. For classes in which inquiries were conducted, just under one-third had 100 percent ELs (in courses such as English Language Development), and just under half overall were high-density EL classes of 33–100 percent ELs (many of which were general ELA classes).

Responsive Inquiry and Scaffolding in the ELA Strand

Inquiry in the ELA strand was framed as responsive to learner needs in a specific teaching context, to particular content area concerns, and to input from a professional community of colleagues, mentors, teachers, and researchers (Athanases *et al.*, 2012a). In responsive inquiry, STs formulate research questions focused on content concerns among their students and not merely generic topics such as note-taking, homework production, and classroom management. We found the focus on content opened the door to pre-service teachers' development of teacher knowledge at the intersection of content and learners (Athanases, Wahleithner, & Bennett, 2012b). Inquiries overall began focused on actions STs might take as instructors and how these might impact student activity and performance. Once into their inquiries, however, most STs discovered they needed to know far more of what their students actually knew and understood. Teaching-focused concerns tended to follow, after STs gained confidence in what they learned of students' engagements with content and then tested methods focused on what they had learned. This trajectory supported the development of inquiries into learning about ELs and their writing.

The STs worked in inquiry groups on ELA issues. Instruction in tools and processes scaffolded inquiry, including a presentation template and ongoing critical feedback. PowerPoint slides and notes detailed: inquiry focus; community, school, and class contexts; research questions; and evidence justifying the need for a study focus and action plan. Inquiries included literature abstracts, a visual of an inquiry plan, data collection and analysis methods, results, and synthesis of learning through inquiry. Scaffolds included mentoring conferences and workshops on pattern-finding in qualitative and quantitative data. Field memos fostered data analysis, pattern-finding, identification of next steps, and articulation of fresh insights. Steven (first author) served as the ELA inquiry instructor, and Lisa and Juliet were outside researchers at the time of primary data collection and later assisted in the inquiry course.

Shaping Inquiries about English Learners and Their Writing

In the responsive inquiry model, STs needed to gather information about their EL students as people and as learners—and then use this information to help shape inquiry about writing.

Documenting the Nested Contexts of Learners

To learn about ELs in their classes, STs collected and displayed demographic details about communities, schools, and classrooms within which they worked. This was important in capturing the diversity of ELs' home languages and home cultures; levels of English proficiency; time since immigration (if applicable); and the racial, ethnic, and socioeconomic dynamics of communities. We found that only slightly over half of STs detailed a community, marking the need for greater attention to documenting and understanding the communities within which classrooms are situated.

Most STs provided details about the schools where they taught and the students in their classes. One ST, for example, reported the demographics of her diverse students. She also provided language proficiency data for ELs and specific data on students with special needs. This included the range of standardized test scores to demonstrate how learners crossed the spectrum from far below basic to advanced. She closely observed student work and performance and conducted analyses to determine educational needs. The teacher noted that, "Despite the vast educational differences within this class, the students have shown they work well together and have shown they are socially adaptable." This kind of detailed classroom attention, supported by additional community data, demonstrated the inquiry expectations.

Using Demographic Information to Shape Inquiry

In our research, we found that moving from documenting demographics to thoughtful use of such data was not always easy. In one transcribed conversation, for example, the instructor (Steven) prompted an ST to consider ways he might tap students' cultural resources in his teaching and inquiry. Despite the ST's careful documentation of students' immigration data, he struggled to figure out ways to draw on those experiences, even as he tried to develop narrative essay work that would foster the students' voice in their writing. Through the mentoring conversation, the ST began to develop a writing assignment that could mine the richness of those immigration stories.

For some STs, reporting demographics of contexts helped frame inquiries and research questions fairly directly. For instance, Nadia, a Latina, taught in a rural farming community 25 miles north of a major city. The school in this community was 52 percent Latino, 40 percent Caucasian, 3.9 percent Asian, and 1.8 percent African American. Nadia taught a ninth-grade Transition English class for Early Advanced, Spanish-speaking ELs. She explained that, "The focus of Transition English is to guide students in acquiring the foundational competencies necessary to move on to Strategic English and ultimately a mainstream class." She explained that her students needed to improve as readers, writers, listeners, and speakers of English, and "strengthen skills in analytical thinking and writing." Nadia reported these contextual characteristics in preparation for planning her inquiry. She explained, "Anyone that sets an ear in this class would assume that they were listening to the conversations of a mainstream English class. It is the writing tasks . . . that make the student EL designation evident." She added: "My students have a very difficult time elaborating on their ideas, especially in written form." Nadia expressed concerns about her students' coherence and clarity in guided writing assignments, and these early observations guided her inquiry planning.

As noted, a responsive inquiry deals with specific content concerns. Questions that focus on what is occurring at the nexus of EL students and writing provide opportunities for teachers to learn from their students about their specific writing needs. Nadia demonstrated this potential when she asked the research question, "How does focused instruction of prewriting skills, such as brainstorming with word webs, affect the quality of Early Advanced English language learners' independent writing tasks?" Nadia explained that her students struggled with writing and frequently stopped to ask if what they were writing was correct. In response, she focused her inquiry on tools that would help students become more independent in prewriting, organization, and elaborations in their writing. Her question enabled her to learn about ELs' writing development as well as pedagogical tools with the potential to address the writing needs of ELs. By targeting ELs and their writing needs through focused research questions, teachers began their own deep learning about content and students.

The Role of Data in Responsive Inquiry

Well-prepared teacher inquirers collect and analyze a variety of data to answer research questions. Each dataset targets and potentially illuminates a particular issue when aligned with the research questions. We found ELA-specific data collection tools fell into four assessment modes (Stiggins, 1994): selected response (multiple choice, matching); essay (written responses); performance (observed demonstrations of understanding); and personal communication (student self-reports and informal gathering of student perspectives). In our analyses of inquiries into ELs and their writing, the essay was unsurprisingly the dominant mode, and selected response was rarely used. The essay mode included many forms that captured a range of writing processes and products. These included short answer responses, note-taking sheets, graphic organizers, prewriting forms, outlines, drafts, paragraphs, longer essays, and revisions. All of these forms of student work held potential to shed light on English learners' developing writing. New learning about ELs' writing development was dependent on solid analysis, which was demonstrated through thorough explanation of how data connected to the overall purpose and research question, clear examples of data collection and analysis tools and what they generated, and depth and complexity of interpretation and analysis. Both breadth of data collection and depth of analysis were key.

Breadth of Data Collection

The degree to which inquiry affords the opportunity to explore and potentially develop understanding of ELs and writing is dependent upon the breadth of data collection. The accountability climate has led teachers, more than ever, to equate assessment with testing and data with test scores. Inquiry into student learning requires a broader definition of data. Varied purposes require diverse methods, tools, and measures, with multiple, meaningful data sources enabling a balanced understanding of achievement, ways to represent data, and what data can and cannot yield. Teachers have privileged access to all forms of student writing-related work and access to insider perspectives of student life from daily contact. Such opportunities yield data for those with the methods, tools, and motivation to gather them and those who play ongoing roles as both teacher and researcher. This is key in learning the individual needs of diverse ELs, to see beyond one-size-fits-all instruction, beyond deficit perspectives, to capture learning that is there. Without multiple measures and levels of data, teachers (like all researchers) can reach faulty conclusions (Love, 2004). We found that STs who varied modes and/or used many data types may have had more opportunities to learn to represent and triangulate data through measures that together created a more complete picture of their ELs and their writing (Athanases, Bennett, & Wahleithner, in press).

While it is important to collect multiple instances of product data on writing, product data alone are insufficient—teachers wanting to develop contextualized EL writing knowledge also benefit from collecting process data on students' beliefs, attitudes, and values related to writing. STs repeatedly reported values of gaining emic understanding of diverse student needs. This is done through surveys, interviews, questionnaires, and focal student data collection. For example, Neil, a White male, taught a Transitional Writing class for students in grades 9–12. He sought to understand the effect that timed writing would have on his EL students' attitudes toward and skills with writing. To learn about his EL students and writing, Neil conducted a preliminary survey, collected multiple timed in-class writing assignments, and administered a final attitudinal survey. The collection of multiple timed essays, on a variety of prompts, enabled Neil to gauge student progress over time and make cross-writing comparisons. He furthered his ability to learn about his students as writers by targeting four focal students and highlighting them throughout his inquiry. Surveys enabled Neil to understand his students' attitudes before the inquiry and to discover if his students' views about writing changed as a result of their participation.

Depth of Data Analysis

After collecting data, teacher inquirers must engage in analysis that enables them to develop new insights about their EL students as learners and about teaching the content of writing. Without careful analysis, student work collected by teachers serves only as potential data; analysis turns piles of work into data, rich for mining new understandings. Careful analysis requires repeated review of data supported by tools and processes to glean information. Data such as essays, discussions, and presentation notes are not amenable to easy scoring. Analysis includes using a priori categories to code data, rubrics to quantify success in hitting targets, or repeated readings and analyses to track emerging themes. Also key is recognizing the relevance and credibility of data and critiquing tools for fit and capacity to capture nuances.

Data Analytic Processes for Learning about English Learners as Writers

We documented and analyzed data analytic processes STs used as they conducted inquiries into ELs and their writing processes and development. These include (a) documenting the achievement that is there, (b) asking and listening beneath the surface, (c) pattern finding, and (d) predicting performance to guide instruction (Athanases et al., in press).

Documenting the Achievement That Is There

Fundamental to learning about ELs and their writing processes is learning to examine writing closely for nuances and variations. This goes well beyond simply marking papers or checking writing for what students did and did not do correctly. It involves carefully analyzing what students are doing in a given piece of writing or writing activity and trying to understand why they make the moves they do. A key challenge many teachers have in understanding the writing of students who are developing proficiency in the English language is focusing on ideas and content rather than errors in standard English usage. Part of this work is moving beyond a deficit perspective to *documenting the achievement that is there*. When teachers use this process, they focus on what students can do and use this as a starting place for taking them further in their learning, rather than focusing their attention on what they cannot do.

Elaine, an African American woman, taught a two-period basic seventh-grade ELA class with 30 students, ten designated as English learners. The focus of Elaine's inquiry was discovering how creative scaffolds might help students think more deeply about using appropriate evidence and analysis to prove their ideas. The writing students did was related to their study of *The Giver* (Lowry, 1993). Elaine selected four focal students to follow throughout her inquiry. Two were ELs— Ana, a Latina, and Xee, a Hmong male. In her analysis of baseline writing samples, Elaine described Ana's work: "She often restates a lot of the prompt . . . as if she's feeling her way through the piece, hoping she'll stumble onto something that looks like analysis." Elaine details what Ana does, making efforts to understand rationales behind her actions. Similarly, when describing Xee, Elaine notes that he "struggles with grammar and mechanics; however, his reading comprehension is extremely high and this is displayed in the content of his writing." Again, she details what Xee can do, providing a starting point for where to focus her instruction to move him to the next level.

Students continued to write during their study of *The Giver*, and Elaine used rubric scoring. However, she continued to look past the scores alone. For one paragraph, Ana scored a one, meaning she had no analysis. Still, Elaine made an effort to understand the reasoning behind the paragraph Ana wrote on the novel's protagonist:

(Ana) appears to have been lost from the very start of the paragraph and so decided to write a restatement of the prompt. I think her next statement was an attempt on her part to show a change in Jonas based on the memories. However, she apparently did not have time to finish.

Elaine is careful to document exactly what Ana did in her paragraph rather than focus her analysis just on what is missing or the problems with Ana's writing. This process of *documenting the achievement that is there* allows teachers to gain insights into their students as learners. Elaine developed an understanding of some of the challenges English learners face as they learn to use evidence and analysis to develop their ideas.

Asking and Listening Beneath the Surface

When conducting inquiries, STs often asked questions leading them to collect data beyond student work. Many used tools such as surveys, interviews, and observations to learn more about their students and their perceptions of content. Collecting data in this way leads to a different analytic process as teachers *ask and listen beneath the surface* of classroom activity.

Working in an eighth-grade class of SDAIE (Specially Designed Academic Instruction in English), Benita, a White woman, focused her inquiry on learning how to advance students' persuasive essay writing. Persuasion was a grade-level expectation for her school. Benita had worked in various ways on argument, counterargument, rebuttal, and audience. She also was careful in her inquiry to document development of students' compositions through multiple drafts. However, she grew bewildered in trying to understand why growth across drafts was minimal. She crafted interview questions for her four focal students to explore their understanding of persuasive writing elements, as well as their reflections on their writing processes and the kinds of support they sought and needed for their writing. Benita learned a great deal from these interviews and reflected on them in a five-page, data-based memo in which she looked closely at each student's responses, noted links across focal student interviews, and distilled a set of themes.

For example, despite repeated attention in class to rebuttal, one student reported to Benita that he had never heard the word before. Benita noted that his response was especially puzzling:

> he attempted to add a rebuttal in the very first draft of his essay. Then, in his second draft, both his counterargument and rebuttal were completely removed. When asked about this, he confessed that he "left that part out because that part didn't really make sense to [him]."

Benita realized through interviews that she had not adequately taught and illustrated rebuttal and the other elements of persuasion. However, the issue was also related to what Benita learned about students' difficulty in working with audience in their essays. In various cases, students revealed that they did not understand certain terms and functions of jobs and roles in society for individuals Benita had supplied as hypothetical readers/audiences for persuasive letter writing. These included manufacturers and their job functions and senators and their relationship to the making of laws. Benita came to realize the need for more in-class time to process various functions and components of persuasion. She also learned the need for greater attention to "academic language on multiple levels." Interviews helped Benita realize some of her students' underlying issues related to writing in a challenging genre and helped her reflect on ways she could move ahead with this group and with her ELs in future teaching contexts focused on writing.

Pattern Finding

Key to developing new knowledge through inquiry is the ability to see patterns in data, a process not altogether natural to teachers (Korthagen, 2010). Multiple processes allow teachers to *find patterns and uncover trends* in students' learning. These were taught, modeled, and practiced in the ELA inquiry course through data analysis workshops and through field memo writing on emerging trends in data analysis. A teacher might note students' scores in order to track various rubric attributes in a table. In other cases, a teacher might graphically represent scores to uncover patterns. In still others, a teacher might categorize student work into piles based on commonalities observed and then conduct further analyses on each pile to understand what made the pieces of data included similar and what the implications of those similarities might be for future instruction.

Nadia (as noted) taught ninth-grade Transition English for Early Advanced, Spanish-speaking ELs. She focused her inquiry on explicitly teaching prewriting strategies: brainstorming, creating word webs, and categorizing information from word webs into lists. Nadia collected data on students' processes of moving from constructing word webs on the topic of their choice, to organizing word web details into categories, and writing compositions using their word webs and categorizations as guides. Nadia's analysis uncovered three trends: (a) students not categorizing details but including them in later writing; (b) students brainstorming ideas but listing them all in one category and then writing all the details in one very long paragraph; and (c) two students "who drew out really detailed and rich word webs (and) also used the list categorization I taught them." Finally, Nadia included one "anomaly" who began the word web to brainstorm ideas but jumped straight to the writing, elaborating on the ideas in his composition. By finding patterns, Nadia developed a deeper understanding of the role of word webs in guiding students' writing. She also discovered students' use of varied processes to guide their writing: "a few students seemed to metacognitively categorize their details from the brainstorm to their compositions without the need for using lists as scaffolds." Nadia began to understand that while some students need the scaffold of categorizing ideas, others can jump successfully from brainstorming to writing.

Nadia then analyzed students' compositions. She scored them using a rubric with three categories (complete sentences, specific details, and topic addressed), four score levels per category. After scoring, Nadia created a table to display scores for each feature. Because the rubric aligned with her baseline data rubric, Nadia created bar graphs and reviewed them side-by-side. Displaying data in this way allowed Nadia to *see patterns in students' growth*. Most notably, students went from mainly baseline scores of one and two to scores of three and four. Finding patterns in her students' work provided new insights for Nadia into EL students' developmental trajectories as writers. She also gained deeper insights into which specific scaffolds for teaching writing led to improvements in students' writing scores.

Predicting Student Performance to Guide Instruction

Elaine, as already noted, taught a seventh-grade ELA class with 10 of 30 students designated as ELs. An additional inquiry analysis process evident in Elaine's work to develop her knowledge of writing and adolescent ELs is *predicting student performance to guide instruction*. Often, teachers use what they learn from noticing patterns in students' performance to predict and plan for students' successes, problems, and resistance. New understanding of their students helps them to plan appropriate instructional activities to guide students' next-steps development. Elaine's work highlights the role *predicting* plays in analysis.

After *documenting achievement* for each focal student, Elaine used this information to predict what instruction might move students' learning and development forward. After reflecting on the achievement she saw in the work of her focal students on the second data collection event, Elaine predicted what she could do to set students up for future success. Elaine noted that students might have been thrown off by what evidence they could or could not use to support their ideas. Consequently, she made plans to "help them write their topic sentences and discuss with them possible pieces of evidence that they can include in their paragraphs so that their focus will be solely on writing their analysis." Elaine predicted that by adding the scaffold of focused attention on topic sentences and evidence as a class, students would then be able to give their individual attention to developing their analysis, thus leading them to develop their ideas more convincingly.

Also, after gaining a deeper understanding of Ana as a writer from analyzing her second piece of writing, Elaine commented that she thought she needed to spend more time with Ana to help her understand writing prompts. Elaine predicted that, "Armed with a focused argument from the very beginning, I am confident that she can write the kind of analysis that adequately supports her topic sentences." In this case, Elaine predicts what type of instruction Ana needs to be more successful with her writing and what she thinks Ana will be able to do once she has a better understanding of expectations. By using her analysis of student work to *predict student performance*, Elaine furthered her knowledge of writing and adolescent ELs. She realized that, as students develop new skills as writers, some skills they have may be temporarily lost as they focus attention on the new skill or process. For this reason, teachers must provide extra scaffolds for students. In this case, Elaine realized she needed new scaffolding to support the writing of analysis.

Synthesis and Next Steps Instruction

The goal of responsive inquiry is the development of new understanding about phenomena within one's teaching context. As teachers reflect on their analyses, they begin to develop new schema for understanding what is happening with their learners. When teachers look across data sets, they begin to synthesize their findings and develop deepened understanding. Synthesis can occur in many forms—across work samples of a single student, across students, and across teaching contexts when pre-service teachers partner in exploring particular foci. In the case of ELs and writing, data collected in different phases of the writing process can reveal ELs' unfolding writing processes, but discoveries can take time as data are collected, analyzed, and synthesized. One value of close analyses of focal students and their writing, supported by breadth of data collection, is that it enables examination of students' writing development at multiple data points over time. Nadia examined how word webs did and did not lead to "category lists," which did and did not shape compositions. It was in her synthesizing that Nadia gleaned some understanding of ELs' writing processes. Written products, of course, can reveal only so much. Benita illustrated how analyses of writing development can guide the crafting of interview questions that ask and listen beneath the surface. It was Benita's linking of data (papers and interviews) and her synthesizing of analyses that enabled her to uncover some themes and deepen her understanding of ways in which *some* English learners may engage *some* writing tasks at *some* times.

The arc of responsive inquiry fostered not only these syntheses but explicit reflection on next steps. STs in our work reported how their inquiries led them to see ways in which their future writing instruction with ELs would likely benefit from more focused attention in writing tasks, greater attention to academic language, and one-on-one guidance. Responsive inquiry is a recursive process. Teachers who engage in this form of inquiry implement a plan–act–reflect cycle on an ongoing basis in their teaching contexts. Questions lead to actions, which lead to findings that in turn inspire new questions about student learning. Often, a preliminary finding will push a teacher to respond with additional data collection events or with new analyses of existing data.

Discussion and Conclusion

Too often, English learners get cast as a uniform group and writing pedagogy relies on formulaic, one-size-fits-all instruction. For teachers to understand the varied writing needs of their EL students, they must learn to focus on and learn from them. We have found that responsive inquiry promotes that deepened focus. Through careful attention to nested demographic data, research questions that target needs of particular students, and the collection and analysis of a wide range of data about students' writing development, pre-service teachers in our studies learned to uncover nuances of students' individual writing processes, as well as trends across students and classes. This enabled planning of logical next-steps instruction (Shepard, 2000) for a range of students and for groups of students with similar needs. By focusing on learners, teachers learned to develop and implement pedagogy that was responsive to their particular learners, rather than developing a generic curriculum that may or may not meet the needs of linguistically diverse learners.

Several analytic processes in particular supported exploration of ELs and their writing. By *documenting achievement that is there*, STs learned to target and build upon student strengths rather than look at students through a deficit lens. This is particularly important for the teaching of writing because writing processes and development are varied and complex, and much of the good thinking and creative ideas embedded in the writing of ELs require that a teacher look closely, sometimes unraveling prose, to see the strengths in the work. *Asking and listening beneath the surface* provided teachers with their EL students' perspectives about writing. *Pattern-finding* promoted a new depth of understanding about EL writing challenges, and *predicting* enabled teachers to plan appropriate next-steps instruction based on current student work. We found that careful data analysis enabled teachers to monitor ongoing learning and to respond. Moreover, such careful work with classroom-based data can bring equity issues to the fore, enabling teachers to disaggregate data to understand which individuals and groups are performing at which levels on dimensions of writing; what issues are shaping students' successes, problems, and resistance; and what kinds of differentiation and further scaffolding are needed. When teachers learn early in their careers to collect and analyze data in these ways, they may internalize these processes so that they can draw on them throughout their teaching careers. This is the kind of professional learning that may especially equip teachers to learn about and meet the writing needs of their English learners.

References

Athanases, S. Z., & de Oliveira, L. C. (2008). Advocacy for equity in classrooms and beyond: New teachers' challenges and responses. *Teachers College Record, 110*(1), 64–104.
Athanases, S. Z., & de Oliveira, L. C. (2011). Toward program-wide coherence in preparing teachers to teach and advocate for English language learners. In T. Lucas

(Ed.), *Teacher preparation for linguistically diverse classrooms* (pp. 195–215). New York: Taylor & Francis.

Athanases, S. Z., & Martin, K. J. (2006). Learning to advocate for educational equity in a teacher credential program. *Teaching and Teacher Education, 22*(6), 627–646.

Athanases, S. Z., Bennett, L. H., & Wahleithner, J. M. (in press). Fostering data literacy through preservice teacher inquiry in English language arts. *The Teacher Educator.*

Athanases, S. Z., Wahleithner, J. M., & Bennett, L. H. (2012a). Learning to attend to culturally and linguistically diverse learners through teacher inquiry in teacher education. *Teachers College Record, 114*(7).

Athanases, S. Z., Wahleithner, J. M., & Bennett, L. H. (2012b). Preservice teacher inquiry and content knowledge for teaching. Paper presented at the American Educational Research Association Annual Meeting, Vancouver.

Athanases, S. Z., Wahleithner, J. M., & Bennett, L. H. (in press). Learning about English learners' content understandings through teacher inquiry: Focus on writing. *The New Educator.*

Bartolomé, L. I. (1994). Beyond the methods fetish: Toward a humanizing pedagogy. *Harvard Educational Review, 64*(2), 173–194.

Brisk, M. E., & Zisselsberger, M. (2011). "We've let them in on the secret": Using SFL theory to improve the teaching of writing to bilingual learners. In T. Lucas (Ed.), *Teacher preparation for linguistically diverse classrooms* (pp. 111–126). New York: Taylor & Francis.

Bunch, G. C., Aguirre, J. M., & Téllez, K. (2009). Beyond the scores: Using candidate responses on high stakes performance assessment to inform teacher preparation for English learners. *Issues in Teacher Education, 18*(1), 103–128.

Coady, M., Harper, C., & de Jong, E. (2011). From preservice to practice: Mainstream elementary teacher beliefs of preparation and efficacy with English language learners in the state of Florida. *Bilingual Research Journal, 34*(2), 223–239.

Cochran-Smith, M., & Lytle, S. L. (2009). *Inquiry as stance: Practitioner research for the next generation.* New York: Teachers College Press.

Dana, N. F., Yendol-Hoppey, D., & Snow-Gerono, J. L. (2006). Deconstructing inquiry in the professional development school: Exploring the domains and contents of teachers' questions. *Action in Teacher Education, 27*(4), 59–71.

Darling-Hammond, L., Chung, R., & Frelow, F. (2002). Variation in teacher preparation: How well do different pathways prepare teachers to teach? *Journal of Teacher Education, 53*(4), 286–302.

de Oliveira, L. C., & Athanases, S. Z. (2007). Graduates' reports of advocating for English language learners. *Journal of Teacher Education, 58*(3), 202–215.

de Oliveira, L. C., & Shoffner, M. (2009). Addressing the needs of English language learners in an English education methods course. *English Education, 42*(1), 123–138.

Dresser, R. (2007). The effects of teacher inquiry in the bilingual language arts classroom. *Teacher Education Quarterly, 34*(3), 53–66.

Enright, K. A., & Gilliland, B. (2011). Multilingual writing in an age of accountability: From policy to practice in U.S. high school classrooms. *Journal of Second Language Writing, 20*, 182–195.

Faltis, C., Arias, M. B., & Ramirez-Marin, F. (2010). Identifying relevant competencies for secondary teachers of English learners. *Bilingual Research Journal, 33*, 307–328.

Fuller, F. (1969). Concerns of teachers: A developmental conceptualization. *American Educational Research Journal, 6*, 207–226.

Gándara, P. C., Maxwell-Jolly, J., & Driscoll, A. (2005). *Listening to teachers of English language learners: A survey of California teachers' challenges, experiences, and professional development needs.* Santa Cruz, CA: Center for Future of Teaching and Learning.

Hammond, J. (2006). High challenge, high support: Integrating language and content instruction for diverse learners in an English literature classroom. *Journal of English for Academic Purposes, 5,* 269–283.

Kagan, D. M. (1992). Professional growth among preservice and beginning teachers. *Review of Educational Research, 62*(2), 129–169.

Kiuhara, S. A., Graham, S., & Hawken, L. S. (2009). Teaching writing to high school students: A national survey. *Journal of Educational Psychology, 101*(1), 136–160.

Korthagen, F. A. J. (2010). Situated learning theory and the pedagogy of teacher education: Towards an integrative view of teacher behavior and teacher learning. *Teaching and Teacher Education, 96*(1), 98–106.

Lew, A. (1999). Writing correctness and the second-language student. In S. W. Freedman, E. R. Simons, J. S. Kalnin, A. Casareno, & The M-CLASS Teams, *Inside city schools: Investigating literacy in multicultural classrooms* (pp. 165–178). New York: Teachers College.

Love, N. (2004). Taking data to new depths. *Journal of Staff Development, 25*(4), 22–26.

Lowry, L. (1993). *The giver.* New York: Bantam.

Lucas, T. (Ed.) (2011). *Teacher preparation for linguistically diverse classrooms: A resource for teacher educators.* New York: Taylor & Francis.

Lucas, T., & Grinberg, J. (2008). Responding to the linguistic reality of the mainstream classroom: Preparing classroom teachers to teach English language learners. In M. Cochran-Smith, S. Feiman-Nemser, & J. McIntyre (Eds.), *Handbook of research on teacher education: Enduring issues in changing contexts* (pp. 606–636). Mahwah, NJ: Lawrence Erlbaum.

Lucas, T., Villegas, A. M., & Freedson-Gonzalez, M. (2008). Linguistically responsive teacher education: Preparing classroom teachers to teach English language learners. *Journal of Teacher Education, 59*(4), 361–373.

Merino, B. J., & Ambrose, R. C. (2009). Beginning teachers' inquiry in linguistically diverse classrooms: Exploring the power of small learning communities. In C. J. Craig & L. F. Deretchin (Eds.), *Teacher Education Yearbook XVII: Teacher learning in small group settings* (pp. 242–260). Lanham, MD: Rowman & Little.

Nevarez-LaTorre, A. A. (2010). *The power of learning from inquiry: Teacher research as a professional development tool in multilingual schools.* Charlotte, NC: Information Age Publishing.

Ortmeier-Hooper, C., & Enright, K. (2011). Mapping new territory: Toward an understanding of adolescent L2 writers and writing in US contexts. *Journal of Second Language Writing, 20,* 167–181.

Pawan, F. (2008). Content-area teachers and scaffolded instruction for English language learners. *Teaching and Teacher Education, 24,* 1450–1462.

Schleppegrell, M. J. (2004). *The language of schooling: A functional linguistics perspective.* Mahwah, NJ: Lawrence Erlbaum.

Shepard, L. A. (2000). The role of assessment in a learning culture. *Educational Researcher, 29*(7), 4–14.

Sowa, P. A. (2009). Understanding our learners and developing reflective practice: Conducting action research with English language learners. *Teaching and Teacher Education, 25*(8), 1026–1032.

Stiggins, R. J. (1994). *Student-centered classroom assessment*. New York: Merrill/Macmillan.

Valdés, G. (1999). Incipient bilingualism and the development of English language writing abilities in the secondary school. In C. J. Faltis & P. M. Wolfe (Eds.), *So much to say: Adolescents, bilingualism and ESL in the secondary school* (pp. 138–175). New York: Teachers College Press.

Walker, C. L., & Stone, K. (2011). Preparing teachers to reach English language learners: Pre-service and in-service initiatives. In T. Lucas (Ed.), *Teacher preparation for linguistically diverse classrooms* (pp. 127–142). New York: Taylor & Francis.

Walqui, A. (2011). The growth of teacher expertise for teaching English language learners: A socio-culturally based professional development model. In T. Lucas (Ed.), *Teacher preparation for linguistically diverse classrooms* (pp. 160–177). New York: Taylor & Francis.

11

UNDERSTANDING HOW PRE-SERVICE TEACHERS DEVELOP A WORKING KNOWLEDGE OF L2 WRITING

Toward a Socioculturally Oriented Postmethod Pedagogy

Lisya Seloni

The linguistic and sociocultural makeup of the K–12 classrooms in the United States has drastically changed in recent decades as a result of record-high immigration. According to U.S. Census Bureau data (2007), in the United States over 55 million people (i.e. one in five) speak a language other than English. Among these 55 million people, the number of school-aged children rose from 4.7 to 11.2 million between 1980 and 2009 (Aud et al., 2011). While bilingual learners constitute a sizable population in any classroom, teachers usually have limited preparation on and knowledge of how to address the needs of an ethno-linguistically diverse student population.[1] In this context, a variety of issues related to linguistically diverse students' literacy needs become salient in teacher education. Questions over pre-service and beginning in-service teachers' knowledge and beliefs about second language learning (particularly second language literacy acquisition and the best ways to effectively address the reading and writing needs of culturally diverse students) provide the substance of many interdisciplinary discussions, including second language teacher education as well as general teacher education. While debates around second language teacher education include topics such as what content knowledge should be at the center of pre-service teachers' knowledge base and how best to teach it (e.g. Freeman, 2002; Johnson, 2006; Leki, Cumming, & Silva, 2008; Yates & Muchisky, 2003), debates in general teacher education include issues such as promoting culturally relevant teaching practices and accounting for linguistic differences (e.g. Commins & Miramontes, 2006; de Oliveira & Athanases, 2007; Goodwin, 2002; Sleeter, 2001; Ward & Ward, 2003). Fundamental to both discussions is that all teachers regardless of their main disciplines should be prepared to address the reading and writing needs of individuals whose first language is not English.

Using findings from a semester-long study on four pre-service teachers, this chapter attempts to illustrate the dynamic relationship between pre-service teachers' knowledge construction and theory building in the teaching of second language reading and writing. A close analysis of the pre-service teachers' narratives on how they construct knowledge about teaching second language writing not only sheds light on how the teachers come to know what they know, but also provides suggestions in regard to curricular changes needed in English education and teaching English to speakers of other languages (TESOL) undergraduate programs.

Problem Statement: The Lack of Second Language Writing Research in Teacher Education

Granted the diversity of today's classrooms, much literature in teacher education is devoted to understanding cross-cultural issues (e.g. Igoa, 1995; Olsen, 1997), and the discussion mostly centers on culturally responsive pedagogy (e.g. Ladson-Billings, 1994). Within this literature, we specifically see a focus on culturally relevant teaching where teachers search for ways of tapping into immigrant children's "funds of knowledge" (Moll, 1990) both to bridge school and home discourses and to raise teachers' awareness of their own cultural backgrounds (Sleeter, 2001). Given the varying educational backgrounds of immigrant children, differentiating instruction has also been one of the main threads of debate in this literature. Although attention has been given to the importance of all teachers' familiarity with addressing the linguistic and cultural diversity of immigrant students, Goodwin (2002), in his examination of 579 articles published in the *Journal of Teacher Education* between 1980 and 2001, reports that not a single article concretely discusses the skills, strategies, and content knowledge that teachers should possess in order to work with students whose first language is not English. In this context, the teaching of second language reading and writing remains invisible in many teacher education courses as a result of a tacit assumption: teaching English language learners is "a matter of pedagogical adaptations that can easily be incorporated into a mainstream teacher's existing repertoire of instructional strategies for a diverse classroom" (de Jong & Harper, 2005, p. 102). This "just good teaching" (de Jong & Harper, 2005) concept may lead teacher education programs to overlook pre-service teachers' need for a concrete understanding of second language literacy issues such as responding to second language writing, teaching issues related to textual ownership, or teaching second language reading strategies. On the other hand, the "social turn in second language acquisition" (Block, 2003) has brought various critical examinations and greater awareness of the social contexts of the second language learners (e.g. Kumaravadivelu, 2001, 2006; Canagarajah, 2002; Norton & Toohey, 2004); much attention has been given to social and political aspect of language learning and the relationships among language, communities, and power (Hall & Eggington, 2000). Manifestation of the social and critical theoretical underpinnings in second language teacher education necessitated an understanding of linguistics and second language acquisition (SLA) (Yates & Muchisky, 2003), situating this knowledge in everyday practices (Johnson & Golombek, 2011) as well as understanding the multiple cultural and sociopolitical complexities of the teaching context (Hall & Eggington, 2000). In response to what should constitute second language teacher education, some argue that teachers "must understand their own beliefs and knowledge about learning and teaching" (Freeman & Johnson, 1998, p. 412) and "must begin to recognize the situated and interpretive nature of teaching" (Johnson, 1996, p. 767). Others, on the other hand, argue that that attention should stay on the "core subject areas of language and [second language acquisition] research" (Yates & Muchisky, 2003, p. 144).

Critiquing Freeman and Johnson (1998) who call for reflective teaching and more congruency between classroom practice and SLA theory, Yates and Muchisky (2003) argue that SLA research has different goals from language teaching in that "we do not expect SLA researchers to be under the obligation to us to articulate how to apply their findings to language teaching pedagogy" (p. 140). To agree with Yates and Muchisky (2003) that not every theoretical foundation can have immediate pedagogical application does not require that a particular theory and knowledge base be "irrelevant to language teaching" (p. 143). However, the field of second language writing provides complex theories, which are at the crossroads of its parent disciplines such as applied linguistics, composition, and rhetoric studies, giving it a more critical orientation (Leki & Silva, 2004). Therefore, the translation of a specific L2 writing-related knowledge domain to teacher education entails reflective and practitioner knowledge and requires that pre-service teachers examine the linguistic, cultural, and sociopolitical realities of their local teaching settings. In this context, the ability to teach second language reading and writing is one of the key components of being an effective and transformative language teacher, at all levels. Although second language writing scholars have been exploring various issues related to the second language writing development of students from non-English language backgrounds, issues related to pre-service teachers' evolving knowledge base for teaching second language literacy are mostly left unexplored. Despite a multitude of improvements in second language writing theory, many K–12 teachers still find themselves not knowing how to address the reading and writing needs of diverse student populations in their classrooms.

Toward a Socioculturally Oriented Postmethod Pedagogy Perspective on Teaching Second Language Literacy

In this study, I specifically draw on a postmethod pedagogy (Kumaravadivelu, 2003) and sociocultural perspectives of teacher education (Johnson, 2006). Both theoretical underpinnings of teacher education emphasize the concept of teachers as reflective practitioners as well as transformative intellectuals. It also focuses on contextually appropriate praxis (Freire, 1970) in which pre-service teachers are given opportunities to theorize from everyday practices. To prepare autonomous and transformative teachers of second language literacy, I argue that teacher preparation programs need to equip pre-service teachers with context-sensitive knowledge, which "has to emerge from teachers and their practice of the everyday" (Kumaravadivelu, 2001, p. 538). I also argue that the ability to develop one's working knowledge relies on the interplay between the discursive practices that shape pre-service teachers' knowledge base (e.g. theory construction) and their experiences with language teaching and learning everyday practices.

It is salient to explore how pre-service teachers form their knowledge base on second language writing and what issues they wrestle with before they are out in the field teaching English language learners. To encourage second language (L2) teachers to become reflective practitioners, Ramanathan (2002) suggests that teachers critically mediate between the "discipline's social practices" and their "individual participation in these practices." One way to achieve this is by

> reflecting on how their professional goals are tied to the goals of their disciplines, how debates in the discipline(s) percolate down to the smaller contexts of their individual classrooms, how they contribute to text types and genres remaining stable or changing in their disciplines, and how "basic facts" and "truths" in their disciplines can, from another point of view, be regarded as highly questionable.
>
> *(p. 7)*

Through reading theory and discussing issues related to praxis, pre-service teachers constantly negotiate meaning, accepting or rejecting certain interpretations.

Theory in second language writing has been the focus of discussion for the past couple of decades (Silva & Matsuda, 2010). Despite the attention given to theory building in second language writing, how these important issues were addressed in teacher education programs with theory-in-practice received little attention. Aiming to fill this gap, this chapter portrays pre-service teachers' ways of knowing, which is shaped by various texts, people, and events. The study's main research focus is how pre-service teachers reorganize their lived experiences with language, culture, and text, and how they mediate between what they learn in their coursework on teaching second language literacy and what they see in the field from senior teachers.

Context of the Study

This study was conducted at a public university in the Midwest. The TESOL program in this university is housed under the English department, which follows an English Studies model that gives students multiple opportunities to integrate various areas of English Studies such as composition, literature, writing, and linguistics. At both the graduate and undergraduate level, students can major in English while concentrating on various areas such as writing, TESOL, children's literature, and English education. The program also offers TESOL endorsement, a TESOL minor, and graduate TESOL certification for students who plan on teaching in public schools. Data for the study were collected over one semester period where pre-service teachers completed a required TESOL methods and materials course (hereafter the "methods" course) while also completing their 100-hour fieldwork experience with a practicum course. The department did not offer a regular second language writing course at the undergraduate level, so various weeks of both courses were devoted to discussing readings on teaching second language reading and writing.

Participants

The participants of this study include four pre-service teachers: Norah, Maggie, Jake, and Katie,[2] all enrolled in the methods course. These students were selected to be participants because during the course of this study all of them were engaged in some level of field experience while they were taking the methods course. Norah was the only master's-level student in the group; the rest of the participants were senior-level undergraduate pre-service teachers in majors such as Spanish, English education, and Latina studies with a TESOL minor. The details of the participants can be seen in Table 11.1.

TABLE 11.1 Research Participants' Background

Name	Major	Level of education	Goals	Languages
Maggie	Latina studies with TESOL minor	Senior	Interested in teaching ESL at secondary level	Native speaker of English, Spanish (advanced)
Jake	Spanish education with TESOL minor	Senior	Interested in teaching in Latin America, then teaching ESL in public school	Native speaker of English, Spanish (advanced)
Katie	English education with TESOL minor	Senior	Interested in teaching high school	Native speaker of English, Spanish (beginner), Italian (beginner)
Norah	TESOL and linguistics with second language writing emphasis	MA	Applying for Ph.D. programs	Native speaker of English, Spanish (intermediate)

Data Collection and Data Analysis

The data for this research were collected from multiple sources: (1) students' blog entries about their field observations and classroom discussions, (2) interviews conducted after both courses were over, and (3) students' final ethnographic papers. The interviews were open-ended and semi-structured in nature and ranged from 30 to 45 minutes in length. All interviews were audiotaped and transcribed to conduct data analysis. Students wrote learning logs prior to each discussion on the class readings and after their observations in the field. They also submitted a final paper for the practicum course in which they wrote an ethnographic analysis of their field experiences. All student artifacts (i.e. blog entries, final papers) were used as data sources in this study.

Thematic analysis was conducted to make sense of the student artifacts and interview transcriptions. As thematic analysis emerges from "the deep familiarity with the data that comes from categorizing" (Rossman & Rallis, 2003, p. 282), data were read carefully and repeatedly over time until meaningful themes were found. Data analysis was done by carefully looking for patterns, themes, and relationships throughout all the data sources. While searching for central themes emerging from the data, I specifically asked, "What broad statements can be made that meaningfully bring all of these data together?" (Hatch, 2002, p. 156). Looking at multiple sources of data and making sense of the emerging themes helped me to "uncover teachers' interpretations of the activities they engage in" (Johnson, 2006, p. 242).

Findings

The findings of this study demonstrate that pre-service teachers' understanding of second language literacy is complex, multilayered, embodied in specific histories, and influenced by various actors, texts, and events. More specifically, the results indicate that pre-service teachers' working knowledge was shaped and mediated by four main practices: in-class theory building, observations in public schools, their own foreign language learning experiences, and their teaching trajectories (Figure 11.1).

As illustrated in Figure 11.1, pre-service teachers were observed to be constantly mediating various meanings and forming their perceptions about second language writing through these multiple layers. As detailed below in documenting pre-service teachers' experiences, three central themes emerged as pervasive in their beliefs and inquiries. These themes included (1) exploration of second language writing praxis through ethnographic experience, (2) evolving theories and higher awareness of second language writing while making meaning of various literacy events, and (3) foreign language learning experiences as a tool of inquiry.

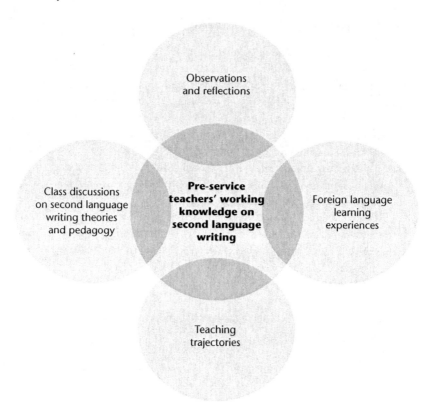

FIGURE 11.1 Pre-service Teachers' Working Knowledge on Second Language Writing Instruction

Theme #1: Exploration of Second Language Writing Praxis through Ethnographic Experience

During their fieldwork, pre-service teachers were encouraged to act like ethnographers while sorting out various schools of thought and approaches to language, culture, literacy, and second language reading and writing. The ethnographic approach created opportunities to reframe, negotiate, and expand on the theories they learned in their methods classes. Acting as ethnographers meant conducting careful observations of literacy events in the ESL classroom, taking copious field notes, keeping an observation diary on their blogs, collecting artifacts from the field, and, finally, writing an ethnographic paper based on their observations in the field.

Through field experience and other hands-on practices in the methods class, their knowledge of second language literacy was not only "populated with their own intentions and in their own voices, but teachers also become active users and producers of theory in their own right, for their own means and as appropriate for their own institutional contexts" (Johnson, 2006, p. 240). The experiential knowledge gained in the field also helped problematize the privileged status of professional knowledge and gave students more ownership to construct local knowledge (Canagarajah, 1999, 2002). Although pre-service teachers in this study occasionally had only a vague understanding of what constitutes ethnography or theory in second language reading and writing, I encouraged them to look at the threads of literacy "practices" they see in the field to make meaning of the instructional practices in class. This grounded theory (Lincoln & Guba, 1985) perspective coupled with reflection-on-action (Edge, 2011) not only helped the pre-service teachers to look for emergent praxis in relation to second language writing events in their observation sites, but also gave them an opportunity to take an active role in the field.

Maggie, who is a Latina studies major with a TESOL minor, conducted 100 hours of observation at a local public school's ESL program where sixth- and eighth-grade students were placed in the same class. Maggie pointed out in her ethnographic write-up the importance of various roles she took during her field experience.

> Through my ethnographic field experience, I was able to take the role of an observer, a learner, a teacher, and a friend. I observed the teacher's methods of teaching second language literacy and mannerism in the classroom, so that I can get an understanding of the approaches that are effective for the English language learners. On the other hand, I was also a learner and a teacher. I was a learner because I was able to put myself in the shoes of the English language learners, and experience learning from their perspective. I was a teacher in that I took the opportunity to get up in front of the classroom as well as work with students on their writing individually. I have gained so much insight from this experience in terms of what exactly it means to be a part of an ESL classroom. I have learned that it is a learning community, co-managed learning process (between the teacher and the students), but most importantly, I have learned that the ESL classroom becomes a family— students of all languages and cultures come together and grow together and succeed together.

The multiple roles Maggie took as a participant observer gave her various opportunities to participate in the classroom events. As this excerpt indicates, Maggie forms a community-oriented approach to ESL learning where she observed that the teaching of writing is situated in larger social frameworks, not in isolated patterns. Some of the pre-service teachers' core practices as classroom ethnographers included closely observing and writing about literacy activities that took place in the field. Such close observations of texts and literacy events seemed to raise pre-service teachers' awareness of the multiple ways of teaching L2 writing in everyday ESL classrooms. The excerpt below from Maggie's ethnographic experiences demonstrates this point:

The two classrooms of Mrs. Dolores and Mrs. Collins both display material and projects on the walls that promote the cross-cultural make up of the class. Each teacher strives to encourage each other's cultural backgrounds to make sure that the classroom has a safe environment in which the students can feel comfortable taking risks and using the language. The students are arranged in a seating chart that encourages them to converse with others around them who do not speak their native language. In the classroom of Mrs. Dolores, the support of multi-culturalism and multiliteracies is clear from the start. There is a crossword with a globe of the world in the background, and in the crossword the names of all the students are intertwined to complete the puzzle. On the other side of the room are displayed the "Facebook profiles" that each student created at the beginning of the school year, and on them is all of the information about each individual: where they are from, what languages they speak, activities they enjoy doing, favorite part about school, etc.

The ethnographic field experience also led some pre-service teachers to situate themselves as teachers of writing. Katie, who conducted her fieldwork at a community high school where ESL classes were divided into four levels, observed how teachers incorporated students' first language into writing assignments. In her interviews, she indicated that one of her teaching trajectories as a future ESL teacher would be to facilitate classroom discussions and assign writing activities where students' first language would be utilized and integrated.

Through classroom observation experiences, I created a future plan to pay special attention to each individual's writing background in my classroom. Through my field experience, I found that when students were asked to write or prompted to share with others how to say a specific phrase in their native language, they responded more often at other times as well. As a future teacher, I plan on doing so in every lesson. Creating writing assignments, such as asking students to present on their cultures, provides benefits not only for the presenter him/herself by placing value and respect on their home language and culture. It also provides a learning opportunity for other students in the class.

What was interesting in such comments is that students were more receptive to the theories that they thought were germane when they noticed some kind of implication of that theory in the ESL classes they observed. Pre-service teachers' narratives of their fieldwork indicate that they learned to ask critical questions to respond to linguistic diversity in an ESL context. More specifically, observing literacy events in various settings and engaging with L2 writing immersed students in the complex literacy practices that go on in ESL classrooms and prompted them to act as ethnographers of classroom communities. Katie in her fieldwork worked with an ESL student where she "helped her become a better writer" through reading and responding to her writing individually.

Along the same lines, Norah emphasized the benefit of the practice-oriented second language writing activities that she did in her TESOL methods course. In the class she refers to in this interview, students had watched the documentary *Writing Across Borders* and provided her written responses to an ESL student writing following lively discussion about providing comments on ESL writing and focusing on form versus organization and content. Norah stated:

> Preservice teachers should really understand the second language acquisition process and what the ESL students are working with. As far as second language writing goes, I think how you assess and evaluate second language writing is really important to know. You especially want to know what level of literacy they are at in their L1 and what level of proficiency they are in their L2. It is always good to examine actual second language writing just like we did in the previous class . . . because you can only read so much about what you are supposed to do but until you actually do it yourself and see what some of the things are . . . that really is important for me. . . . For example, it would also be interesting to do some sort of project where preservice teachers work with second language writers themselves . . . maybe not even face to face . . . maybe using googledoc they could upload their work and then analyze real ESL writing. Maybe if you get a willing secondary education teacher to work with preservice teachers—that could be a project throughout the semester.

In her narrative, Norah also emphasizes specific activities and practices that could promote her understanding of second language writing. She indicates the importance of active learning, engaging in the process of responding to L2 writing, and building community projects with the public schools. As seen below, collaborating with various actors (e.g. ESL students, cooperating teachers) while participating in their TESOL courses had a significant impact on students' working knowledge of second language literacy and helped them gain a higher awareness of the practice of second language writing.

Theme #2: Evolving Theories of Second Language Writing: Higher Awareness of Second Language Writing

The impact of pre-service students attending school-based communities in diverse settings and collaborating with various actors was visible in their ways of making meaning from their experiences. Some pre-service teachers in this study reported how their expectations and beliefs about second language writing have changed as a result of being in the ESL classroom. The main theme in their perceptions seemed to include a multidimensional view of second language writing theory.

They observed the manifestations of two lines of theory base: writing as a cognitive act and writing as a contextual and situated activity. Students often referred to the importance of genre knowledge acquisition as well as employment of L2 reading and writing strategies. Their evolving views on teaching second language writing mirror the writing theories they have been reading and discussing in class. In methods class discussions, pre-service teachers were cautioned against too easily fitting these theories into each instructional practice and teaching of writing contexts. Specifically, we discussed the dynamic relationship between theory and practice by underscoring the importance of program goals, learner needs, and social and political roles of the institutions. Some of the main topics of the weeks where second language writing and reading were discussed included intercultural rhetoric (previously known as contrastive rhetoric), focus on form versus content, and moving from process-based to genre-based writing theories. Maggie, who specifically observed writing ESL classes during her fieldwork, indicated that her views on second language literacy have evolved from a focus on form to a focus on the content and context of the writing,

> Teaching second language writing is obviously imperative in the ESL setting: writing relates to all other disciplines of English just like reading, speaking and listening. I think it is important as an ESL teacher not to focus on grammatical correctness always or focus on form, but rather focus on what the students do know and what the content of their paper is. I think it is important to emphasize to the students that I am not looking for perfection at any stage, since native speakers do not write perfectly either. It is also necessary to teach students different genres of writing such as persuasive, expository, and creative. Also, as an ESL teacher, we have to recognize that students' cultural backgrounds are going to affect their writing, and we have to make sure that we understand how they have previously learned to write and find a way to compromise with the "American ways of writing."

This excerpt carries important traces of not only Maggie's reflections on some of the intercultural rhetoric theories she read in class on the connection among language, culture and thought in writing, but also her reflections on what happened in the field when the cooperating teacher compromised students' culture with "American ways of writing." In her account, one can also see a clear emphasis on her interest in genre-based writing instruction and emphasis on the social and cultural writing environments in which L2 writers specialized.

While the social context of writing was emphasized in this instance, Maggie also noted where the cognitive process aspect of writing was underscored through strategy development in reading and writing activities. In her class observations, Maggie emphasized that she was not aware that teaching writing and reading strategies constituted an important part of second language writing. She repeatedly said in her blog entries and in her interview that "the teaching of writing should be centered in teaching of strategies and teaching of how to write in different genres." Here, Maggie experiences the multiple facets of second language reading and writing instruction, which include a wide range of theories. In this case, the social functions of writing (e.g., genre-based instruction) and cognitive process (e.g., strategy teaching) are not necessarily opposed. She notes in her paper a few examples she observed in the field:

> Since there is such a high level of expectation of independent learning that is required by the schooling in the United States, Mrs. Dolores and Mrs. Collins seek to prepare their students to be autonomous learners, in that they are able to take control over their own learning. One of the ways in which they do so is by incorporating learning strategies that support literacy into each and every one of their lessons. The students apply learning strategies to determine the meaning of words or phrases that they cannot understand. By using a "find the meaning" strategy, students look at surrounding words or sentences to determine what an unknown sentence or word means. When she was also teaching different ways of organizing your thoughts for her advanced ESL writing class, she first presented the material and had them take notes about each organizer. Not only is this effective because students are learning about organizers, but they are also explicitly learning how to take notes while listening to the teacher talk—a behavior that is expected by many teachers. Once the students have completed the notes, they are each then put into groups in which they compare their notes to create a poster that they will present to the class.

Another pre-service teacher who reported multiple approaches and instructional practices in teaching second language writing was Jake. In his interviews, he juxtaposed both genre-based instruction and process-oriented approaches to teaching writing. Like Maggie, his views on second language writing instruction were partially shaped by the various literacy activities that emphasized ESL students' socialization into various discourses through the acquisition of various genres. Jake's working theoretical orientation towards responding to ESL writing appears vividly in his post-observation reflections:

> I think that students should be exposed to different types and genres of writing for various scenarios that they may encounter, as well as be able to give both written and oral feedback at all stages of writing. So long as the student's paper is comprehensible, there does not necessarily need to be a focus on grammar—especially in the first drafts of a paper. Focus should be placed on progress, not on 100% accuracy.

Referring to his fieldwork, Jake quotes one of his cooperating teachers and explains how she adopts a process-oriented approach to teaching second language writing.

What is interesting is that in his narrative Jake does not differentiate much between genre-based and process-oriented approaches and the paradigm shift that occurs in the field, and refers to them as complementing one another.

> Mrs. Smith's writing program for the beginner ESL strives to make the students competent writers. She says "We want our students to see themselves as writers who can creatively and effectively express their thoughts, feelings, and opinions through writing." The teacher also mentioned the importance of the process of writing, even commenting that it is as important as the final product. In regards to the last comment, I would have to mainly agree in the context of ESL. In order for students to create a final product, it requires steps to get there, and since these [students] are beginning learning of the language, it is a process to understand not only the grammar and vocabulary, but also to know the structure of writing. The aim of this program is to instill the process [of] writing into the students. Therefore, the students learn about prewriting, drafting, revising, editing, and publishing. They have done this though various genres including journaling, short stories, letter writing and giving directions. In the future, I also want to scaffold my students into becoming good writers, through journals and creative writing exercises that will apply their understanding of the writing process.

Jake's reflexive account in this excerpt exemplifies some of the second language writing theories he read and extensively discussed in his methods class. Literacy practices he observed in the field seem to reinforce his knowledge of second language theory and sense making in why teachers do what they do in class.

These examples demonstrate that pre-service teachers gain a higher awareness of terminologies and concepts related to second language writing, especially how practice occurs in a specific context of instruction, rather than a critical examination of such practices. Although it is impossible to tell how much of the pre-service teachers' working knowledge translates into practice in future teaching contexts or how much theory building students will be engaged in once they are out in the real world, these accounts show that being in the ESL classroom and engaging in various second language writing-related topics lead pre-service teachers to a space where they begin to join the disciplinary dialogues on various complex issues regarding second language reading and writing instruction.

Theme #3: Foreign Language Learning Experiences Creating Opportunities to Make Meaning of Second Language Literacy Theories

It is observed that part of how pre-service teachers know what they know about second language reading and writing derives from their experiences with other foreign languages, whether the language is learned formally in a classroom context or is culturally inherent in the student's heritage language which was spoken in the family while they were growing up. As participants were making sense of the second language literacy-related theories, they often referred to their own foreign language reading and writing practices, which mostly came from their experiences in a foreign language classroom, interacting with a native speaker of that language in their communities or study abroad experiences. The intertextual links the pre-service teachers establish to their use of a foreign language demonstrate the interconnectedness of their linguistic and cultural background to their working knowledge base on teaching second language literacy. Pre-service teachers in this study also indicated that their foreign language knowledge has been beneficial not only for establishing a greater level of empathy with English language learners but also for enriching their understanding of the complex nature of second language literacy acquisition. Maggie, in one of the interviews, underlined the connection between speaking and writing by juxtaposing a personal anecdote about her acquisition of Spanish literacy and literacy practices that she observed in the ESL setting:

> Well, for me when I was acquiring Spanish, I would write what I said first and then I would say it, especially when I was at the level in which I could not produce the language on top of my head. A lot of times I would have to write what I said and then I would be able to say it. In the ESL context what I have seen from the practicum is that speaking is just always occurring: students are talking about what they are writing, they are talking about why they are writing it and they are talking about how they are writing it, so really speaking is part of writing and the students are making an understanding of what they are doing.

As the excerpt indicates, Maggie resonates with what goes on in the ESL classes she observed due to her first-hand experiences with Spanish. Similarly, Maggie's responses in her class blog also included traces of references to her Spanish literacy acquisition. The post below is an example where she was discussing the reading strategies for ESL students.

> To give an example, when I was learning how to read in my L2, I was taught that it is never necessary to know every single word that you read. In other words, my teacher told me, "Put the dictionary down, stop looking up every single word that you cross that you do not know, and just try to read the sentence and understand it without using the dictionary." This is exactly what I did, even when I was not very proficient in the language, I would just read the sentences without barely using a dictionary. She taught me the skills that I needed to infer what some of the words meant by looking at the other context of the sentence in terms of words that I already knew. This

technique proved to be very successful to me in my second language reading abilities. Strategic reading is also very important in an L2 setting although it is much more than that. It is important for the students to know that they must read with a purpose: that is to infer, predict or to understand what the author means; rather than just simply reading the words on the page.

It is significant to recognize the impact of Maggie's linguistic experiences with reading in Spanish on her interpretation of ESL reading. In this excerpt, her use of a dictionary and her teacher's comments on this is translated to her second language literacy knowledge base as "strategic reading," a vocabulary that she picked up in the course readings as well as in her fieldwork experience. Similarly, Jake, whose heritage language is Italian and who is a second language learner of Spanish, has been exposed to diverse foreign language learning situations, which helped him to relate to what went on in the field. Jake's experiences with both Spanish and Italian seem to play an important role as he forms his knowledge base on second language teaching.

> I thought that it [teaching L2 writing] was all going to be teaching grammar. So, like "this is how we form passive sentences," but it is not at all like that in ESL classes. I guess what I do is compare a lot of how I acquired Spanish as a foreign language to how these students acquire English as a second language. Also, growing up for the most part, I would understand only Italian. We grew up in an Italian neighborhood. So, like, back when I was younger, I was very quiet just because I was afraid of speaking English. If you spoke Italian in class, you would get a slap on the wrist. I feel that we still sort of do that. Almost every class I have been to there's always one student who speaks Spanish. Usually teachers use Spanish and embrace that with that student, but when it comes to a French-speaking, Korean-speaking [student] and the other languages, they are asked not to use it. It's one of the ways that ESL kids lose their heritage language.

In this excerpt, due to his own language loss, Jake always appeared to be empathetic to the ESL students who had yet to develop an awareness in English and whose first language was not recognized or incorporated by the teacher as opposed to the first language maintenance of many Spanish-speaking ESL students he had observed.

Both Maggie's and Jake's reflections on their foreign language acquisition demonstrate that pre-service teachers' constructs of second language literacy could be highly influenced by the interplay of a range of other language learning experiences and by their realization of the dissonance between their own experiences and the ESL students' literacy experiences. This experience seemed to encourage students to look into the diversity inherent in their linguistic and cultural background and reformulate their ideas on teaching second language writing.

Discussion and Conclusion

Documenting the reflections of pre-service teachers on L2 writing theories and their observations on how these theories are manifested in the everyday classroom could provide invaluable insights on the various cultural resources pre-service teachers draw upon to shape their perspectives and beliefs on language, culture, and literacy. The findings of this study demonstrate that second language writing in the context of teacher education can be seen as an embodied and socially situated activity in which pre-service teachers should be tracing their own working knowledge. Close analysis of participants' field-based observations present important "telling cases"[3] (Mitchell, 1984) as to how observing real classroom settings with real literacy activities enabled them to gain a greater sense of what goes into teaching and learning L2 writing. The reflections on these observations through their ethnographic papers and blog journals also created opportunities for them to identify and then articulate various L2 writing-related issues such as process-writing, genre-based approaches, and focus on form versus content. This reflection process allowed students to see practice as embedded in theory, and theory as generated from practice. As Atkinson (2010) puts it, "teachers are not technicians . . . teachers are also mediators, mediating between institutional requirements and students, curriculum and students, textbook and students, specialist knowledge and students, assignments and students, grading rubric and students, even students and students" (p. 14). Just like in-service teachers, pre-service teachers should also be seen as mediators of various actors and practices within the teacher education program of which they are a part. As seen in the narratives of Jake, Norah, Maggie, and Katie, pre-service teachers usually mediate between the course readings, their observations of ESL teaching, and their own literacy socialization in a foreign language. The findings show that they were constantly forming, reformulating, negotiating, and appropriating various second language-related issues by observing everyday practices, participating in these practices, and making sense of the class readings. In other words, pre-service teachers, through their reflections, illustrate that they "consciously mediate what they know including but not only what they have discovered for themselves through the act of teaching, and rework, redirect, and redistribute it in ways that allow learning to go on" (Atkinson, 2010, p.14). Using the observations and class discussions as tools of inquiries, their narratives were filled with multiple types of disciplinary knowledge in which they displayed their knowledge of L2 concepts and process knowledge in which they come to unpack and examine their own ways of knowing about second language literacy in general. While the great bulk of general teacher education research on preparing pre-service teachers for today's diverse classrooms has explored multicultural issues such as culturally relevant teaching, this chapter specifically documented and explored the ways in which pre-service teachers come to know what they know on L2 writing and how they build a greater awareness using some disciplinary knowledge. The absence of second language writing courses in this specific

TESOL program at the undergraduate level made it more difficult to introduce important cross-cultural writing theories. Therefore, the methods course was used as a way to develop some understanding of L2 reading and writing theories. Looking at the absence of a concrete focus on second language writing research in the teacher education literature and in teacher education programs gives one a sense of urgency to develop curricular changes and insights focused on second language literacy education.

Teacher education has a critical role to play in preparing pre-service teachers for the needs of L2 writers across the curriculum. The reflections of the pre-service teachers in this study led me to explore an important curricular question: What curricular adjustments do TESOL programs need to better prepare pre-service teachers for the writing and reading needs of language-minority K–12 students? While fieldwork and methods courses can inform many experiences that define pre-service teachers' identities (Farrell, 2001), specific L2 literacy-related issues need to be included within the cross-cultural curriculum. Programs that offer a TESOL minor or endorsement need to reconsider incorporating and institutional-izing second language reading and writing courses in a more concrete way. Given that each teacher education context is particular in that it is embedded in its own particular institutional and sociopolitical goals, it is impossible to provide a generic set of practices that would work for every local institution. However, the following recommendations could provide points of discussion for curricular decision-making in teacher education programs.

Take Time to Unpack Pre-service Teachers' Assumptions about Second Language Writing

An important goal of every teacher education program is professional development, which aims to improve the quality of pre-service teachers' learning and expand their knowledge base in the content area. As all pre-service teachers bring with them various values, beliefs, and assumptions about the nature of language and culture, unpacking their assumptions can help them recognize relevant teaching issues. Casanave (2004) suggests that a good place to begin unpacking pre-service teacher' beliefs about teaching and learning L2 writing is to ask them to craft their own literacy autobiographies. In them, students can examine various sources of their beliefs such as their own second language learning and literacy acquisition histories. Revealing pre-service teachers' assumptions and philosophies could help further their understanding of the new concepts and theories they are developing. Extending Casanave's suggestion on literacy autobiographies, I argue that reflection on second language writing should be ongoing and interactive through various tools of inquiry. Pre-service teachers in this study were asked to discuss their dispositions on class readings as well as their field observations by keeping weekly blog journals, which they brought to each class session to discuss with fellow classmates. Students' individual blogs proved to be fruitful spaces where examining one's working knowledge was done continuously. As seen in the data, the participants made constant references to their first and second language writing experiences both in the classroom space as well as within their blog entries. Another way to unpack pre-service teachers' assumptions on second language writing is to give them ongoing short surveys about their beliefs and perceptions on various L2 writing issues. Casanave (2004) provides a short survey which L2 teachers can use to examine and reflect on some of the answers to complex L2 writing questions. Some of her questions include "In the context of your own teaching and/or learning of L2 writing, how do you characterize 'improvement' in writing? Try to define what you believe each of the following improvements consist of, adding your own" (p. 96). This survey can be appropriated by the teacher educator and serve as a useful tool in the beginning of a teacher education class. Inspired by this idea, the students in the methods class, which included the participants in this study, were given a short survey on their current perceptions and knowledge on teaching of second language writing (see Appendix).

Create (Post)Method Courses With a Specific Reading and Writing Emphasis

In addition to knowledge of how to teach, pre-service teachers also need to build a strong foundation on the content of their subject areas. To best prepare pre-service teachers to work with ESL students effectively, teachers need to have a good grasp of second language writing concepts and theories and an understanding of the unique nature of second language writing (Silva, 1993). In many TESOL programs, this knowledge base is provided within the methods courses, where a wide range of language-centered (e.g. audio-lingual method), learning-centered (e.g. natural approach), and learner-centered methods (e.g. communicative language teaching) are introduced. The idea of method as a prepackaged and decontextualized set of skills mostly suggested by experts in the field rather than as a reflection of teachers' everyday practice has been problematized. Methods in language teaching as accumulated entities (Rutherford, 1987) are not only seen as "interested knowledge," which "diminished rather than enhanced our understanding of language teaching" (Pennycook, 1989, p. 597). The postmethod era, which signified "an alternative to method rather than an alternative method," gives more voice to practitioners, and underlines how they construct personal theories by everyday practice (Kumaravadivelu, 2003). Approaching teaching L2 writing from a postmethod condition gives pre-service teachers "a sense of plausibility" (Prabhu, 1990) and autonomy in which teachers could personally seek "context-sensitive, location-specific pedagogy that is based on a true understanding of local linguistic, sociocultural, and political particularities" (Kumaravadivelu, 2003, p. 37). An empowering curriculum is not a curriculum that simply includes methods and strategies that can be easily transferred and delivered, rather it emphasizes a dialogic process in which pre-service teachers act as autonomous meaning-makers who critically examine the political and social issues revolving around teaching second language literacy. An empowering second language literacy curriculum in the context of teacher education critically engages its pre-service teachers with issues related to monolingualism, monoculturalism, ethnocentrism, and normalization through analyzing real-life examples where such ideologies permeate. Moving from a method to a postmethod approach to teaching second language literacy can create conditions for critical engagement which could enable pre-service teachers to monitor their own belief and create situation-specific and personal theories. This process should be an integral part of any courses geared towards TESOL and bilingual education.

Teach Second Language Writing as an Ethnographic and Socially Situated Endeavor

Ethnographic approaches can help teacher educators look into multiple social contexts that pre-service teachers enter and help them gain greater critical language awareness. Instead of looking at pre-service teachers as individual cases of analysis, we should be looking at the different kinds of courses they take, the kinds of activities embedded in such courses, and, especially, students' "thick description" of their own professional growth and evolving epistemologies around teaching L2 writing. Implementing meaningful activities and engaging student dialogues on their own language learning experiences could be the key in diversifying pre-service teachers' disciplinary knowledge, unpacking assumptions, and promoting more autonomy.

Pre-service teachers' adopting an ahistorical and apolitical method-based approach to teaching second language writing where they may associate teaching L2 writing with any kind of "good teaching" act should be replaced by ethnographic and sociopolitical approaches which will draw their attention to discussions of broader ideological, relational, linguistic, and cultural aspects of the teaching of writing. Writing carries features of linguistic differences and is interlocked with various social, gender-based, linguistic, and cultural features. Preparing pre-service teachers for this complex and fluid domain of teaching second language writing, TESOL courses should be seen as spaces where a change of attitude to language variations could begin. Engaging pre-service teachers in dialogues about linguistic minority students' cultural and linguistic resources could help them move away from the idea that these students are "lacking" certain linguistic abilities, educational background, and thinking skills, and encourage pre-service teachers to understand the interplay of power, identity, and culture in L2 writing (e.g. Kubota, 2003; Luke, 1997). Helping pre-service students unpack possible writing stereotypes by encouraging them to be ethnographers of writing could help them move away from essentialist approaches to second language literacy which solely identify any kind of L2 writing differences with first language transfer and national culture interference, disregarding many other important aspects such as educational background, sociocultural context, and genre characteristics (Connor, 2011). Therefore, critical discussions around the concept of culture and L2 writing can liberate pre-service teachers from limited understandings about teaching writing to linguistic minority students.

Thinking through a reconceptualization in teacher education means seeing and looking into alternative practices. Such practices can begin with small local changes in current teacher education courses. It may first of all mean taking on the responsibility of alternative ways of thinking, believing, knowing, speaking, and listening (Gee, 2000) to teaching L2 writing in teacher education programs. Goodwin (2002) writes, "If teacher education is to change, teacher educators will have to be the first to do some changing. Are we ready?" (p. 170). One question that we can add is: Are we ready to invest time and energy to create some radical curricular and pedagogical opportunities across the curriculum in teacher education where linking pre-service education to the community could be an essential component to promote cross-cultural competence? Finally, are we ready to give more voice and autonomy to TESOL faculty to create a curriculum that includes more topics such as L2 writing, L2 reading, and intercultural rhetoric?

Appendix

Area of Specialty/Major:
Languages:
Teaching Experience:

The purpose of this survey is to understand pre-service teachers' values, beliefs and personal theories on teaching of second language reading and writing. Please read the following statements. Based on what you learned about post-method pedagogy so far in this semester, decide whether you **(5) strongly agree; (4) agree; (3) neither agree nor disagree; (2) disagree or (1) strongly disagree.**

1. Regardless of their language level and educational context, English language learners greatly benefit from explicit instruction when they learn how to write in academic English.
   5   4   3   2   1

2. ESL students across grade levels and disciplines should learn how to self-edit their own writing.
   5   4   3   2   1

3. When responding to a second language writing, it is important to prioritize the comments.
   5   4   3   2   1

4. Teachers should not be concerned about accuracy in earlier stages of student writing in an ESL class.

5   4   3   2   1

5. It is highly important that I mark every grammatical error in student writing regardless of what stage students are in their writing process.

5   4   3   2   1

6. There is an important connection between reading and writing.

5   4   3   2   1

7. There is an important connection between writing and speaking.

5   4   3   2   1

8. Culture is the most important determinant in students' second language writing success.

5   4   3   2   1

9. While giving writing assignments, it is important that materials are relevant to students' cultures and lives in general.

5   4   3   2   1

10. Conducting classroom research with ESL students is an important part of my pedagogy.

5   4   3   2   1

11. Teaching second language literacy is closely connected to sociopolitical and cultural issues.

5   4   3   2   1

12. It is important to go beyond the professional methods conceptualized by theorists and construct my own personal theory.

5   4   3   2   1

13. Teaching second language writing at school is primarily the ESL teachers' job.

5   4   3   2   1

14. Second language reading can best be learned through content-based teaching.

5   4   3   2   1

15. It is important to expose students to multiple genres when teaching second language writing.

5   4   3   2   1

16. Knowledge of descriptive grammar is the most important aspect of good second language writing.

    5   4   3   2   1

17. In the case of an extensive reading, ESL students should be allowed to select what they want to read.

    5   4   3   2   1

The focus of the questions below is your personal reflections on your pre-service teacher education.

1. Teacher education curriculum should offer courses that specifically deal with teaching of second language literacy.

    5   4   3   2   1

2. Practicum experience should be embedded within every TESOL course that aims to address second language reading and writing.

    5   4   3   2   1

3. I learn more from class discussions than teacher lectures in TESOL courses.

    5   4   3   2   1

4. I learn more from the class readings when I write personal reflections (e.g. blogs).

    5   4   3   2   1

5. At this stage of my teacher development, I feel confident in teaching second language writing.

    5   4   3   2   1

6. At this stage of my teacher development, I feel confident in teaching second language reading.

    5   4   3   2   1

Notes

1   While 41 percent of teachers nationwide report that they have English language learners (ELLs) in their classrooms, only 12.4 percent of these teachers indicated that they had participated in eight or more hours of professional development related to English language learners in the past three years (http://www.nea.org/home/13598.htm).
2   All names are pseudonyms.
3   A telling case (Mitchell, 1984) can be defined as a case that is representative and illustrative of a phenomenon under study.

References

Atkinson, D. (2010). Between theory with a big T and practice with a small p: Why theory matters? In T. Silva & P. K. Matsuda (Eds.), *Practicing theory in second language writing* (pp. 5–18). West Lafayette, IN: Parlor Press.

Aud, S., Hussar, W., Kena, G., Bianco, K., Frohlich, L., Kemp, J., & Tahan, K. (2011). *The Condition of Education 2011* (NCES 2011-033). U.S. Department of Education, National Center for Education Statistics. Washington, DC: U.S. Government Printing Office.

Block, D. (2003). *The social turn in second language acquisition.* Washington, DC: Georgetown University Press.

Canagarajah, S. (1999). Resisting linguistic imperialism in English teaching. Oxford: Oxford University Press.

Canagarajah, S. (2002). Reconstructing local knowledge. *Journal of Language, Identity, and Education, 1,* 234–259.

Casanave, C. (2004). *Controversies in second language writing: Dilemmas and decisions in research and instruction.* Ann Arbor: University of Michigan Press.

Commins, N., & Miramontes, O. (2006). Addressing linguistic diversity from the outset. *Journal of Teacher Education, 57,* 240–246.

Connor, U. (2011). *Intercultural rhetoric in the writing classroom.* Ann Arbor: University of Michigan Press.

de Jong, E., & Harper, H. (2005). Preparing mainstream teachers for English-language learners: Is being a good teacher good enough? *Teacher Education Quarterly, 32,*101–124.

de Oliveira, L., & Athanases, S. (2007). Graduates' reports of advocating for English language learners. *Journal of Teacher Education, 58,* 202–215.

Edge, J. (2011). *The reflexive teacher educator in TESOL: Roots and wings.* New York: Routledge.

Farrell, T. (2001). English language teacher socialization during practicum. *Prospect, 16,* 49–62

Freeman, D. (2002). The hidden side of the work: Teacher knowledge and learning to teach. *Language Teaching, 35,* 1–13.

Freeman, D., & Johnson, K. L. (1998). Reconceptualizing the knowledge-base of language teacher education. *TESOL Quarterly, 32,* 397–417.

Freire, P. (1970). *Pedagogy of the oppressed* (M. B. Ramos, Trans.). New York: Continuum.

Gee, J. (2000). *An introduction to discourse analysis: Theory and methods.* New York and London: Routledge.

Goodwin, A. L. (2002). Teacher preparation and the education of immigrant children. *Education and Urban Society, 34,* 156–172.

Hall, J. K., & Eggington, W. G. (Eds.) (2000). *The sociopolitics of English language teaching.* Cleveland, OH: Multilingual Matters.

Hatch, J. A. (2002). *Doing qualitative research in education settings.* Albany: State University of New York.

Igoa, C. (1995). *The inner world of the immigrant child.* New York: St. Martin's Press.

Johnson, K. E. (1996). The role of theory in second language teacher education. *TESOL Quarterly, 30,* 765–771.

Johnson, K. (2006). The sociocultural turn and its challenges for second language teacher education. *TESOL Quarterly, 40/1,* 235–255.

Johnson, K., & Golombek, P. (2011). A sociocultural theoretical perspective on teacher professional development. In K. Johnson and P. Golombek (Eds.), *Research on second language teacher education: A sociocultural perspective on professional development* (pp. 1–12). New York: Routledge.

Kubota, R. (2003). Unfinished knowledge: The story of Barbara. *College ESL, 10,* 11–21.

Kumaravadivelu, B. (2001). Toward a postmethod pedagogy. *TESOL Quarterly, 35,* 537–560.

Kumaravadivelu, B. (2003). *Beyond methods: Macrostrategies for language teaching.* New Haven, CT: Yale University Press.

Kumaravadivelu, B. (2006). Postmethod perspective on English language teaching. *World Englishes, 22,* 539–550.

Ladson-Billings, G. (1994). *The dreamkeepers: Successful teachers of African American children.* San Francisco: Jossey-Bass.

Leki, I., & Silva, T. (2004). Family matters: The influence of applied linguistics and composition studies on second language writing studies: Past, present, and future. *Modern Language Journal, 88,* 1–13.

Leki, I., Cumming, A., & Silva, T. (2008). *A synthesis of research on second language writing in English.* New York: Routledge.

Lincoln, Y. S., & Guba, E. G. (1985). *Naturalistic inquiry.* Beverly Hills, CA: Sage.

Luke, A. (1997). Genres of power: Literacy education and the production of capital. In R. Hasan & G. Williams (Eds.), *Literacy in society* (pp. 308–338). London: Longman.

Mitchell, C. J. (1984). Case studies. In R. F. Ellen (Ed.), *Ethnographic research: A guide to general conduct* (pp. 237–241). London: Academic Press.

Moll, L. (Ed.) (1990). *Vygotsky and education: Instructional implications and applications of sociohistorical psychology.* Cambridge: Cambridge University Press.

Norton, B., & Toohey, K. (Eds.) (2004). *Critical pedagogies and language learning.* Cambridge, UK: Cambridge University Press.

Olsen, L. (1997). *Made in America: Immigrant students in our public schools.* New York: New Press.

Pennycook, A. (1989). The concept of method, interested knowledge, and the politics of language teaching. *TESOL Quarterly, 23,* 589–618.

Prabhu, N. (1990). There's no best method: Why? *TESOL Quarterly, 24,* 161–176.

Ramanathan, V. (2002). *The politics of TESOL education: Writing, knowledge, critical pedagogy.* New York: Routledge.

Rossman, G., & Rallis, S. (2003). *Learning in the field: An introduction to qualitative research.* Thousand Oaks, CA: Sage Publications.

Rutherford, W. E. (1987). *Second language grammar. Learning and teaching.* London: Longman.

Silva, T. (1993). Toward an understanding of the distinct nature of L2 writing; The ESL research and its implications. *TESOL Quarterly, 27,* 657–677.

Silva, T., & Matsuda, P. (2010). *Practicing theory in second language writing.* West Lafayette, IN: Parlor Press.

Sleeter, C. (2001). Preparing teachers for culturally diverse schools. Research and the overwhelming presence of whiteness. *Journal of Teacher Education, 42,* 94–106.

U.S. Census Bureau (2007). Language use in the United States: American community survey reports. Retrieved March 1, 2012, from http://www.census.gov/prod/2010 pubs/acs-12.pdf

Ward, M., & Ward, C. (2003). Promoting cross-cultural competence in preservice teachers through second language use. *Education, 123,* 532–538.

Yates, B., & Muchisky, D. (2003). On reconceptualizing teacher education. *TESOL Quarterly, 37,* 135–147.

CONTRIBUTORS AND EDITORS

Steven Z. Athanases, University of California, Davis
Lisa H. Bennett, University of California, Davis
Luciana C. de Oliveira, Purdue University
Kerry Anne Enright, University of California, Davis
Alan Hirvela, Ohio State University
Amanda Kibler, University of Virginia
Ditlev Larsen, Winona State University
Juliet Michelsen Wahleithner, University of California, Davis
Melissa Niiya, University of California, Irvine
Christina Ortmeier-Hooper, University of New Hampshire
Lisya Seloni, Illinois State University
Jennifer Shade Wilson, Rice University
Tony Silva, Purdue University
Mark Warschauer, University of California, Irvine
Youngjoo Yi, Georgia State University
Binbin Zheng, University of California, Irvine

INDEX

academic language 150
academic trajectories 27–42, 47
academic voice 112
academic writing 28–9, 41, 77, 98, 104, 105, 111–14
accountability policies 27, 28, 31, 38, 42, 150–1, 155
achievement gap 28
activity theory 47
affinity spaces 109
after-school programs 96, 97
argument as moves approach 79–80
argument is everywhere approach 79, 83
argument schema 67–8, 76, 77, 80
argument stratagems 76, 77
argumentative writing 67–83
arguments to convince 79
arguments to explore 79
arguments to inform 79
arguments to make decisions 79
arguments to meditate or pray 79
assessment of student writing 31, 38–9, 47, 60, 73, 127–8, 133, 140–1, 145–6
assimilation of language 107
audience 141
audience-oriented approach to argumentative strategies 78–9, 83
audio-lingual method 183
authenticity 141
automated writing evaluation (AWE) software 113–14

behavioral engagement 99
blogs 104, 105–6, 107, 112–14, 171, 172, 176; preservice teachers 182–3
Brown Education Alliance report 73

caring, concept of 94, 97
church-based literacy 96–7
code-switching 107
cognitive strategies approach to argumentative strategies 77–8
"Cognitive Strategies Reader's and Writer's Tool Kit" 78, 82
collaborative reasoning approach to argumentation 76–7, 81, 82
collaborative writing 141
Common Core Standards 68, 70, 73, 74–5, 82, 83
communicative language teaching 183
communities of practice (CoP) 89, 97
computer-mediated communication (CMC) 105–7
Conference on College Composition and Communication (CCCC) 135
content area writing 27
content literacy and learning 41
contrastive (intercultural) rhetoric 71–2
corpus technology in argumentative writing 72
cultural dissonance 12
cultural theories of identity 14

Daily Sparks 139, 147–8

data analysis 156, 157–61, 171; ask and
listen beneath the surface 158–9, 162;
documenting the achievement that is
there. 157–8, 162; pattern finding
159–60, 162; predicting student
performance to guide instruction
160–1, 162
demographic information 154–5; breadth
of data 155–6; role of data in 155–6
developmental trajectory of new teachers
149
digital media 104–14
Digital Underground Storytelling for
Youth (DUSTY) in California 95, 98
disciplinary grammars 150
disclosure, paradox of 20–2, 23–4
disengagement 12
dissonance: loss of, writer's engagement
and 19–20; in teacher–child
relationship 17–19
duty 15

Ecological Systems Theory 87, 90
email 90, 104, 105, 106
emotional engagement 99
enactments of identity 57
engagement in writing 99
essay writing 31, 34, 39, 47, 53–5, 55–7,
58, 60, 111, 155, 158; argumentative
67–83
ethnic theories of identity 14
ethnographic approaches 184–5
ethnographic experience 172–5

Facebook character project 139, 140
families 90
fanfiction 109
"five-and-dime" version of instruction and
writing norms 40
foreign language learning experiences
178–80
"Freedom Writers" project 111

genre-based writing theories 176, 178, 181
genre conventions 150
genres of writing 40
Georgia High School Graduation Tests
133
Georgia High School Writing Testing 133

histories of participation 59

identity 98

identity assertions 12
identity, digital media and 108–11;
multiple modalities 109–10; peer
feedback 108–9; writing the word and
the world 110–11
identity formation 89
identity texts 110
informal fallacies 69
interactional histories approach see
longitudinal interactional histories
approach
interactions: impact of 55–7; lack of 51–3;
while creating text 53–5
I-R-E (teacher Initiates, student
Responds, teacher Evaluates response)
sequences 38
iterative writing 113–14

language broker 91
language complexity 106–7
language-centered approach 183
learner-centered methods 183
letter writing 57, 159
library skills 142
literacy broker, adolescents as 91
literacy studies 88
logical reasoning 75, 76
longitudinal interactional histories
approach (LIHA) 48–58, 60

MinneTESOL 128
MSN 92
multimedia, use of 109–10
MySpace 92, 98

National Council of Teachers of English
(NCTE) 135
natural approach 183
neighborhood relationships 95–8
next steps instruction 161–2
No Child Left Behind 31
noticing and adopting language 107–8

on-the-job learning. 127, 129
one-to-one laptop research 111–12, 113
opinion pieces 75

patterns of inferences 69
peer feedback 108–9
peer socioliterate interactions 92, 95
personal responsibility 53
placements, teacher training 152
plagiarism 112

postmethod courses 183–4
postmethod pedagogy in teacher education 168–80; ethnographic experience 172–5; foreign language learning experiences 178–80; higher awareness of second language writing 175–8
pre-service teachers: assumptions 182–3; challenges and concerns for writing pedagogy 141–2; knowledge construction and theory building in 166–87; knowledge of and beliefs in writing and writing pedagogy 140–1; limitations 125–6; preparation 119–29; remedies 127–8; sense of preparedness 137, 138
problem solving approach to argumentation 80–1, 83
process-based theories 176, 178, 181
Project FRESA 110–11
punishment, writing as 142

rapport 23
Readers' Theater projects 139, 141, 143
recognition of achievements 16
reflective writing 76
refugees: demography 9; needs and complexities of 10
Report of the National Literacy Panel on Language-Minority Children and Youth 73
research, writing as 111–12
responsibility, personal 15, 16
responsive inquiry 149–62
rhetorical triangle 79

scaffolding 153
school relationships 91–5
script writing139
self-identity 12, 13
self-study, trial and error 127
siblings 90

situated approaches to literacy 29
snowball phenomenon 76–7
social relationships 87–98; home 90–1; neighborhood 95–8; school 91–5
social responsibility 53
socio-political identity 14–17
sociocultural theory (SCT) 14, 89
socioliterate relationships 87, 91, 92, 98
stasis system 69
strategic reading 180
STRUGGLE 95–6, 97
syllogisms 69
Symposium on Second Language Writing 135
synchronicity 17
syntax 114

teacher–child relationship, synchronicity in 17; affective-intellectual "space" 17; dissonance in 17–19
teacher education program curriculum 124–5
teacher identities 143–5, 146
teacher perceptions of multilingual writers 11
teacher preparedness 124–5, 137, 138
teacher–student relationships 93–5
textual self 95
thematic analysis 171
Toulmin model of argumentation 69–70, 75–6, 81
trust 23, 98

Venn diagrams 69
vocabulary development 114
Voices, Inc. 98

Welcome to Buckeye City 98
wikis 104
Writers' Workshop techniques 143
writing 'shutdown' 11, 12
written language functions 150